Joseph Glicklich and fellow Jewish officers in the Polish army, 1924. Courtesy of Rosalie Baker.

Destruction of Bilgoraj
(Biłgoraj, Poland)

Translation of
Khurban Bilgoraj

Original Book Edited by: A. Kronenberg

Originally published in Tel Aviv 1956

A Publication of JewishGen, INC
Edmond J. Safra Plaza, 36 Battery Place, New York, NY 10280
646.494.5972 | info@JewishGen.org | www.jewishgen.org

Destruction of Bilgoraj (Biłgoraj, Poland)
Translation of *Khurban Bilgoraj*

Editor of Original Yizkor Book: A. Kronenberg
Project Coordinator: Moses Milstein
Emerita Coordinator: Rae Meltzer
Layout and Name Indexing: Jonathan Wind
Reproduction of Photographs: Sondra Ettlinger
Cover Design: Nina Schwartz

Printed in the United States of America by Lightning Source, Inc.

Library of Congress Control Number (LCCN): 2022930806

ISBN: 978-1-954176-31-7 (hard cover: 270 pages, alk. paper)

About JewishGen.org

JewishGen, an affiliate of the Museum of Jewish Heritage - A Living Memorial to the Holocaust, serves as the global home for Jewish genealogy.

Featuring unparalleled access to 30+ million records, it offers unique search tools, along with opportunities for researchers to connect with others who share similar interests. Award winning resources such as the Family Finder, Discussion Groups, and ViewMate, are relied upon by thousands each day.

In addition, JewishGen's extensive informational, educational and historical offerings, such as the Jewish Communities Database, Yizkor Book translations, InfoFiles, Family Tree of the Jewish People, and KehilaLinks, provide critical insights, first-hand accounts, and context about Jewish communal and familial life throughout the world.

Offered as a free resource, JewishGen.org has facilitated thousands of family connections and success stories, and is currently engaged in an intensive expansion effort that will bring many more records, tools, and resources to its collections.

Please visit https://www.jewishgen.org/ to learn more.

Executive Director: Avraham Groll

About the JewishGen Yizkor Book Project

Yizkor Books (Memorial Books) were traditionally written to memorialize the names of departed family and martyrs during holiday services in the synagogue (a practice that still exists in many synagogues today).

Over the centuries, as a result of countless persecutions and horrific atrocities committed against the Jews, Yizkor Books (Sefer Zikaron in Hebrew) were expanded to include more historical information, such as biographical sketches of famous personalities and descriptions of daily town life.

Following the Holocaust, the idea of remembrance and learning took on an urgent and crucial importance. Survivors of the Holocaust sought out other surviving residents of their former towns to memorialize and document the names and way of life of those who were ruthlessly murdered by the Nazis. These remembrances were documented in Yizkor Books, hundreds of which were published in the first decades after the Holocaust.

Most of these books were published privately, or through landsmanshaftn (social organizations comprised of members originating from the same European town or region) that still existed, and were often distributed free of charge. Sadly, the languages used to document these crucial histories and links to our past, Yiddish and Hebrew, are no longer commonly understood by a significant percentage of Jews today. As a result, JewishGen has undertaken the sacred responsibility of translating these books into English so that the culture and way of life of these communities will be preserved and transmitted to future generations.

In 1986, a group of farsighted JewishGenners started a project to pool their efforts together in groups based upon their ancestors from each town and donate money to get the Yizkor books of their ancestral towns translated into English. As the translated material became available, it was made accessible for free at www.JewishGen.org/Yizkor. Hardcover copies can be purchased by visiting https://www.jewishgen.org/Yizkor/ybip.html (see below).

It is our hope that the translation of these books into English (and other languages) will assist the countless Jewish family researchers who are so desperately seeking to forge a connection with their heritage.

Director of JewishGen Yizkor Book Project: Lance Ackerfeld

About the JewishGen Press

JewishGen Press (formerly the Yizkor Books-in-Print Project) is the publishing division of JewishGen.org, and provides a venue for the publication of non-fiction books pertaining to Jewish genealogy, history, culture, and heritage.

In addition to the Yizkor Book category, publications in the Other Non-Fiction category include Shoah memoirs and research, genealogical research, collections of genealogical and historical materials, biographies, diaries and letters, studies of Jewish experience and cultural life in the past, academic theses, and other books of interest to the Jewish community.

Please visit https://www.jewishgen.org/Yizkor/ybip.html to learn more.

Director of JewishGen Press: Joel Alpert
Managing Editor - Jessica Feinstein
Publications Manager - Susan Rosin

Notes to the Reader

The images in the original book were reproduced from photographs from the time of the first edition. These reproductions were already of poor quality, being pre-war and at least 30 or more years old. As a result the images in the book are not very good and the best achievable.

A reader can view the original scans of the book on the websites listed below.

The original book can be seen online at the Yiddish Book Center web site:

https://www.yiddishbookcenter.org/collections/yizkor-books/yzk-nybc317983/kronenberg-avraham-hurbn-bilguray

To obtain a list of Shoah victims from Bilgoraj (Biłgoraj) the reader should access the Yad Vashem web site listed below; one can also search for specific family names using family name option. These lists are continually updated by Yad Vashem, so it is worthwhile to periodically search these lists.

There is more valuable information (including the Pages of Testimony, etc.) available on this website: https://yvng.yadvashem.org/

A list of all books available from JewishGen Press along with prices is available at: https://www.jewishgen.org/Yizkor/ybip.html

Acknowledgements

I would like to thank JewishGen, and Yizkor Book Director, Lance Ackerfeld, for giving me the opportunity to translate the testimony, and memoirs of the survivors of the Jewish community of Bilgoraj.

Thanks also to Sara Mages, and Jerrold Landau for their help in translating the Hebrew portions of the book.

Moses Milstein
Pemberton, British Columbia
February 2022

Credits and Captions for Book Cover

Front Cover:

Machla (Maya) Stempel with her brother, Leibel (Areyeh), 1938. Courtesy of Harold Baum.

Moshe Sharf in his family's sawmill yard, c.1935. Courtesy of Israel Bar-On and the Israel Bilgoraj Society.

Hudes (Hadassah) Mercer, left, with a friend, Bilgoraj, c.1938. Courtesy of Esti Szpitalnik Eilam.

Farewell party for Binyamin Warshaviak, 1922 departing for Eretz Israel. Courtesy of Rosalie Baker. Warshaviak, probably in shirtsleeves at center. Third row, second from right: Joseph Glicklich, Rosalie Baker's father. Back row, second from left: Moishe Tajer.

Background: 1916 Map, from Karte des westlichen Russlands. Public domain. Source: Topographic Maps of Eastern Europe, easteuropetopo.org, held by Geography and Map Division, Library of Congress.

Back cover:

Main square of Bilgoraj, c.1917. Public domain. Source: National Library of Israel.

Machla (Maya) Stempel, right, with two friends, 1938. Courtesy of Harold Baum. The women are in front of Machla's family home, 6 Lubelski Street.

Fajerman family, c.1904. Courtesy of Rosalie Baker. Joseph Glicklich, age 2, his mother Chana Machle Fajerman Glicklich, his aunt Dvora Fajerman Lax (left), his uncle Tavel (Tobias) Fajerman, and his grandmother Hudes Ruchla Fajerman.

Re-scans of book photos courtesy of Israel Bar-On and the Israel Bilgoraj Society.

GeoPolitical Information

Bilgoraj, Poland is located at 50°33' N 22°42' E 138 miles SSE of Warszawa

	Town	District	Province	Country
Before WWI (c. 1900):	Biłgoraj	Biłgoraj	Lublin	Russian Empire
Between the wars (c. 1930):	Biłgoraj	Biłgoraj	Lublin	Poland
After WWII (c. 1950):	Biłgoraj			Poland
Today (c. 2000):	Biłgoraj			Poland

Alternate Names for the Town:

Biłgoraj [Pol], Bilgoray [Yid], Bilgorai [Rus], Biłgora

Nearby Jewish Communities:

Frampol 9 miles N
Goraj 12 miles N
Zwierzyniec 12 miles ENE
Tarnogród 13 miles S
Szczebrzeszyn 16 miles NE
Józefów 16 miles ESE
Chrzanów 17 miles NNW
Łukowa 17 miles SE
Janów Lubelski 17 miles NW
Krzeszów 19 miles SW
Ulanów 20 miles WSW
Turobin 20 miles N
Zdziłowice 20 miles NNW
Kuryłówka 20 miles SSW
Cieplice 21 miles S
Chłaniów 21 miles NNE
Modliborzyce 21 miles NW
Rudnik nad Sanem 21 miles WSW
Krasnobród 22 miles E

Cewków 22 miles SSE
Dzików Stary 23 miles SSE
Leżajsk 23 miles SSW
Ułazów 24 miles SE
Nisko 24 miles W
Żółkiewka 25 miles NNE
Pysznica 25 miles W
Wysokie 25 miles N
Wola Żarczycka 26 miles SW
Sieniawa 27 miles S
Zamość 27 miles ENE
Jeżowe 27 miles WSW
Grodzisko Dolne 28 miles SSW
Rozwadów 29 miles W
Cieszanów 29 miles SE
Zaklików 30 miles WNW
Kamień 30 miles WSW
Tarnogóra 30 miles NE
Oleszyce 30 miles SSE
Narol 30 miles ESE

Jewish Population: 3,486 (in 1897), 4,596 (in 1931)

Map of Poland with **Bilgoraj** indicated

TABLE OF CONTENTS

Melamdim and Cheders

People

Bilgoraj Community Activists

Destruction of Bilgoraj
(Biłgoraj, Poland)

50°33' / 22°42'

Translation of *Khurban Bilgoraj*

Edited by:

A. Kronenberg

Published in Tel Aviv, 1956

———

Acknowledgments

Project Coordinator:

Moses Milstein

Emerita Coordinator: Rae Meltzer

This is a translation from:

Khurban Bilgoraj;
Destruction of Bilgoraj, ed. A. Kronenberg, Tel Aviv, 1956.

[Page III]

Introduction

by I. D. Mittlepunkt

Translated by Moses Milstein

The style of these memoirs, as recorded by their authors, is a warm, folksy one, and this alone is already a holy effort.

An unfamiliar page, exposing the most tragic experiences of the Bilgoraj Jews who carried the burdens of the ghetto with spiritual dignity.

The compiler of these memoirs, A. H. Kronenberg, has through this labor, doubtless helped add a stone to the coming monument that future historians will someday erect by immortalizing through their writing Jewish martyrology in the dark days of Hitlerism.

Tel Aviv, Adar 25, 5716[1]

———

Translator's footnote:

    1.   March 8, 1956

———

[Page IV]

Where There's a Will, There's a Way

by Abraham Kronenberg

Translated by Moses Milstein

Although difficult, we succeeded through collective effort to create a monument to our martyrs who perished at the hands of the German murderers.

The work was hard, but we did not give up. We collected, created, begged, and made requests of everyone, and the majority of our community did indeed make a significant contribution, and we succeeded in creating a monument in the form of a book of almost 400 pages. But what are 400 pages compared to our precious Jews, killed by the German murderers. There is no end to what can be written about them, and therefore, we had to satisfy ourselves with bringing out the most salient.

We have collected pictures of events where no remembrance exists but the photo itself, and we have presented these so that future generations should not forget that there were once precious Jews, pious and "free," merchants and tradesmen; they were all dear to us, and beloved, and all perished because they were Jews.

We worked hard and produced a picture of our city and its dear Jews, its parties, institutions, and personalities. May we not forget what we had, and what will never again be.

We beg that we may not be judged too harshly for omitting names from the lists of the dead, because it was not our fault. We turned to our co-citizens many times about this, and received very few responses. But even those missing from the list, will always remain in our memories.

[Page V]

A heartfelt thank-you to the committee for publishing this book, and for their work. And to the shuldiner Abraham Yakov for his assistance in compiling the list of the dead.

It was difficult to obtain these pictures of our city and its parties, as well as the only surviving, damaged, picture of "Chalutz." But, where there's a will, there's a way.

[Page VI]

Modest Words for Great Deeds

by Book Committee

Translated by Moses Milstein

There was once a shtetl, Bilgoraj, like all cities in Poland, with the same buildings and appearance, establishments and institutions, the same jobs and professions, and above all, the same people, the same dear, warm-hearted Jews. And it was just like all the Jewish shtetlach, similar one to another, and annihilated by the same circumstances and terrors, a fate shared equally by our home town of Bilgoraj.

The shtetele and its Jews is no more! It disappeared in horror and pain, taking with it everything of value, everything created through the work of many generations, and ending in destruction in the last generation.

Only a small handful of Bilgoraj Jews were saved who, because of various circumstances, are now spread and scattered throughout the world.

We, the surviving Bilgorajers in Israel are not concentrated in one area, as is the case with other landsmanschaften. The majority of Bilgorajers are scattered in cities and villages throughout the country. Contact between us is difficult to attain, aside from the one yizkor evening where the majority of us come together in order to remember, and mourn our martyrs.

In this way, about ten years went by where at various gatherings the subject of a monument in the form of a yizkor book was discussed and planned. A book which should be found in every house of our former co-citizens. At the moment when longing would gnaw at the heart of a Bilgoraj son or daughter, he could open this book, and between its pages, find his old home, the shtetele and its streets, buildings and institutions, its people and all its hues, the various figures and personalities, their work and professions, their actions and their existence, and the last, the martyrs way, the sad end.

[Page VII]

And this very task of creating a monument was undertaken by our friend, Abraham Kronenberg. Beginning at aleph, he connected with the Bilgorajers in Israel and abroad. He mobilized more than forty people who contributed various articles such as memories and tales of the past. He collected photos of people who had died, and had left no traces behind, who had left no survivors to remember their names. He inscribed and immortalized their names and images in this monument, and worried about the organisation of the book, its historical worth and literary style.

It has to be said that he did this work indefatigably, every day after physical exertion until late at night. And thanks to his work we succeeded in immortalizing, in words and in pictures, the past of the shtetl and all its times until the elimination of the last Jew.
We do not thank him for his great deed, because our words would be inadequate. We dedicate to him a few modest words.

Committee for creating the book:

> Shlomo Weinberg
> Shimon Obligenhartz
> Mordechai Rapaport
> Shmuel Bron
> Itzchak Rapaport
> Moshe Tayer
> Israel Geist

———

[Page 1]

My Shteteleh

by A. Kronenberg

Translated by Moses Milstein

In Congress Poland, hard by the old border with Austria, not far from Zamosc, Lubliner district, was the city of Bilgoraj.

It was a city of 12,000 residents, 65% of them Jewish. Everywhere you went, you heard Yiddish. Almost all the businesses and crafts were in Jewish hands.

The streets were full of our beautiful Jewish children. Bilgoraj had a thousand charms, because everything reflected the glow of Yiddishkeit. It was a city of Jewish culture and development hundreds of years old.

The antisemitism that raged in Poland was barely felt in Bilgoraj almost up to the outbreak of World War II, because it was so heavily Jewish. Jewish influence was everywhere. The new Christian shops even failed to attract their own coreligionists.

It was a pleasure to see our people sitting on city council, with yarmulkes on their heads, and patriarchal beards, representing all the Jewish parties, from right to left.

The Christians put up a big fight during city elections. To prevent a Jewish majority, they registered the peasants from the surrounding villages. By doing so, they tried to avoid being ruled by a Jewish majority.

Bilgoraj possessed many synagogues, Chasidic *shtiblach*, a yeshiva, cheders, a Yavneh cheder, a Beit Yakov, several Jewish banks, many goodwill organisations, and many Jewish parties. It was a city that breathed Yiddishkeit, with pure Jewish living. A city that had a rabbinical dynasty of the most respected *godl hador*[1] in hundreds of years, of whom the last rebbe was the son of the Belzer rebbe, R' Mordechai Rokeach, *z"l*.

[Page 4][2]

Bilgoraj was a city of Torah and greatness like no other. And then the Nazi murderers came and exterminated everything so that no trace remained–except for the small *sha'arit haplitah*[3] who survived in various parts of the world.

Sometimes when you remember the tragedy, it seems unreal, like it must have been a dream. But, unfortunately, it was a sorrowful reality. The Nazis transformed a deeply embedded Jewish community hundreds of years old, into a huge mountain of ashes which always swims before our eyes. We, and the coming generations, will never forget the call of our sacred martyrs, "Remember what Amalek did to you!"

Our enemies did not succeed in exterminating the Jewish people. The remaining glowing embers reignited themselves, and the chain weaves itself once more, and in our own land.

May this book serve as a monument to a Jewish community destroyed by the German murderers.

Honor for the memory of our beloved shtetl, Bilgoraj.

———

Translator's footnotes:

1. One of the greatest men of his age.
2. Page numbers, although out of sequence in some cases, are presented as printed in the original text. The text itself is sequential.
3. Survivors of the war in Europe.

———

[Page 3]

A Monument to My Shtetele

by I. Ch. Kronenberg

Translated by Moses Milstein

Bilgoraj, my shtetele,
Where I spent my youth
The place where those nearest to me perished
And their children slaughtered before their eyes.

I plant a tree in your memory:
A monument for your mass grave.
Sky-blue silk arching above in the daytime

And with glowing children's eyes be-starring the
night.

In the wind blowing through the branches, I hear
The voice of my dear ones,
In the rustle of the leaves–their whispered
words,
And in the sad song of the bird among the
monument-leaves--,
The weeping of the nursing babes.

In the dawn, as the sun emerges over the dew-
covered fields,
The bright children's eyes disappear–the stars,
With those of the leaves of the tree, the dew
drops–their tears.

———

[Page 5]

Rabbis of Bilgoraj

by A. Kronenberg

Translated by Moses Milstein

According to the historical evidence, Bilgoraj is a very old city, which can also be seen in the style of construction of the houses: one on Third of May Street, a second on the shul street, and a third on Pilsudski Street. The little windows and the stout round doors, and the style of the chimneys are evidence that they originated from the time of the Tartar invasions. Due to the number of fires that had occurred in Bilgoraj, only a few houses remained.

But when the Jewish community of Bilgoraj was founded, we can't determine, because the community Pinkas was destroyed along with the community.

Bilgoraj as a city was mentioned as far back as 1648. The book, Yon Metzilah, states: "When the Cossacks attacked Zamosc, they ranged over the whole region and murdered and plundered the cities of Bilgoraj, Tarnogrod, Frampol, and others…" which were not fortified. And actually, because of this, they used to build the shuls in the form of a fortress.

A Jewish community in Bilgoraj in 1731 is noted in the "Pinchas Arbei Artzot."

It is also known that in the old cemetery, on Third of May Street, there were tombstones more than 200 years old. And there was even an older cemetery, near the shul, where there were two tombstones whose dates could not be made out.

Without the Pinkas, we have no way of knowing exactly who the rabbis were who occupied the Kisei Harabbanut with the emergence of the Bilgoraj community.

[Page 6]

Therefore, we have to make do with what we do know:

The gaon, R' Moishe Tzvi, the son of the Zolkver[1] rebbe, R' Shimshon Meizlish[2], was the rabbi in Bilgoraj. For a long time, he had no son. When a son, who they named Avigdor, was finally born to him, the bris was celebrated with great simcha, and the townspeople expressed the hope to the rabbi and rebbetzin "that their son would take over as rabbi for a hundred years." The parents answered, "Amen!"

When R' Shimshon Meizlish died, the Zolkver community invited his son, R' Moishe Zvi, the Bilgoraj rabbi, to take over his father's place. After he left Bilgoraj, we have no information on who, if anyone, was the Bilgoraj rabbi. But when Avigdor reached 18 years of age, and was widely known for his Torah knowledge and wisdom, representatives of the Bilgoraj community came to Zolkow and asked him to become their rabbi. He was, however, very close to his parents, and did not want to leave them, and he turned down the request. The representatives then went to the Zolkver rabbi and reminded him of the wish they had blessed him with to which he had answered, amen.

The young R' Avigdor had no choice therefore, and on his father's command, he traveled to Bilgoraj where he served as rabbi until he was very old, and had grandchildren and great-grandchildren.

After him, his son-in-law, R' Itzchak Nathan Nuteh Berliner[3], occupied the Kisei-Harabbanut. He was the son of R' Hershele Berliner, the Berlin rabbi. He was rabbi for about 50 years in Bilgoraj. He died on 14th of Iyar, 5624.

[Page 7]

After him came his son-in-law, R' Nachum Palast, who was known as a great tsaddik.

After the death of R' Nachum Palast, there were several rabbinical candidates, and as is usual, there were quarrels among their supporters. They finally ended up electing R' Shmuel Engel as rabbi, the son-in-law of R' Shmuel Mendl Weissman, who stemmed from an important business family in Bilgoraj.

R' Shmuel Engel was a great scholar, and later became renowned as the Radomishler[4] rabbi. But even after his election as Bilgoraj rabbi, the quarrels continued until they came to the attention of the Russian authorities who expelled alien residents, and seeing as R' Shmuel was from Galicia which belonged to Austria at the time, he was arrested and led to the Austrian border. With that, the quarrels around the Kisei Harabbanut in Bilgoraj ended.

After, the great sage, R' Yakov Zilberman[5], who was referred to as the Matziver[6] Ilui, became rabbi. He would sit and study night and day. Many rabbis consulted him with questions and requests that were printed in various books. He was Bilgoraj's rabbi for many years.

During the First World War, 17th of Tammuz, 5675, when the Austrian army was occupying Bilgoraj for the second time, the rabbi went to Lublin where he died in the cholera epidemic which was raging throughout the entire region.

The rabbi's son, R' Yosef, who was dayan while his father was alive, remained in Bilgoraj.

[Page 8]

When the Austrian army occupied the Bilgoraj region, and battles took place at the river San, the shtetl Kreshev[7], was burned down from the artillery shells. The Kreshev Jews who were homeless now, mostly came to Bilgoraj, among them the Kreshever rabbi, R' Chaim Hoichman.

When the Austrian army entered Bilgoraj, it brought with it the cholera epidemic. From 17th Tammuz until Tisha B'Av, 5675, three weeks, more than 500 people died of cholera in Bilgoraj. Large numbers of people from cholera-infected homes were quarantined in special buildings on the "sands." Among the victims was the Bilgoraj rebbe's son, R' Yosef. Consequently, the Kreshever rabbi became the Bilgoraj spiritual representative to the occupation authority. Whenever something happened to a Jew, he would rush to intervene on his behalf, notwithstanding his advanced age, and usually with success.

When R' Yosef recovered and became city rabbi, the Kreshever rabbi stayed on in Bilgoraj.

After R' Yosef Zilberman died suddenly one Friday evening, 13th Adar, 1926, the gaon and tzaddik, R' Mordechai Rokeach, zt"l, brother of the Belzer rabbi, shlit"a, was appointed rabbi.

He sat on the Kisei Harabbanut until the outbreak of WWII, in the year 5699, when all the Jewish communities were annihilated including Bilgoraj's.

———

Translator's footnotes:

1. Zolkiewka
2. Elsewhere spelled as Majzels, or Meizels.
3. Also known as Nathan Perlmutter of Shebreshin
4. Radomysl
5. Grandfather of Isaac Bashevis Singer
6. Maciejow, Ukraine
7. Krzeszow

———

HaRav HaGaon, R' Yakov Mordechai zt"l
(Served as Rabbi of Bilgoraj until the First World War)

by HaRav R' Yitzchak HaCohen Hoberman

Translated by Sara Mages

HaRav HaGaon HaTzadik, R' Yakov Mordechai son of R' Yosef and his wife Fradil, was born in the city of Mezhirichi. At that time, HaGaon HaKadosh, R' Eliezer Charlap, may his virtue stand us in good stead, who was accustomed to receiving payment for his blessings, served in the rabbinate of this city. When R' Yakov Mordechai was three years old, he asked his mother to give him a three Grosze coin and went to the aforementioned *tzadik* rabbi to receive his blessing. The *tzadik* blessed him and said that he would be a great Torah scholar and God–fearing.

HaRav HaTzadik, R' Yakov Mordechai *zt"l*, studied in his youth with a melamed [teacher] who was a Kotzker Hassid. After his marriage, this melamed was in Kotzk and the Holy Kotzker Rebbe *zt"l* asked him to think which of his students were the best, and he gave him all of them. Among them was R' Yakov Mordechai, and he praised him for being a great genius. In this conversation, the melamed told the Kotzker Rebbe *zt"l* that R' Yakov Mordechai married [the daughter] of a rich man from the city of Michov. The Rebbe sighed and said: it's a pity that he fell into a place that is not a place of Torah.

Sometime later, he came to visit his parents in Mezhirichi, and by chance, the Kotzker Rebbe was there. The Rebbe sent for him, but since he was then a great opponent of the Kotzker way, he did not want to visit the Rebbe.

And when the rabbi told me about it, he sighed and said that to this day he regrets not going to see the Kotzker Rebbe *zt"l*.

And he also told me that after his wedding, he began to behave in the ways of Hassidut and Torah with fasting and solitude, according to the customs of *tzadikim kadmonim*[1]. Since then, he found shelter with His Holiness, the *Trisker Maggid*[2], and when he was in the Beit HaMidrash with a group of yeshiva students, an old man, who he did not know, came and told him that he needed to talk to him about an important matter, and this old man said to him in these words: "If you have neglected the Torah, you shall have many who bring you to neglect it" [*Perkei Avot* 4/10], and immediately disappeared from his sight. Since then, his father–in–law, who was a very rich man, became impoverished and was no longer able to support him, and for that reason he had to take on the burden of the rabbinate. At first, he was very upset and cried when a question was brought before him, because after every ruling he was afraid that he had made a mistake in a matter of *Halacha*[3].

On his greatness in the Torah: HaRav HaGaon, R' Shneur Zalman *zt"l*, *Av Beit Din* of Kehilat Lublin, said, that in the entire district he had no one to talk to on *Divrei Torah* except for the Rabbi of Bilgoraj, and the Rabbi of Szczebrzeszyn HaRav HaGaon R' Shmuel Zak *zt"l* who was later appointed Rabbi of Biala Podlaska. In his childhood, when he studied with the Rabbi of Poritsk [R' Mordechai Mardush], author of "The Innovations of the MaHaRam Schiff," he wrote *sheelot u–teshuvot* [responsa] for the HaRav HaGaon, R' Yosef Shaul Nathansohn, which was printed in "*Avnei Nezer*" ["Stones of the Crown"] with great honor.

On 17 Tamuz 5675, the rabbi fled to Lublin after the second conquest of Bilgoraj by the Austrians. The rabbi, may his virtue stand us in good stead! died along with thousands of other Jews in the cholera epidemic that broke out throughout the area.

Translator's footnotes:

1. *Tzadikim kadmonim* – *tzadikim* (righteous) from ancient times.
2. The Trisker Maggid – Ha'Admor Rabbi Avraham Twerski, *zt"l*
3. *Halacha*, is the "way" a Jew is directed to behave in every aspect of life, encompassing civil, criminal and religious law.

[Page 9]

The Last Bilgoraj Rabbi

by Shmuel Feller

Translated by Moses Milstein

The Bilgoraj rabbi, Harav R' Mordechai Rokeach, *ztz"l*, son of the Belzer rabbi, Harav R' Issachar Dov Rokeach, *ztz"l*, and a grandson of the old Belzer rabbi, Harav R'Sholem, *ztz"l*, and also a brother of today's Belzer rabbi, *hamavdil bein chaim l'chaim*, R' Aaron Rokeach, *shlit"a*, who is in Israel today, was appointed Bilgoraj rabbi in 1927.

[Page 10]

He occupied the *kisei harabbanut* until the devastation in Poland, where he left Bilgoraj for Belz, and from there together with his brother, today's Belz rabbi, *shlit"a*, wandered from place to place including the Bochnia ghetto near Cracow, and from there, after great efforts by Hungarian Jews, headed by the Satmar rebbe, *shlit"a*, who is now in America, and also from the Sanzer rebbe's son, R' Yishayele the Tzechoiver rabbi, they succeeded in getting to Budapest, and with his brother the present Belzer rabbi, made it to Israel in the year 5704[1]. Unfortunately, after several years there, he died in the year 5710[2] leaving his second wife a widow with a child 2 years of age.[3]

The Bilgoraj rabbi was the son-in-law of the rabbi of Kobryn. After the outbreak of the war, the rebbetzin [his wife] and her child fled to her parents in Kobryn, and perished there with all the other martyrs of Kobryn.

The Bilgoraj rabbi, R' Mordechai Rokeach, *ztz"l*, was one of the most respected rabbis Bilgoraj had had in modern times. Being a son of the Belz court, he was respected by the Bilgoraj population which was made up of a lot of Belzer Chasidim. A lot of people from the surrounding area also came to Bilgoraj during the holidays. He was beloved by the Bilgoraj people, and they bought him a house near the besmedresh and the shul. There he carried out his rabbinate with dignity and a firm hand.

The Bilgoraj rabbi, as a *gaon* of Torah, had in him both *chsides* and Torah. He had a silver tongue, was a good orator, and gathered around him all levels of Bilgoraj society: Chasidim, scholars, tradesmen, and just plain Jews.

Everyone heeded him, and always found in him a counselor and a helper in all things, both in community matters and in personal matters.

In his time, many religious institutions were set up, like the three-story tall cheder building which was known throughout the whole region, and a Beit Yakov school.

[Page 11]

They were very well developed, and of a high standard, and were supported by the Vaad headed by the rabbi.

The Bilgoraj rabbi was a community leader, concerned with all the institutions in the city, a mediator between all the various parties, and remained apolitical as rabbi, so that all parties treated him with respect.

As mentioned, the Bilgoraj rav, *ztz"l*, was a great scholar, and was able to find new interpretations of complicated issues which he wrote about every day. There are a great many of his manuscripts remaining, *chidushim* on Talmud and Torah.

The Bilgoraj rebbe kept a diary of everything that happened to him every day, including during the war. He continued writing, even while he was wandering homeless, until his death. The diary is in the possession of his widow.

The surviving Bilgorajers mourn all the martyrs, and especially their unforgettable rebbe, who even in Israel headed the Bilgoraj committee, and was the driving force behind it. He concerned himself with all of the surviving Bilgorajers, and was in contact with all the Bilgoraj committees worldwide, and enjoined them to provide help for needy Bilgoraj Jews.

Even the yohrzeit for the Bilgoraj martyrs, 22 Marcheshvan, was established by his reckoning.

He died suddenly after a difficult illness, 25 Marcheshvan, 5710.[4]

Translator's footnotes:

1. 1944
2. 1949
3. Yissachar Dov Rokeach. Raised by his uncle the fourth Belzer rabbi, he became the fifth Belzer rabbi.
4. November 17, 1949

[Page 12]

Bilgoraj

by I. Ch. Kronenberg

Translated by Moses Milstein

The city of Bilgoraj resembled all the other mid-sized cities in Poland–low wooden, one-story houses, mostly with shingled roofs, surrounded by walls. The market was a large square in the center of town, surrounded on all four sides by Jewish houses and stores, the Jewish merchants in their stores waiting for customers.

Years ago, there was a city garden in the center with two pumps on the sides where the people would draw water. The market had not yet been paved, and when it rained the market became one vast mud pile in which people slopped around up to their waists.

The single pharmacy and the two optical dispensers were also found near the market.

In the middle of the market there were three rows of stores arranged like the letter, *chet*. Most of them sold salt, naphtha, and iron. There were also grain mills there. In front, in R' Shmuel Eliyahu Shwardsharf's house (the house was a gift from the governor, and later he sold half to the municipality) was city hall. Nearby was the most recently built cinema. In the middle of the "*chet*," where the garden once was, stood the firemen's tower and its siren. Every Sunday, they would conduct exercises there, and when a fire occurred in the city, this siren did indeed wail the alarm.

Most recently, a row of stores was erected right by Kosciusko Street, and these were called the Polish stores, because they were in fact all Christian stores, with the Polish co-op there as well.

[Page 13]

Behind the stores, Jewish women market merchants sat at their stalls selling all kinds of good fruits, and the Goraj *lezhelkes* the kids loved.

A little farther on, the big, strong Jewish porters sat on their wagons, ropes wound around their chests, waiting for a client. They were constantly on the lookout for wagons arriving at Yechezkel Kandel, Lippe Wakshal, and the Leichters, or trucks with goods the Bilgoraj Jews would bring from Warsaw. It was not unusual for them to sit all day with hardly anything to show for it at the end.

On the other side of the market, were the butcher shops, mostly Jewish, other than the few Christian pork butchers.

Right before WWII, they erected a row of stores opposite the butcher shops, which sold pork and beer.

Up until WWI, Bilgoraj belonged to Russia, and a division of Cossacks was quartered there, from whom Bilgoraj Jews profited handsomely.

The main street, Kosciusko, ran through the center of town. Previously it was called the Tarnogrod road, or as the Jews called it, the promenade street, where the city gardens, called the promenade gardens, were also found. It joined Pilsudski Street, previously the Zamosc road, and so it made a straight line, like a backbone the entire length of the city and stretched to the road to Tarnogrod. It had been called "the sands" for years, which signified the outskirts of the city.

[Page 14]

The market (Kaminer side and Harman side)

Pilsudski Street (Grossman's house)

[Page 14 (sic)]

All kinds of stories were told about "the sands," as if they were at the ends of the world. People were afraid to walk there alone. Cheder kids who lived there would not go to cheder in the evening, or the melamed would accompany them with a lantern. It was also where the Cossacks were quartered.

Later, beautiful, tall houses were built there, the city *electravnyeh* with its beautiful plaza, where Jewish youth would enjoy themselves until late into the night. It was also the site of the kolejka[1] which took people to the wide-gauge railroad in Zwierzyniec.

* * *

Bilgoraj had a beautiful, calm river, which snaked lazily along the entire length of the city, with green meadows and trees on both banks of the river whose willow branches were used for Hoshana Rabah. The nearby neighbors would wash their dishes after meals, and do their laundry there. There were three good places on the river to bathe: the so-called "cut-off river," Lasse-Guri, and the "hut river." There it was very deep, and only good swimmers bathed there. People would enjoy the warm summer days at the river.

The sole two Jewish millers also used the river to power their mills.

And although Bilgoraj had a river, nevertheless divorces were not permitted in Bilgoraj. This was because Tsar Nicolai had the notion to change the name of the river, which ended up being called the Lada. (According to the laws, a divorce can only go ahead in a place by a river with a definite name). And as a result of this, Bilgoraj couples rarely divorced, because on their way to Goraj to get a divorce, they often made up, and returned in harmony.

Bilgoraj had no water management. There were pumps which provided plenty of water, but for tea water, people went to Yishaye Nuteh's pump, even in the depths of winter.

[Page 15]

Every Friday, it was the scene of a big line up and arguments. Erev Pesach, you could see men in satin *kapotes*, with basins in their hands, getting matzah water. (*Mayim shelanu*). People would also get tea water at the well near the river. Women believed the well water was a good treatment for eye problems. Women also used it to wash their hair.

The sport grounds were also near the river. Competitions between Jewish and Christian clubs took place there, as well as games between only Jewish teams. Near the sport grounds was the tennis area.

* * *

The bridge street (Lubelski) was completely Jewish, and even the few Christians who lived there could speak Yiddish just like Jews. All the houses on the street were low wooden houses, with shingled roofs. It was densely populated; families with many children in one small room. Almost all of the poverty in Bilgoraj was found by the bridge. The women did their work sitting on the stoops of their houses.

The side streets of the bridge, the so-called *Zabashta*, were where only poor working people lived. It was so densely inhabited that it felt like one vast room. Wagons, horses, chickens, goats with long beards, wandered among the children. At any moment, a child whose small piece of bread was snatched by a goat could be heard to cry, quickly followed by the mother wielding her broom. But the goat could defiantly stand his ground, brandishing his horns ready for combat, and the mother would have no choice but to withdraw.

A lot of the sieve workers lived there.

[Page 16]

All the women workers would sit outside and thread the hairs. The high-pitched screams of the children, and the racket from the mothers went on all day. But when night came it became deadly quiet, dark so deep that you couldn't see anyone. Many houses didn't even have electric lights, only the glow from lanterns through fogged up windows lit the darkness.

And when it rained it became a circus. It was simply impossible to walk there. More than one person left their galoshes in the mud there, and barely made it out alive.

In the winter, when the big frosts came, it got busy there. All day long, the peasants brought wood for the Jewish wood merchants at their places near the kolejka station. At night, the children from all over the city would come there with their sleds, and slide down the hill that was the bridge street. When one sled collided with another, and both capsized, you could hear the shouts and laughter carrying far.

More than one carriage driver would become a victim of this. A gang would steal his sled, and in the morning, it would be found broken in pieces.

Erev Pesach, when the women took to whitewashing the rooms, everything was carried out to the street. Old cupboards, wooden beds stood outside. The women kept on pouring naphtha on everything. The bedding was arrayed on the chairs, and beaten with a wooden paddle to get the dust out.

The women, smeared with whitewash, their heads covered with kerchiefs, would polish the windows, wash the floors, hang up the sheets, all requiring great effort, and every house would acquire a *yomtovdik* appearance.

[Page 17]

The Bilgoraj river and beach

The *starostva* building (an additional story was added later)

[Page 17 (sic)]

It was truly a wonder how a poor Jewish woman could manage to expel the disorder of winter, and bring a little light into the small rooms.

The bridge street was lively on Rosh Hashanah. The whole city went to the river singing to perform *Tashlich*, and the residents around the bridge used to stand by their houses, dressed in their holiday best, and greeted the crowds with celebration.

* * *

Bilgoraj's forest was renowned throughout the region. It was rich in blueberries, *valakhes*, mushrooms, and burdock. The forest reached practically to the city and stretched from Janow to Zamosc.

The road into the forest was Pilsudski Street (Zamosc). It was an avenue with trees on both sides. Young people would gather there until late at night. Couples in love would sit there and dream about their happy future. The singing of the young people could be heard in the whole city.

The forest was a place of great enjoyment for Bilgoraj residents. The pleasant dry air of the pine trees, and the chirping of the birds carried to the whole city. Shabbes, the forest was full. Almost the entire town's Jews were there. You could even encounter pious Jews, kerchiefs around their necks, bringing along a small child to carry a religious book (because the forest was outside the *tkhum*[2]), lying at ease on the soft earth, looking into a religious book, and partaking of a Shabbes nap.

The younger people would take walks through the forest, often going to Wola where there was a big Jewish sawmill, and then come through the Bagner forest where the small mill was which also belonged to Jews.

Translator's footnotes:

1. Narrow gauge railroad
2. The distance (about 2/3 of a mile) observant Jews must not exceed on Shabbes when walking out of town.

[Page 18]

The Synagogue Courtyard

by A. Kronenberg

Translated by Moses Milstein

The spiritual center of Yiddishkeit, the shul courtyard, stood at the beginning of the bridge street.

To the left of the entrance was the besmedresh, the most beloved and cherished place for Bilgoraj Jews.

Come evening, Bilgoraj Jews dropped everything and went to the besmedresh to get in a *kedushah v'borchu*. Many arrived a little early, looked into a religious text, some studying a chapter of Mishnah, or *Ein Yakov*. On the other side, men stood around R' Pinchas listening to the news and politics as he read from the daily newspaper.

Seated around the tables, young men facing open Talmuds and Gemaras studied with a ringing, sweet Gemara rhythm that carried through the whole besmedresh, until late at night.

Whenever the *magid*[1], R' Baruch-Tebl, came to town, the shul would fill up with people from all the besmedreshim come to hear him. The audience loved his sermons and parables about the coming of the messiah, who, he demonstrated via various verses of scripture and gematria, was just about on the outskirts of the city.

Between the two tables, R' Mordechai-Yosef stood at his lectern, his face covered by a red kerchief, reading a holy text, making all kinds of gestures, deep in kabbalah. Suddenly, he would raise his heavy cane and start to bang on the lectern shouting, "Gevalt, it's burning." Until a large crowd gathered. Then he would shout even louder, "Gevalt, it's burning," Women are walking around with short sleeves. These alarms over the "fires," he tended to repeat regularly.

[Page 19]

Near the oven, the paupers sat and counted over the day's earnings. Some would be eating dry bread and herring for supper, telling tales from their wanderings through cities and shtetls, and which housewife gave better meals.

By the door, R' Wolf stood with a basket containing: frozen apples, *banikers*, *nont*, hot peas and *brikev*, surrounded by children all shouting at once, "R' Wolf give me, R' Wolf, give me some."

In the besmedresh house (in *Pulish* as it was called) was the tailors shul. In truth, they never davened there. But on Simchat Torah they would do the *hakofes* over there. (Of course, before the little besmedresh was built, they used to daven there, and it became the custom for them to do the *hakofes* over there).

Over on the right, stood the newly built, five story, city cheder, *Zichron Yakov v'Beit Moishe*. (Named after the penultimate Bilgoraj rebbe, R' Yakov Mordechai, *ztz"l*, and the Bilgoraj benefactor in America, R' Moishe Frost, *z"l*).

The cheder was highly esteemed in the whole region. The children sat in nice, comfortable rooms, under the management of a *vaad* on which the Bilgoraj rebbe, R' Mordechai Rokeach sat, *ztz"l*, and under the supervision of the *menahel*, a big scholar.

In order to avoid having to send the children to a government school, which was compulsory, they arranged an agreement with the government to recognize the cheder. Government teachers would come to the cheder and teach the Polish language.

[Page 21 (sic)]

On the top, on the last floor, was the kehila office where the *dozors* used to conduct their meetings and attended to all the needs of the city.

A little further, on the same side, was the little besmedresh, in front a carved *oren kodesh* with a velvet curtain, a *balemer*[2], ringed by pews below, a gift from the great Bilgoraj philanthropist and community activist, R' Shmuel Eliyahu Shwerdsharf, *z"l*. He even bequeathed several stores in the market as charitable endowments so that the revenue could support the besmedresh. Almost all the tradesmen in the city davened there including: tailors, shoemakers, sieve workers, blacksmiths, millers, carriage drivers, butchers, and just plain Jews.

Every evening, after a hard workday, the tradesmen would hurry to finish their work a little early in order to get to the besmedresh and get in a few chapters of psalms before Minche-Maariv.

Friday night, after supper, the whole crowd would get together in the little besmedresh to study Chumash with Rashi with R' Hersheleh Melamed who explained things with very nice examples that gave them much pleasure. They would study until late into the night, and more than a few, tired after a week of hard work, would fall asleep. Afterwards, everyone went home happy.

Opposite the little besmedresh, on a little hill, the city shul stood with its beautiful four-cornered tall building. While the shul was being built, R' Shmuel Eliyahu Shwerdsharf, who had received a diamond ring from Kaiser Nicolai, brought over the governor of Lublin to lay the first stone with a silver trowel.

[Page 22]

The entrance to the shul was through two, wide, doors with colored panes, an inscription in golden letters, "*Ma tovu ohalecha Yaakov, mishkinotecha, Israel.*" Near the door, in a hollow in the wall, was the *Kupat Rambam* where the Bilgoraj Jews would deposit coins for Eretz Israel. There were large, round, windows with stained glass and a Star of David in the middle on all sides of the shul. On the eastern wall, from floor to ceiling was the beautiful, carved, oren kodesh with various animals and inscriptions, and a Leviathan with its tail in its mouth. Children worried that the tail might slip out of its mouth and devastate the world. Older Jews would lick their lips imagining a piece of it. Above, the tablets were inscribed with the Ten Commandments, and a Torah crown. The ark was covered by a beautiful plush curtain donated by various tradesmen.

The walls were covered with paintings from the Tanach from the old days. On the high round ceiling the 12 signs of the zodiac were painted. In the middle, with stairs leading up to it, was the Torah reading area, and Eliyahu's chair which was sometimes used for a bris.

The ner tamid made of several pieces of stained glass, hung at the entrance of the shul, and the women's shul occupied two sides.

Erev Yom Kippur, the whole city gathered at the rebbe's house near the shul yard, Jews in their socks, wearing taliss and *kitl*[3], women carrying *machzors* and *tkhines*, their heads covered by white, silk shawls, wishing each other *ketivah v' chatima tovah*, and the sobbing that could be heard throughout the whole city.

When the rebbe, dressed in white, his head covered by his taliss, left the *beis din* house, which was packed full with people, all those gathered there flocked after him.

[Page 23]

The rabbi entered with quick steps and right at the threshold, he began, "*Or zaruah latzadik, uleyishrei lev simcha.*"[4]

The shul was full to overflowing with people praying. The dancing flames of the candles reached to the ceiling along with the prayers, and the congregation stood in fear and davened.

Many Christians came to shul for kol nidrei, and listened to the prayers with great respect.

The shul was festive on Simchat Torah. Almost the whole city, men and women, came to shul to see the rebbe perform the *hakofes*, and dancing went on until late at night.

When there was a wedding in the city, the shul became the scene for celebration. The in-laws would dance with candles in their hands, accompanying the bride and groom to the chupah right in front of the shul doors.

The shul cost a lot of money to build, and was the jewel of the city. It was renowned in the whole region.

Hard by the wall of the shul was the site of the first Bilgoraj cemetery. Understandably, it was then on the outskirts of the city. Two gravestones remained, but they are illegible. The cemetery was overgrown with grass and goats grazed there. On the side, stood a single tree looking exactly as if it had been left there to stand guard. Children used to say that once, when a branch was broken, a voice was heard–don't tear out my beard–a sign that a great tzadik had been buried there.

[Page 24]

Further down the shul courtyard were the bathhouse and the mikvah. It was the only bathhouse in the city and belonged to the Jewish community. A bath-goy was always employed there. He would turn the wheel when water was needed, and guard the Yom Kippur lights in the besmedreshim, and sell the *chametz* Erev Pesach.

Erev Yom Kippur, the bathhouse was full. After soaking in the mikvah, people hurried off, stopping at all the *tzedakah pushkes* arrayed in the shul yard, putting something in each, and then entering with great zeal, the besmedreshim.

Erev Pesach, the bath was thronged. Children came with baskets full of new utensils to dunk in the mikvah, or to kosher older items in the bathhouse oven.

Just before the last world war, a slaughterhouse for poultry was built in the shul yard, concentrating all the religious activities in one place.

* * *

The second cemetery, which was near Eliezer Mitzner, was once surrounded by a wooden fence. When the fence collapsed, the city wanted to expropriate a piece of the cemetery in order to straighten the road. The Jews were not in favor of this, and there began a series of legal trials between city hall and the community. Not having any choice, the entire Jewish community turned out one night, and overnight, rebuilt the wall with red brick. It became an established fact, and remained so. In the cemetery there were wooden and stone gravestones, completely overgrown with moss, over 200 years old.

[Page 25]

The latest cemetery was on "the sands," far away from town, surrounded by a stone wall, and full of tall trees with black crows' nests. The crows would open their mouths and shriek and their calls echoed far and wide. There were always people in the cemetery whether for a yorzeit, or, in a time of trouble, praying for a sick person. People used to end up at the *oyhel*[5] which was full of *kvitlach*, light a candle, weep bitter tears, sneak out furtively, pick something up from the ground then throw it back, wash their hands and leave with a lighter heart.

The cemetery guard was a Christian who lived by the entrance. Every Friday he would go around the city collecting challahs which he was given with due respect.

* * *

Up until WWI, Bilgoraj was isolated from the rest of the world around it. There was no train. The only communication was via coach (closed carriages) pulled by three or four horses. They drove along unpaved roads until Rejowiec, and from there on by train. A trip like this to Warsaw could take three or more weeks. It was not unusual for a horse to give out in the middle of the journey, and another have to be found, and this at the expense of the travellers. A trip like this was also dangerous, because there were frequent attacks by bandits on travellers. People would return from such trips *bentching goyml*[6]. For that reason all the besmedreshes had panels hanging with the *goyml* blessings displayed.

Even the mail was delivered by wagons guarded by soldiers. Arriving in the city, they would sound the trumpet informing everyone that the mail had arrived, later to be delivered by letter carriers.

[Page 26]

In WWI when Bilgoraj was occupied by the Austrians, a small gauge railway was built to connect to Zwierzyniec and from there to Rejowiec.

As a result, Bilgoraj developed a broader connection with the surrounding world. The whole transport lumber business went by this small train. Up to the outbreak of WWII, Bilgoraj had an extensive network of bus connections to the surrounding cities and shtetls.

Until recently, information was communicated through town criers banging on a drum. Kasibucki went around banging his big drum until a large crowd gathered. Then he put on his glasses, read out the news from a paper, adding his own comments that the crowd very much enjoyed.

Translator's footnotes:

1. Itinerant preacher
2. Reading desk from which the Torah is read
3. long white linen coat worn on holidays
4. Light is sown for the righteous, and gladness for the upright in heart
5. Monument over the gravestone of important figure
6. Blessing said in the synagogue after escaping great danger

[Page 29]

Trade and Industry

The Lumber Business

by Sh. Y. Shper

Translated by Moses Milstein

The Bilgoraj region contained enormous areas of forest that went from Krzeszow to Janow. There was Krasnik, which belonged to Count Zamoyski, and many state–owned forests. Many forests also belonged to peasants who had been given them by "servitude." (The czar, Alexander II, who was very liberal, abolished the "*panszczyzna*[1]" where the peasants were obligated to work for the noblemen. The czar issued a "*ukas*[2]" whereby every peasant would receive 24 acres of land, and a portion of forest. This was called "servitude.") In 1918, after the establishment of the Polish government, parts of the forestlands were distributed to the peasants. This led to the formation of a significant lumber business in Bilgoraj.

The lumber business had been in existence for many years, and was exclusively in Jewish hands. At the top, there were large Jewish firms such as: Harman, Honigboim, Shper, Arbesfeld, and Hirschenhorn.

One of the first lumber merchants was R' Shmuel Eliyahu Shwerdsharf, *z"l*, who used to sell lumber to Danzig. He also had properties of his own, and many woodlots near Frampol which he sold in his later years to Endleman of Warsaw, and finally, they were sold again to Falik Fabricant.

Back then, there was no train service in Bilgoraj, and all the lumber was transported by water.

[Page 30]

In summer, the lumber was hauled by wagons, and in winter by sleighs, to the village of Harasiuki by the river Tanew. (It led to a larger river). The wood was transferred to the river and floated to the river San until Ulanow via Krzeszow. There the lumber was collected, and rafts were made on which people sat and guided them to the Vistula, and with the Vistula to Danzig. The journey took a long time, and was beset with various dangers.

Later, before World War I, in 1901, the German company, Franka, came to Bilgoraj and bought large sections of forest from Count Zamoyski. (According to Russian law, a German company could not be involved. So all the business was carried out in the name of R' Itzi Flamenboim, who was employed by the company). They hired many people, among them Jews like Yechezkel Arbesfeld who was called Yechezkel the German's. He later became a big lumber merchant himself.

In those days, a terrible thing occurred. In 1913, before Pesach, Moishe Edelshtein, an employee of Franka, tried to cross the river which was in flood. The bridge in Osuchy was covered in water, and he fell into the river and drowned. His body could not be found. His parents sought out rabbis who proposed the following remedy: They were to get a loaf of bread, place a lit candle in it, and put it in a skiff, and launch it in the river.

[Page 31]

Where the skiff stops, the drowned man will be found. After lengthy searches he was found.

At the outbreak of World War I, the Franka company was liquidated. All the German employees returned to Germany. It was later rumored that the company had been established for espionage purposes.

After World War I, the lumber business came back to life. Rich Jewish merchants bought up large tracts of forest from the state and from Count Zamoyski. They produced various kinds of building materials and railroad ties. The peasants from the surrounding villages were employed, some as carpenters, some as foremen in the transportation of the lumber.

After working with the wood, the merchants sold it to large firms, or to the state for railroad ties. A lot of wood was also exported outside the country.

There were a lot of small–scale merchants who used to buy a few trees from a peasant's servitude, turn them lumber products, and sell them to the bigger merchants in town.

The frosts of winter were a time of great activity in the lumber business. Only sleighs could get to the trees. They prepared the wood, and then brought it out from the forests to the Jewish merchants who had places at the "Rapa station."

From there, the wood was loaded onto wagons and carried to the train at Zwierzyniec.

[Page 32]

The porters (*grustchikes*) who loaded the wood on the trains were also Jews.

There were also merchants who had wood sawed at the two Jewish sawmills. One was Sharf's steam mill, and the other, Grinapple, in *der kleiner volyeh*[3].

A tragic event took place in Bilgoraj that upset the entire community. A small merchant, Fuchs, had purchased a few trees from some peasants. When the time came for them to bring the wood to him, they failed to appear. So he went off to see them and demand either the wood, or his money back. The peasants, wishing to rid themselves of this problem, lured him into the woods, ostensibly to show him other trees for sale, and killed him there. When he failed to return, the police were summoned, and an investigation was begun. Then the antisemitic city notary butted in, and stated that the Jews were instigating a libel against the peasants, and that he himself had seen Fuchs in Warsaw. The murderer was later captured, and the peasants who confessed were sentenced severely.

Translator's footnotes:

1. Feudal service, corvée
2. Decree
3. Probably the nearby village of "Wola Mala" which means "little Wola" in Polish

————————

[Page 35]

The Netting[1] Business
A Bilgoraj Industry Specialty

by M. Tayer

Translated by Moses Milstein

The exact date when the netting business developed in Bilgoraj is not known, but Bilgoraj is recorded as the city of netting in the oldest historical records of the city.

In this, Bilgoraj distinguished itself from other cities. It was the only city with this reputation, not just in Poland, but also in Europe.

Until the First World War, the industry was based entirely on hairnets, and the only market was in Czarist Russia.

With the outbreak of World War I, and later, with the establishment of the government of Poland, the Russian market was cut off. It was widely believed that this would mean the end of the business.

People who had supported themselves in this industry quickly began to look for other employment. But this situation did not last long. The dynamism of the netting workers did not permit resignation. The expertise of generations could not be allowed to die.

After the end of World War I, the pioneers of this industry applied their whole energy and boldness to innovations in the trade. They acquired new markets, developed new networks, many times larger, broader and more diversified.

[Page 36]

The industry grew in two different directions: One division organized and developed the internal Polish market. Taking part were: Michal Tayer, *z"l*, (died in Russia), Abraham Harman (in Israel today), the Shier family, *z"l*, (perished in Bilgoraj), and others.

They didn't restrict themselves to just hairnets. They organized and developed a very diversified wire–ware business, on a large scale, that overshadowed the earlier netting production. They produced wire–ware of many different sorts and designs from screens to fences, and to building materials, and to the finest weaves, as well as various filters from copper wire, as well as hairnets.

This production enabled Bilgoraj to become the biggest player in the Polish market. Hundreds of Jews and Christians from the area were employed.

A second, quite separate, part was involved in developing the export market for hairnets. These were: Arish Zilberberg, *z"l*, (died in Bilgoraj), Moishe Weissman, *z"l*, (died in Lemberg), and Zev Tuchman (in Israel today). They developed a big business in exporting hairnets to Europe and elsewhere.

With every year, they acquired new markets in different countries.

Several hundred families, exclusively Jewish, were employed by, and drew their livelihood from, the production of nets for export.

[Page 37]

In 1930, a new branch was developed, a spin–off from the netting line of activity. This was the use of horsehair bristles, so called "*wlosienka*[2]." The organizers of this branch were Avigdor Levinkop, and Moishe Tayer (both in Israel). This branch innovated and grew, finding markets all over Poland. The Bilgoraj *wlosienka* was renowned in the Polish market for its quality.

Hundreds of people, Jews and Christians, were employed in this activity as it grew every year.

A separate branch consisted of dozens of families involved in collecting the raw material (horsehair). Employed in this were the Schnitzer brothers, *z"l*, the Korn family, *z"l*, the Shper brothers, *z"l*, and others (all perished). They used to travel to the bigger cities to procure the hair, clean it, and prepare it for weaving.

There was also a group that was occupied in making violin bows. (*Smitskes*). Involved in this were Berish Feder (in America today), and Eliyahu Dorfman (died in Russia). The products were used in Polish markets, or exported.

The mesh/netting concept in Bilgoraj represented a major creative activity, a broad, diversified important undertaking, which benefited the city and the milieu.

[Page 38]

The brutal eruption of the German volcano whose fiery lava brought death and destruction to Europe, along with the total annihilation of European Jewry, also eradicated this beautifully developed tree and its branches, and tore it out by its roots.

———

Translator's footnotes:

1.   Yiddish "*zip*" translates as sieve, filter, screen, net, mesh. Considering the uses described in the article, it would appear that all the definitions describe the industry in Bilgoraj.
2.   Possibly "haircloth" used in textiles primarily as interlining.

———

[Page 39]

The Jewish Printing Shop

by A. Kronenberg

Translated by Moses Milstein

In 1906, the large print shop owned by R' Nuteh Kronenberg in Piotrkow was moved to Bilgoraj.

Before WW I, Bilgoraj was under Russian administration, and the print shop used to print books for rabbis in all of Tsarist Russia. All kinds of books: *machzors*, *chumashes*, and religious books, as well as secular books. The print shop employed several scores of workers.

Some of the workers in the print shop

With the outbreak of WW I, and the occupation by Austria, all life came to a standstill, including the big Jewish printing business. But this situation did not last long.

[Page 40]

Things began to normalize, and the print shop quickly established contact with the large Jewish publishing houses like: Yosef Schlesinger in Vienna; Simche Freund in Przemysl who had begun to work with religious books such as *siddurs*, *chumashes*, *selichos*, *kinos*, and others. The print shop began to operate on all cylinders, employed many workers, and grew from year to year.

Because of its printing business, Bilgoraj became known worldwide. If someone said to a stranger that they were from Bilgoraj, they would immediately respond, "Ah, the big Jewish printers."

There was virtually no place in Europe or America where the print shop did not have contacts with publishers or with rabbis.

After the establishment of Poland, the print shop came into contact with the big "Shtibl" publishing house in Berlin that had opened a division in Warsaw. The publisher printed hundreds of translations of the best books, as well as the originals–all in Hebrew. They went so far as to send a proofreader to Bilgoraj in order to avoid any delays with the mail.

The print shop had relationships with all the Jewish booksellers in the country and abroad, such as: Central Kletzkin, Gitlin, Cohen and Freid, Munkatch, and others. A large part of Sh. L. Gordon's Tanach was printed in Bilgoraj.

[Page 41]

Rabbis from the whole world had their books printed in Bilgoraj: HaRav Babad, Tarnopol; HaRav Ferlav, Belchow; HaRav Horowitz, Stanislaw; HaRav Michelson, Warsaw; HaRav Levine, Ruszow; HaRav Eiges, Vilna; HaRav Gutman, Romania (in Israel today); HaRav Met, London; HaRav Kalenberg, Metz; HaRav Resnick, Rochester, N.Y.; HaRav Emile, Antwerp (died in Israel); HaRav Dr. Klein, Nuremberg; (when Hitler came to power, he came to Bilgoraj, today in Israel); HaRav Leiter, Vienna; and others.

Another group of workers

In 1923, on a market Thursday, the *Chafetz Chaim*[1], *z"l*, paid a special visit to Bilgoraj to print his book "*Mishnah Berurah*." Friday morning, he asked R' Nuteh Kronenberg, *z"l*, to find him a *minyan* for Shabbes so he could daven early as was his custom. But with one stipulation–that he not reveal that he, the *Chafetz Chaim*, was here in Bilgoraj.

[Page 42]

Being such a humble person, he did not want any special recognition. But the news spread lightening fast through the city. Friday evening, and Shabbes, the whole town turned out for the *davening*, and the Shabbes feasting.

Saturday night people streamed in with *kvitlech*[2], but he refused them all saying he was just an ordinary Jew like any other.

In the middle of the night, he was heard calling R' Hillel (his son–in–law who accompanied him) and discussing learning.

His departure was accompanied by everyone in the whole city, pious or freethinking. They carried him to the *kolejka*[3] in their arms. Going through the Christian streets he was greeted with respectful looks.

Bilgoraj had the honor of hosting the big *gaon* of the last generation.

Later the print shop published itself under the name "*Main*," and issued dozens of religious books, including the well–known siddur, "Beit HaOtsar," put together by the owner, R' Nuteh Kronenberg, *z"l*. The company bought the rights to the book, "*HaElef Lecha Shlomo*," from R' Shlomo Kluger, *z"l*, which was printed in the thousands. The company carried on extensive work and commerce with its own books throughout the world.

The print shop and the book business became very developed and grew steadily. It employed agents who travelled all across Poland selling its books. It became a member of the chamber of commerce in Lublin, for engaging in foreign trade that the Polish government was then strongly supporting. The government gave large incentives for companies that brought in foreign currency.

[Page 43]

The first work, under the name of *Salamandra*, by Isaac Bashevis Singer, who was a grandson of the old Bilgoraj rebbe, and who lived in Bilgoraj for a lengthy period, was also printed in the large Jewish print shop of R' Nuteh Kronenberg, *z"l*.

A group of print company workers, at the end worked in Lemberg

At the outbreak of WW II, some of the type and machinery were buried in the print shop yard, and remained there, undisturbed by anybody. What was not buried, including all the typefaces, worth tens of thousands of zlotys, was destroyed by the German murderers.

[Page 44]

After the war, and the establishment of a new Polish government, a Jewish official, T. I., who had worked in the print shop, went back to Bilgoraj, dug everything up, brought it to Warsaw, and it became the first kernel of a new Jewish newspaper in Poland, "*Dos Nayeh Lebn.*"

And so, R' Nuteh Kronenberg and his great work, the Jewish printing industry, which was renowned world wide, and the Jewish community of Bilgoraj, came to an end.

In more recent times, the brothers, Shlomo and Israel Weinberg opened a print shop that also developed ties with the wider world.

The Mistake

In 1913, the Malkiner rebbe, who was printing his book, "*Oz B'yad*," came to Bilgoraj. As he descended from the carriage which had brought him from Rejowiec, and just as he was coming into the print shop, the head–quartermaster, Meyerbrodi, showed up. He was there to arrest the rebbe. (Because there was already an atmosphere of war. They were looking for spies). They quickly ran to get Sholem Yosel's (Hoichman), who was the petition writer for all government affairs. Mayerbrodi searched the rebbe, and found many manuscripts, a printed Western Wall (*mizrech*)[4], receipts for money collected for *Kupat Rambam*, and a letter from his brother in America. When Mayerbrodi asked him who the letter was from, the rebbe, not knowing any Russian said, "My brother." The quartermaster interrupted,

"How does he know my name is Mayerbrodi?" (To him, *mein bruder* sounded like Mayerbrodi), and he concluded that he was a spy, and the Western Wall print was a map.

With large "*protektsieh*" he was released. They confiscated all his "spy" documents like the *mizrech*, receipts for *Kupat Rambam*, his brother's letter, and his books. They sent everything away to Lublin to the censor. A while later, the rebbe received all his documents back, and the police apologized.

The Test

Out of the blue, the print shop received a letter from a Dr. B in Lemberg asking us to undertake several large projects for him. We took the dawn train, went to Lemberg, and arrived at the address given. At the residence, a Jew with a long beard and curly *payes* answered the door and asked us in.

Soon Dr. B came in and proposed a large quantity of work, on the condition that each work had to be ready at a predetermined time or the print shop would have to pay a given penalty.

The manuscript soon arrived, and when the work was begun it became clear that this was missionary literature. R'Nuteh Kroeneberg took the manuscript to the rebbe, and it was decided not to publish the book.

When the predetermined time period passed without the book having been printed, a letter promptly arrived from a lawyer demanding the penalty money stipulated in the agreement.

R' Nuteh Kronenebrg, as a religious Jew, resisted the temptation and chose to pay the penalty rather than to print the missionary material.

————

Translator's footnotes:

    1.   Rabbi Israel Meir Kagan
    2.   Petitions presented to a rabbi
    3.   Small gauge railway
    4.   An image showing East

————

[Page 47]

A Market Day

by A. Kronenberg

Translated by Moses Milstein

Thursday. Though still dark out, the farmers from the nearby villages are already arriving at the market, their wagons filled with all sorts of things. Some come to buy, and some to sell.

A farmer dragging a cow or a pig on a rope walks slowly along. Behind him, his wife carries a pack on her back with things to sell in the city–chickens, eggs, butter, flax. She wears a bottle on a string to bring back things for the home, naphtha, salt, and other trifles.

The traffic was so great that the streets simply couldn't handle it. The market was so packed with carriages and people that, to the on–looker, everything blended into one black mass.

Jews came from neighboring cities–second–hand clothes tailors, hat makers, shoemakers, haberdashers–because the market was a significant source of business for the Jews. Everyone set up his stall in the places he had rented from the city. More than once, arguments broke out about someone's stall encroaching on another's spot.

Later, when there was no more room in the market, the farmers would set up in the streets around the market.

Jewish horse merchants would try out the horses on the street near the apothecary.

[Page 48]

In negotiating a price they would slap each other's hands. With each slap, one went up and one went down. The slapping went on and on until they reached a deal.

A market day with city hall in the center

The butchers also walked around among the farmers buying cattle to provide meat for Bilgoraj. (In most recent times, the city council moved the horse and cattle market near the mountain).

The noise in the market was so great that you couldn't hear yourself speak.

[Page 49]

The cries of the geese, chickens, ducks and turkeys were deafening. The women went from one farmer to the other looking for bargains, something for Shabbes, and for the rest of the week. Women farmers stood along the sides of the streets with fresh tubs of butter calling for buyers.

Market days were the hardest for the women–carrying a basket of apples, or pears, a fat goose, several chickens, a sack of potatoes. Not to mention erev yom tov, when they simply collapsed after a whole day of shlepping the stuff around.

The Jewish shops were full of farmers, men and women, who bought all kinds of things: boots, suits, dresses, kerchiefs, hats, and scarves for the children.

Every so often a clang echoed through the air as a farmer tested a strongbox at the Jewish iron monger's, or when a bar of iron was cut to fix a wagon.

In the evening, after they had sold their products, or horses or cows, they visited the Jewish taverns like those of Yankel Sender, Yechiel Gershon, Fishl Kalmenovitch, and got down to drinking. The noise and the smell of the beer which drifted out the open windows was enough to make passers–by drunk.

[Page 50]

Often, when the farmers got drunk, they got robbed of all their goods, and after they sobered up, they looked around and realized they had neither the cow nor the money.

And every Thursday we would hear the shouts of the drunk farmers going home until late into the night.

*

The wheat business supported quite a few families in Bilgoraj. The whole business was in Jewish hands. There were big Jewish wheat merchants: Hershele Sheinwald, Shabach Wermut and others who dealt with wagonloads of wheat. They would buy it from the gentry and mill it in the two Jewish mills. They would sell the flour in the stores, or elsewhere in the province.

There were also small–scale merchants who bought wheat from the farmers at the markets in the nearby towns, and sold it to the bigger merchants.

*

Bilgoraj was surrounded by fields and so a big egg business developed in Bilgoraj. There were big egg merchants like Stoll, Kleinmintz and others who used to export wagonloads of eggs throughout the whole country, and abroad. There were also small merchants who bought eggs at the markets and sold them to bigger dealers.

*

[Page 51]

The merchants, Stoll and Leiter, who dealt in hemp, flax, and linen, would buy the merchandise from the farmers mostly at the markets, and a lot also from Jews who traded in the villages. It was later sorted and packed into bales and exported to the rest of the country and abroad.

*

The big stores, like Wagschall and Leichter's, served the whole city and the province, and were always full of customers. You had to wait for hours until you got your turn.

*

Third of May Street was always full of carriages coming to buy from the wholesalers Kandl and Schlafrack: flour, naphtha, herring and salt.

*

The larger wholesale stores, I. Gerstenblit, (iron), H. Leichter, Hirschman, Groisman and others (manufacture), who used to provide goods for Bilgoraj were always full of customers.

*

All the stores in Bilgoraj were in Jewish hands–manufacture, iron, sewing goods, grocery, food, radio (Lang, Teneholz), bicycles (Feder), guesthouses, (G. Grosman, Furer).

*

There were two soda water factories in Bilgoraj. Sholom Rofer (he was also the only seller of hides), and the Boims. They provided a cold drink on hot summer days. It was also the only place where you could get some ice for a sick person.

[Page 52]

The only candy factory in Bilgoraj, on a small scale–where kids used to come to lick the syrup in the jars–was owned by Itzik–Leib Olive.

*

The three mills in Bilgoraj were all Jewish owned. The big water mill that used to belong to Shmuel Worman, was later bought by Hershele Sheinwald. He used to mill wheat for all the merchants and was a big flour merchant himself. Other grains were also milled.

The mill was known in the whole region for the quality of its flour.

The steam mill and its sawmill, which belonged to the Sharfs, used to mill flour for the flour merchants, and also for the farmers in the surrounding area.

The sawmill was always busy sawing wood for the wood merchants and the nearby farmers.

The "little mill," which had previously belonged to the Sharfs before they constructed the steam mill, was bought by the widow Silberfein. It was mostly used by the farmers.

*

The big Jewish sawmill in *der kleiner volyeh*[1] owned by Grinapple, who was a big lumber merchant himself, used to cut boards for others and for farmers.

*

[Page 53]

The two oil factories in Bilgoraj, Y. Grinapple, Shulman, produced various oils, and were Jewish owned.

There were a few hand–operated kasha mills, also Jewish.

*

The one brick factory that supplied Bilgoraj with bricks was owned by Yotze Weintraub.

*

The only lottery ticket sellers, Gergstein, Y. Leichter, and Kalikstein were Jewish. Three Bilgoraj Jews did actually win big.

*

The fish business was in Jewish hands, The fish merchants would buy fish from the wealthy farmer, Czwikla, who had his own ponds near the brick works. On a hot summer Shabbes, Bilgoraj Jews would come to the ponds to enjoy themselves.

Early Friday morning, the fish sellers were already set up with their fish. Fish sellers from nearby towns also came to the market. The shouts–Ladies, wonderful fish for shabbes–used to carry over the whole market.

*

Friday, while still dark, you could hear the voice of Abraham–Itshe the butcher, and the clatter of his wheels on the stone bridge echoing through the empty market, bringing meat for all the butchers.

[Page 54]

The butchers, with their broad stately beards, stood by the chopping blocks, and sliced pieces from the hanging meat. The shouts of the butchers–Ladies, cheap — ladies, a zloty a kilo — ladies, *kapital*–seemed to work, and the women came and bought.

*

While it was still dark outside, the Bilgoraj *dorf geyers*[2] would head out, a sack on their back, and a stick in their hand to ward off the dogs. Each had his villages, and familiar relationships with the farmers from whom he regularly purchased things. It was not unusual for them to trudge around all day, and have little to show for it coming home in the evening.

*

When the grey dawn had relieved the darkness that had enveloped the city, the clang of tin cans was heard all over the city. The milkmen were on their way to the villages for the milking. A door would open, a sleepy face would peer out, look around, and empty a basin, and cover half the street with it.

Coming back with the milk they pass men in *taliss* and *tefillin* on their way to *daven*. They greet them with a hearty good morning.

[Page 55]

The milkmen bring the milk to the houses. In every house they stop and chat about what the farmers are saying, and to brag that their milk is the most kosher.

The milkmen provided Bilgoraj with kosher milk, never being late for a milking.

*

Saturday night, after Havdalah, the agents are already at work making lists, orders for what the Bilgoraj merchants might need. Agents like Feivish Weissman, Pintche Farshtendig, Leibl Feifer, Yokl Bekelman, Mendl Shatz, Ch. G. Eilboim, and Berl Bergerfreund. Every minute the door opens, and a storekeeper comes in and says, "What luck that I just remembered, or I would have been without ribbons, and here, the *choges* (Christian holidays) are almost upon us."

Sunday evening the agents ran laden with packs to the bus, which went to the train at Zwierzyniec.

They came back from Warsaw saddled with heaps of packs, aside from what was sent by trucks that travelled to Warsaw.

Later, they would distribute the goods. If things were going well, they made two trips a week.

The last one to leave was always Pintche. He would get on the train when it was already moving, always having forgotten something back at the inn.

Translator's footnotes:

1. Probably the nearby village, Wola Mala, which can mean "small Wola" in Polish.
2. Literally, village goers. Jews who visited villages to buy and sell.

[Page 56]

Artisans

by A. Karmi

Translated by Moses Milstein

The Jewish tradesmen in Bilgoraj were exceptional people. They were hard–working Jews, almost all with long, stately beards, and round caps like in Congress Poland.

Despite their hard work–days, they almost never failed to *daven shachris*, *minche*, and *maariv* with a *minyan* in the small *besmedresh*. After *minche–maariv*, they used to stroll in groups along the Zamosc road, or sit in the municipal garden and discuss politics.

Every Friday evening, they would gather in the small *besmedresh* to study a *parsheh chumash* with *Rashi* with Hershele Melamed. They were also regular patrons of the city cinema, and the Jewish theater.

There was no institution in the city which they did not support with all their might.

Bilgoraj was a city that possessed many artisans. They were compassionate people. If someone were in need of help, they would drop their work, and go get the help needed.

They were well organized. Even before there were banks in Bilgoraj, they had their own *gemiles chesed* bank that gave small loans to their members without interest. In cases of long overdue installments, it was not unusual for a worker's machines to be seized for failure to pay.

[Page 57]

In those cases, the artisan society would intervene, usually with success.

The artisan society had a representative at the *skarb* (state office for taxes) when they met each year to assess the taxes. He fought courageously for them, and did not permit any abuses to befall the Bilgoraj Jews.

The Bilgoraj artisans were not rich.

They earned their living with great difficulty, yet Shabbes, when the *besmedresh* was full of *orchim*[1], no poor man was left hungry. There was always somebody who would take a poor man home, and share his meager meal with him.

The Bilgoraj craftsmen were models for the entire region. There was not a trade that Jews did not dominate.

There were Jewish smiths, locksmiths, bricklayers, shoemakers, tailors, hat makers, carpenters, painters, upholsterers, glaziers, bookbinders, radio technicians, electrical technicians, pig bristle handlers, tinsmiths, watchmakers, photographers, rope makers, sausage makers, roofers, print workers, even a Jewish chimney sweep.

*

There were several Jewish barbershops, as well as one Christian one run by a *feldsher*[2].

*

The bakery trade in Bilgoraj was exclusively in Jewish hands, except for one Christian one, and latterly, the bakery at the *spuldzielna*.

[Page 58]

The only millinery was owned by a Jewish woman, Lolyeh Hodes.

*

All the carriage drivers, porters and water–carriers were Jewish.

*

The first ones to establish bus communication to the train in Zwierzyniec, as well as motor vehicles to carry merchandise to Warsaw, were Jewish.

*

A special place was held in Bilgoraj for the klezmorim[3] who originated from the Gimpels, and were renowned in the whole area.

There was not one Jewish or Christian celebration that the klezmorim did not play at. Even at the Christian carnivals.

When Abraham–Yekl and his band played at a wedding during the *badekn di kaleh*, and the *badchan*[4] began to celebrate the bride in song, the moving tones of his violin touched everyone's soul and moved them to tears.

And when he broke out in a *frelech*[5] to the *chupah*, the whole crowd, willing or not, had to dance.

In recent times, as the air in all Poland was poisoned by antisemitism, the Bilgoraj klezmorim were affected too. They were boycotted by the Christians who brought in their own musicians from Zamosc, or hired the firemen's band.

*

The only commercial printing facility that Bilgoraj possessed was Jewish and was owned by Y. Kaminer.

[Page 59]

It did work for the whole county and all of its municipalities.

The entire city was surrounded by turnpikes, (they were used by the Jews as an eruv), and the toll collections (the tax for bringing merchandise into the city) were leased out by the city. It was almost always leased by Yosl Wolf Gedalyahu's and Gedalyahu Fech.

*

Bilgoraj had no reason to feel ashamed of its intellectual trades. There were Jewish lawyers, (Brenner, Kaminer), doctors (Rudorfer, Potoker), dentists, (Kaminer A, Nelkin), engineer, (Dr. Reich), *feldsher*, (Judashko, and earlier, Sh. Entenberg), obstetricians, (Entenberg). There were also a few midwives, grandmothers–Ziseleh Bramberg and Miriam–Ruchl–who used to assist the obstetrician, and even sometimes delivered the baby by themselves.

*

The clerks–who the Polish government forced to pass an exam–were all Jewish: Rubinstein, Akerman, Kantor, and Berman.

*

Up until World War I, Bilgoraj had its own Jewish landowner, Falik Fabricant, whose palace was near Sheinwald's mill. He would always come into town in his coach pulled by white horses and made various charitable donations. With the outbreak of the war, it was all destroyed.

Translator's footnotes:

1. Poor people invited for the Sabbath meal
2. Unlicensed doctor
3. Klezmer–a popular form of Ashkenazi Jewish music
4. Master of ceremonies and jokester.
5. A klezmer upbeat musical style.

[Page 60]

Bilgoraj in World War I

by Y. Ch. Kronenberg

Translated by Moses Milstein

Life in Bilgoraj, like in all shtetlech, flowed along placidly. Everything was so homey, close, as if the whole city was one big family. If someone celebrated a simcha, the whole city rejoiced, and if, God forbid, a tragedy befell someone, then everyone grieved along with him. The middle class was endowed with a special folksy charm.

How alive everything still seems to me: Here, Thursday, market day, the big marketplace is filled with farmers' wagons, loaded with all kinds of goods. Jews, small–scale merchants, walk among the wagons, inspect the country merchandise, stop and haggle with the farmers, male or female, over the price of a bundle of flax, eggs, butter, mushrooms, etc. Everyone is preoccupied with his business, as if nothing in the world existed but the farmers and their produce.

But then suddenly, a cry is heard–the bride is being taken to the _chupah_! The small buyer abandons the farmer and his wagons, and runs to celebrate with the _machetonim_ who are leading their children to the _chupah_.

The carriage drivers who waited at the market and carried the merchandise to Zamosc and back were an unassuming bunch, always cheerful, joking and carefree.

[Page 61]

If a driver from a small shtetl fell into their hands, they would give him a hard time about his driving skills.

This was Bilgoraj life in 1914. That year, you could smell the scent of gunpowder in the air. Bilgoraj was not far from the Austrian border. Officers and soldiers appeared and could be seen in the forests, on the roads. They were making measurements and drawings.

A constant flow of news circulated around the oven in the _besmedresh_. Everything going on in the world was known there. Before the newspaper had even arrived from Warsaw (the third day after publication), they had begun to talk of war. They debated world politics, and argued about whether there would be a war or not. There were those who were calmer and argued–"foolish people, just a year ago there was talk of war. They had even held onto those who had completed their service. Yet you see, nothing happened and the soldiers who had done their term went home. Don't speak nonsense." Don't utter the word, war, people said, and spat, just as if they were talking about an illness whose mention alone could be harmful.

And then the shot in Sarajevo echoed around the world, and war became a fact. Along with all the other misfortunes that the war brought, were the loss of the brotherliness and the gentility of the common person in Bilgoraj.

[Page 62]

This happened only a few days after the crown prince and his wife were killed by two Serbian patriots in Sarajevo.

Thursday evening, 7th of Av, 5674,[1] after market day had ended, Starniewski, the town crier, accompanied by several policemen, announced that a general mobilization had been declared and that all men under 40 years of age who had served in the army were required to go to the army mustering area in Zamosc on the following day, Friday, and Saturday.

Heart rending scenes took place during the farewells, as fathers were separated from their wives and children not knowing if they would see them ever again.

Sunday was Tisha B'Av. People gathered in the *besmedreshes* reciting *kines* with broken hearts. Suddenly the city rebbe, R' Yakov Mordechai, burst into the Rudniker *shtibl* and shouted, "*Yidden*, why are you sitting here reciting *kines* when there are so many families with poor women and children whose breadwinner was taken away." Jewish hearts opened and everyone contributed beyond what he could afford.

And even then, there were those who insisted there would be no war. It was just each country trying to scare the others. But that situation did not last long, and the worldwide slaughter became a reality.

Concerned about drunkenness, the Russian government ordered the destruction of all the government alcohol monopolies.

[Page 63]

They dug a hole, threw all the bottles of alcohol in and smashed them. The alcohol filled the hole, and when it flooded over the sides, people filled pitchers with it, and sold it later.

With the outbreak of war, the border guards (*Objeszcikes*) were replaced by mounted patrols from the regular army that rode along the border, and had frequent encounters with the Austrian patrols. More than once, the Jewish population of Bilgoraj was scared to death by a drunken soldier. Once, when a crowd had gathered in the Rudniker *shtibl* for *Minche–Maariv*, a drunk did, in fact bust in, and the crowd stampeded out. Sholom Hochman (Sholom Yosel's) stayed behind with the drunk, and calmed him down until he left.

After the mobilization was announced, the police organized civilians to guard the telegraph poles. Later, they set up watchmen for each street who patrolled every night, because they feared not only spies who could set fires in order to spread panic among the population, but also ordinary thieves who, because of the fires could create a panic in order to carry out their robberies.

Once, some crooks, thinking that everything was in chaos, broke into Mordechai Maimon's and demanded money. The Poles were quickly arrested, and the police maintained that they had the right to immediately shoot in such cases.

The Bilgoraj population did not rely only on police powers.

[Page 64]

City hall established special night watchmen who wore a special insignia of city hall that identified them.

The situation went on like this for two weeks. No Russian soldiers, other than the patrols, were to be seen. It appeared that that the Russian powers were getting out of the Bilgoraj area.

Friday, *Parashat Eikev*, an alarm was raised in the city. Soldiers were seen arriving. It was thought that they were Austrians, but they turned out to be Russian Uhlans[2] with lances who guarded the old border.

After more Austrian troops arrived, a battle took place in the Tarnogrod marketplace. Six Austrian soldiers fell. The Russian army retreated to Bilgoraj, and stopped at the market to rest.

After doing a headcount of his men, an officer sent out a party of soldiers to look for the missing, but they returned with no one, and left.

There were no Russian police in the city. Even the officials had gone. Only the Russian burgermeister remained, and the city watch patrolled the streets.

Friday night, the whole city was awake, and wearily waiting for morning, not knowing what it would bring. At dawn, they ran to shul to finish their davening early, to be ready for new events.

In the *besmedreshes*, they *davened* one *minyan* after another. At 9:00 o'clock, when our *minyan* in the Rudniker *shtibl* had ended, rifle shots were heard.

[Page 65]

People trembled–here now, it's beginning. Is it a warning from the Austrians that they are coming? There was no Russian military here!

Suddenly, a galloping Russian dragoon appeared coming from the bridge (Lubliner) road, and behind him, two soldiers riding one horse. One was killed there, and was buried in the garden near Michalski. Someone asked, what happened? –They're chasing us and catching us! came the reply.

Soon, an Austrian officer rode up at the head of a platoon of Uhlans who paired off, left and right, down every street looking for Russians.

An officer with a platoon riding with swords in hand was looking a map and asked the Jews who were cowering there: Where is the road to "Dobre Wola?" The Jewish man did not understand that he was asking about the village, Wola, which goes through the forest to Zamosc. He thought they were being asked if they surrendered to the Austrians. "Dobra Valni"–dobra valni, dobra valni!–he, in his haste, replied, afraid that someone would interrupt him, and that not he, but another would have saved the town.

At noon, the main army, which numbered in the tens of thousands, began to march.

[Page 66]

They occupied the whole city. They were deployed in all the streets and courtyards, where they stayed until the morning, and then marched further on.

Saturday night, when the Austrians had already taken Bilgoraj, a *balabos* from Zamosc Road, R' Eliezer Vollier[3], as he was called, put on his Russian insignia, and went out to guard the telegraph poles. He was quickly arrested. He sat in jail together with the Russian priest, and the former burgermeister, until the Austrians retreated four weeks later.

The Austrians quickly began their confiscations. From Hersh Sheinwald's mill, they took several thousand sacks of flour. From the sugar merchants, they took sugar. Any products they found they confiscated under military authority. The paid with vouchers which went generally unpaid.

When Hersh Sheinwald appealed to the higher authorities for payment, he was told to go to Frampol where the treasury was located, and he would be promptly paid.

One Sunday, when the Austrians had almost reached Lublin, they were attacked by Russian outposts. A battle ensued by the Goraj mountains. When Hersheleh Sheinwald arrived in Frampol, and heard the artillery fire, and saw the shrapnel flying, he dropped everything in fear and fled, and barely escaped with his life.

[Page 67]

And so, all the confiscated merchandise was lost. Even the bakers were forced to bake bread with their flour, and received the same vouchers.

Bilgoraj, which was renowned for its mesh industry that sent its products all over Russia, was ruined with the outbreak of war. And, indeed, a lot of mesh workers supported themselves by selling tea and cigarettes to the Austrian soldiers marching through.

Merchants began developing ties with Austria. But soon after, the big battle at Trawnik began where the Austrians suffered a major defeat, and retreated in great haste.

Saturday, *Parashat Tavo*, 5674[4]. In exactly four weeks, the Russians returned. Before retreating, the Austrians released the Russian priest, and Eliezer Vollier.

At a time when armies were replacing each other, it was understandable that people avoided the roads. Even the farmers who used to bring fish to the Jewish fish sellers also stayed away.

In order to provide fish for the Jews for Shabbes, Yankel Eliezer Vollier's, went to the farmers he knew in the village to get the merchandise. In the forest, he met a patrol of Russian Cossacks who were on the heels of the retreating Austrian army. They asked him if he had seen any Austrians. Later, he met an Austrian patrol, who asked him if he had seen any Cossacks. As some farmers reported, the Russians saw him talking to the Austrians, and later shot him.

The first Russian patrols appeared coming from the "sands," Tarnogrod Road, and the Russian priest went out and greeted them. He also brought up the fact that, while in jail under the Austrians, the Jews had brought him food. This had a big effect on the Russian troops, who then greeted the Jews with friendship. The Jews lost their fear of these first patrols.

People went out into the streets, set up tables, and distributed *challahs*, bread, cakes, and schnapps. But the next day, Sunday, when masses of military began the march to Galicia, Jews little by little began to get a taste of the Russian whip.

But soon everything stopped. The Russians besieged Przemysl fortress, captured Lemberg, and reached as far as the Carpathians. Jews began to send various kinds of merchandise to Galicia, mostly to Sokolow, and Rzeszow, and from there, brought back things needed in Bilgoraj.

In the meantime, the Przemysl fortress surrendered. The victory was celebrated in Bilgoraj with a big parade in which the Jews and the city rabbi took part.

In spite of that, persecution of the Jews began. They were accused of spying. R' Nathan Maimon, a man who knew nothing about politics, was sent to Siberia.

[Page 69]

Celebration of the taking of the Przemysl fortress by the Russian army in the First World War

[Page 70]

This went on for a whole year. Shavuot time, 5675, the Germans broke through the Russian front at Gorlice, and the Russian retreat began to the river San where battles took place for several weeks. They began to seize people to dig trenches at the Tanew, Kneshpol, and in the Harshekes up to Bilgoraj. Meanwhile, the Germans took Lemberg, breaking through to Tomaszow, and from there, to Zamosc. The Russians, to avoid being surrounded, were forced to evacuate the Bilgoraj area.

Before retreating, they blew up many cellars in the city and stole the hidden merchandise.

Tamuz 17, 5675. The Austrians returned for a second time to Bilgoraj.

Several days before the Russian retreat, a man returned home from digging trenches, and suddenly got sick, and died.

After the Austrians entered, it all became clear. They had brought Cholera with them. The first victim was Akiva Shtrickendrier, from Morow Street. He had suddenly become sick, began vomiting, developed stomach pains, and after three days of heavy suffering, he died. The first cases were sick for several days. Then, the disease took on the characteristic of an epidemic. You could be walking down the street, talking, chatting, and suddenly fall down and die. People fell like flies. The dead were taken away.

[Page 71]

The living were quarantined. As soon as the authorities heard about a sick person, he was immediately taken to the hospital which had been set up in the military barracks on the "sands." The healthy were held in a nearby barn.

If any of the healthy ones made the slightest complaint, they were immediately taken to the hospital from which few came back out. I think that there were only three rare people: R' Yosef the rebbe's, later the rav in Bilgoraj, Yehuda Mercer, and Mendl, Hersh–Mendl–Beder's a grandson.

The houses of the sick were locked shut. After, sanitary workers came and disinfected the houses, and all the household things, such as clothing, were burned. They used civilians, mostly Jews passing through, who they used to catch for the work. They also used to forcibly enlist people to bury the dead that accumulated in large numbers every day.

Parents whose children had died used to wait for the cart carrying the dead to pass by, and quietly, without a moan, placed the bodies on it, and quickly disappeared so that they wouldn't be dragged along to the isolation barn, or to the hospital where death awaited them.

People became despondent, not seeing an end. The authorities forbade getting together in large groups, so as not to spread the disease.

[Page 72]

They assembled in secret to *daven* with a *minyan*, and secretly they prepared the bodies of the dead.

The city was quarantined under military guard. Large signs erected on all sides of the town, declared, "Halt! Cholera epidemic in Bilgoraj." Nobody was allowed in or out. Commerce was completely paralyzed. Workers didn't work. Grass grew in the market. There was no one to be seen in the street. The only business that existed was in food. They drank whisky, and ate a lot, as much as they could. People regularly snuck out of town by side streets to buy things to eat. They now understood the Talmudic expression: *chatof v'echol, chatof v'ishti, ki machar namut*. Grab and eat, grab and drink, because tomorrow we die. This lasted for three weeks, from 17th Tamuz until Tisha B'Av 5675.

In those three weeks of national sorrow, about 500 people died in Bilgoraj. They took to resorting to all kinds of remedies. People remembered that, years before, a cholera epidemic had raged through Poland, but Bilgoraj was not touched. A board had been nailed into the southeast corner of the shul. So now, when the tragedy occurred in Bilgoraj, they hammered in another board. (There were actually two small boards nailed into the southeast corner). They tried various other remedies. They hung a sign on the door that said, "No one lives here." At that time, they also resorted to a well–known remedy. They held a wedding in the cemetery.

[Page 73]

The married Yechezkel Viotch to *Der Shtumer* Matl,[5] and the cholera epidemic ended.

There were still fatalities after Tisha B'Av, but only among those who were already sick.

Life slowly took on a normal character. Tradesmen returned to their work, store owners to selling. However, many people were unemployed, particularly the workers in the mesh industry. The road to trade with Austria had not yet opened.

Many people brought wood from the forest, or picked mushrooms in order to support themselves. Many took on manual labor. Road building was beginning then. It was mostly Jews who worked on building the railway line in Zwierzyniec.

Slowly, trade with Austria developed. Merchants found markets. The retail trade developed. Hunger reigned in Austria, so Bilgoraj merchants began to bring foodstuffs to Galicia, and brought back industrial articles.

Since everything was under the supervision of the provisioning office, which confiscated all the food even in the settled areas, a smuggling business went on to Galicia and back. It was necessary not to be dependent on the carriage drivers, because the Austrians often confiscated not only the merchandise, but also the horse and wagon. So the merchants began to buy their own horses so that practically all of the merchants became carriage drivers, owners of horse and wagon.

[Page 74]

The occupation powers were always detaining people for different kinds of work. One Sunday, while the Jews were praying in the *besmedresh*, the gendarmes encircled the building, and seized Jews for work. They even tore the *teffilin* off their heads. They gathered together a group of Jews and sent them off to Ludmir to work.

Later, when it was becoming difficult to make a living, and the Typhus epidemic was raging, they sent the sick to the hospital they had set up in Tarnogrod.

This epidemic was not as terrible as the cholera epidemic, but it took enough victims.

The food supply became very tenuous. Not only sugar, but every piece of bread was carefully weighed and measured. Some Jews, in order to lessen the difficulty of finding food sources, started to buy cows. It was impressive to see the young Gentile boys, hired cowherds, leading a whole bunch of cows which gradually got smaller as each cow went into practically every open gate. Early in the morning, they went back out to pasture.

It is worth noting an episode from that time. The printer, Nuteh Kronenberg, had, at the time, trade relations with the firm, Yosef Schlesinger, in Vienna. He would often visit the company. Once, while in Vienna, Schlesinger's daughter came to see him with another girl who she introduced to the printer, Kronenberg, from Bilgoraj.

[Page 75]

This previously unknown girl asked him to take a package to her cousin who was serving in the occupation authority as a prosecutor. Kronenberg brought the parcel to the prosecutor who begged the printer that should the need arise, he should come to see him. Thereafter, every time he travelled to Vienna, he brought back packages for him.

At that time, Ephraim *Chazer–hor–kemer's*[6] brother–in–law, Hershele Magram from Sieniawa (Galicia) which was under Austria, lived in Bilgoraj, and was an Austrian citizen. He had two grown sons who had to go to the army. Wanting to avoid going to war, they hid in Bilgoraj with acquaintances in Bagner street. But as deserters, they faced harsh punishment. They could not remain where they were, so they went over to their uncle, Ephraim whose house was near the Russian Orthodox church. At that time, Nuteh Kronenberg lived there, and had his print shop there. But it turned out that the wrong people found out about it.

It was Saturday night, the first night of Shavuot. Nuteh Kronenberg came home quickly from *davening* because of the war situation. No civilians were allowed to be out late at night. Near his house, he noticed some suspicious looking people. When he entered the house, he saw the two deserters, the Magrams. They had come in to ask for some cigarette paper, and seeing a newspaper on the table, they had sat down to read it.

[Page 76]

It seems that the spies had seen them through the window. No sooner had they left with the cigarette papers, and as Nuteh Kronenberg was preparing to make Kiddush, than suddenly, the door was torn open and the gendarme, Szecko, burst in with gun in hand. Other gendarmes followed him. They searched all the rooms, found nothing, and left.

They went off to Ephraim *Chazer–hor–kemer* where they found both young men, and arrested them. They came back later, and arrested Ephraim, and also Nuteh Kronenberg.

At the inquiry, both the boys argued that they had been taken away by the Russians, and had been wandering a long time, and had just arrived in Bilgoraj. Naturally, they were not believed. After the inquiry, Ephraim was accused of hiding deserters, but Kronenberg stated that this was the first time he had seen them.

The Kronenberg family reminded the prosecutor of his promise, and Ephraim was soon released. The two boys were sent to the army.

After the cholera and Typhus epidemics, a lot of orphans were created with no one to care for them. With the initiative of a Jewish officer in the Austrian army, the orphans were gathered together, and an orphanage was created for them, as well as a low–cost kitchen for the needy.

And thus the years of the First world war flowed by, in which the idyllic way of life was destroyed.

[Page 77]

The conduct of people to one another became different. Notwithstanding the emergence of a great civilization, and the development of technology, morale fell. People became cruel, money–hungry. That may be the reason why so many charitable institutions were established in those days, because as people became worse in this respect, they sought to improve the social life.

During the war years, the Russian government promised to reestablish Polish independence. To that end, the polish legion was founded under the leadership of general Dowbor Musnicki. How Jews suffered from the legionnaires is something to tell.

Then Austria and Germany declared Graf Szeptycki as regent in Poland. The Poles began to recruit members for the Polish legion, who were transferred to the leadership of Josef Pilsudski (later field–marshal of Poland).

This lasted until the breakup of the Austrian and German armies. The Polish legionnaires and volunteers took control immediately. These little *shkootzimlech* threw fear into the occupation powers from whom they requisitioned weapons.

A certain Piotr, the hunchback, a shoemaker by trade, who was always drunk, went up to an Austrian gendarme (Szecko) who used to make the whole city tremble, and took his rifle away in the middle of the street.

[Page 78]

Jews also responded to the call for legionnaires. In Bilgoraj, a certain Moishe Shirota, and others. Moishe fell in the war with the Bolsheviks.

After the establishment of the Polish state, Jews from Russia began to return to Bilgoraj: Itamar Fefferman, Warshaviak, Shloime Rubinstein, Antshel Shur, and Eichenblat who had left for Russia with the Russian retreat from Poland.

With the outbreak of the war between Poland and the Bolsheviks, Poland suspected the returnees of being Communists. Two of the most prominent businessmen, Shloime Rubinstein, and Anshel Shur were arrested, and taken in chains to Zamosc. They were later freed.

This is how a Jewish community that is no more survived the First World War.

Translator's footnotes:

1.   August, 1914
2.   Cavalrymen
3.   Goiter
4.   1913–1914
5.   Deaf Matl
6.   pig–hair–comber

[Page 81]

Institutions and Parties

The Kitchen and the Orphanage

by Shoshana Lerman

Translated by Moses Milstein

Bilgoraj suffered a serious economic crisis during WWI when the Austrians occupied it. Everything stopped, the factories didn't operate, and there was no commerce other than in foodstuffs. It was so bad that the Jewish population of Bilgoraj was running out of food.

This situation gave the prominent people of the city no rest. With the initiative of Monik, Kubeh, and Esther Brafman, Perl and Golda Honigboim, Roize Shwerdshaft, Broche and Chaneh Groisman, Yakov Mermelstein, Shrentze Shapiro, and Hershke Goldbrenner, a public kitchen was created which provided lunches for any needy Bilgorajers.

There was a Jewish, Austrian army officer in Bilgoraj at the time, Schranz and his wife. They took over the entire initiative.

In order to fund the kitchen, a drama club was formed under the direction of a certain Matzek from Zamosc. They presented King Lear for the first time in Bilgoraj to great acclaim. They frequently put on various shows and this did in fact enable the kitchen to continue.

There was even a song composed about it.

[Page 82]

The cholera and typhus epidemics that raged through Bilgoraj claimed many adult lives leaving many orphans behind. This same committee moved the kitchen which had been at Deskaches (Weiss), on Szewski Street, into David Furer's big building, and established an orphanage there. They brought the children there, treated them as if they were their own. They were bathed, received haircuts, cleaned up and were dressed in identical uniforms.

The children at the dinner table

A large segment of youth was recruited to the work, and they put their heart and soul into it. They were divided into groups, and each group had to go on a given day to the kitchen to prepare the food.

[Page 83]

Before Pesach, the same committee organized a "*lat*," (baking matzos) which drew almost all the youth of the city.

Erev Pesach, every needy Jew in Bilgoraj received matzos and wine for Pesach.

Thanks go to the group of activists whose actions describe a beautiful chapter in the history of Bilgoraj. With the emergence of the Polish state, which had begun to look after social issues, the kitchen and the orphanage were closed.

The committee and the orphanage

[Page 84]

The Zionist Movement in Bilgoraj

by M. Oberhant, M. Groisman, A. Kronenberg

Translated by Moses Milstein

Before WWI, Bilgoraj belonged to Russia, and every freedom movement was forbidden. With the outbreak of the war in 1914, Austria occupied Bilgoraj, and soon after, Bilgoraj Jews began to feel like free people, and social life began to reawaken.

There were many Zionist Jewish officers in the Austrian army, and in 1916, the first Zionist organization in Bilgoraj was founded, and headed by Oizerkes (a one-time Austrian officer), Aharon Berman; Shper. Sh., Y.; Honigboim; Bramberg, Leib; Brafman; Groisman, Eliyahu, and others. The Zionist organization continued to grow and attracted a large part of the population.

In 1917, the Zionist organization in Bilgoraj put together a very impressive celebration of the Balfour Declaration. The city took on a festive appearance, many houses decorated with pictures of Dr. Herzl, and almost all the houses flying blue-white flags with Zionist slogans.

A procession marched all through the city and ended at the city shul where the whole crowd recited *Hallel*. There were many speakers and presentations. The celebration brought together the whole city population, so that in time, the Zionist organization became the leading force behind social life in Bilgoraj.

[Page 85]

A drama club was created with: Hershke Goldbrenner, Roize Shwerdsharf, Yakov and Aharon Kaminer, Esther and Manes Brofman, Libeh Shatz, Broche and Chaneh Groisman, and Perl Honigboim. They presented theatrical plays in the Jewish cinema hall at Kaminer's. All the revenue went to support the public kitchen and the orphanage that were created and supported by the Zionist organization.

At the same time, all the Zionist collection funds stood at a high level. Practically every house had the little blue-white box hanging there. They also conducted various meetings, parties, as well as theatrical presentations, and the earnings went to KK"L[1]

In 1918, with Polish Independence, when war against the Bolsheviks began, the Zionist organization in Bilgoraj was dissolved.

After the war, the Zionist organization reestablished itself under the direction of: Oizerkes, Oberhand, Moishe; Groisman, Eliyahu; Shwerdsharf, Nuteh; Bromberg, Abraham; Honigboim, Moishe; Bromberg, A. Y.; Ilish, Itzhak Meir; Hodes, Meir; Oberhand, Chaim; Fuks, Hindeh; Shvester, Mitler; Bergstein Kayle; Yegergarn; Rubinstein, Feige; and Teneholz, Tuvyeh. The Zionist organization created a "*Chalutz V'Hashomer*, and a rich library of various Yiddish and Hebrew books. They also introduced Hebrew classes for youth and adults. They formed a drama club under the direction of Groisman, Eliyahu, which frequently gave performances. A music group was also formed which gave concerts from time to time.

[Page 86]

The Zionist organization in the year 1919-20

Later, a youth group was created, *Ze'evim* (Viltchukes), which attracted around it a large number of youngsters, boys and girls.

At the head of the *Ze'evim* were Oizerkes, Groisman, Eliyahu, and Moishe Oberhand. Oizerkes, as an erstwhile officer, gave the *Ze'evim* a military character. They presented courses in Hebrew, geography of Eretz Israel, and Jewish history.

[Page 87]

They learned Zionist songs, and at every yom-tov celebration, the youth marched through the streets of Bilgoraj.

The desire to take part in the theater was widespread among the young, and a drama section of youngsters was formed with the following people: Yosef Shlechterman, Hodis Kornblit, Chantche Hodes, Rochl Yegergaren, Neitche Honigboim, Ettl Bromberg, and others, under the direction of Nuteh Shwerdsharf, and Meir Hodes. The drama section frequently put on plays that had broad appeal.

A group of girls in the Ze'evim (Viltchuk)

[Page 88]

In 1920, the first pioneer to leave Bilgoraj for Eretz Israel was Eliyahu Groisman.

The pioneer ideology spread among the youth of Bilgoraj. The Zionist movement grew from day to day. From 1921 to 1923 emigrants included Teitelboim, Shloime; Meir Hodes; Nuteh Shwerdsharf; Moishe Honigboim; Abraham Bromberg; Binyamin Yegergaren; Tuvieh Tenenholz, and Binyamin Warshaviak.

Practically the entire town was at the kolejka (small train) to see them off. The Zionist songs echoed through the whole city, and inspired the Zionist ranks.

Zionist ideology also penetrated the walls of the besmedresh. By 1920 there was already a Mizrachi in Bilgoraj, that was composed entirely of besmedresh boys: Moishe Zilberman, Moishe Horndrexler, Itzchak Singer (today's well known writer in America under the pseudonym of Itzchak Bashevis), Yosl Glicklech, Binyamin Brezel, and others.

A group of young people, such as Abraham Kronenberg, Moishe Tayer, Ephraim Stern, Yehoshua Schwartz, Chaim Shur, and others, who were already organized, made overtures to Mizrachi. Mizrachi took the group in and created a Chalutz Hadati. Two battalion chiefs were chosen: Moishe Horndrexler and Itzchak Singer who led the group in political Zionist work.

[Page 89]

The Chalutz Hadati took part in all the Zionist fundraising, through its representative, Shloime Zilbermintz, who was on the committee of KK"L, collecting the money in the blue-white boxes every month.

Later, all the older ones from Mizrachi joined the Zionist organization. The "Shomer Hadati" remained and continued to carry out the Mizrachi activities in Bilgoraj.

There were always Zionist speakers coming to Bilgoraj, like: Funt, Bialopolski, and others. They would draw huge numbers of Bilgoraj Jews.

The desire for aliyah was very strong among Bilgoraj youth. The central office of Hechalutz then instituted the so-called "*hachshara*" which everyone who wanted to go on aliyah had to pass through for a certain amount of time. This consisted of chopping wood for the city tradesmen. This did not scare off the Bilgoraj youth. Boys and girls went around the city chopping wood.

Later, they organized groups to go out to the villages to the Polish aristocrats and do agricultural work. Moishe Horndrexel and Binyamin Brezel went on aliyah.

The same year, Itzchak Wirtzer came to Bilgoraj and threw himself passionately into the work of Mizrachi in Bilgoraj. He, and Yoineh Kronenberg, Aharon Grossman, and others created a Mizrachi party which continuously grew and attracted people of all classes in the city.

[Page 89 (sic)]

That same year, Mizrachi created the first "Payen bank", and because of this, its prestige grew from day to day, and the party grew and became the most prominent in the city.

In 1925, when the university in Jerusalem was inaugurated, a magnificent celebration was held in Bilgoraj. The Zionist local organized a march from the *knochns*, on the sands, to the city shul in which the Zionist organization, Ze'evim, Mizrachi, HeChalutz HaDati took part. Also taking part were the Jewish children from the government school, who were given the day off from school for this.

A holiday spirit reigned in the city. The houses were decorated with blue-white flags and Zionist slogans. The large banner in the parade, "*Ki mitzion taytzeh Torah u'dvar adonai mi yerushalayim*," swept up the entire city's residents who joined in the parade.

In the year 1925, Abraham Kronenberg received the first certificate from HeChalutz Hadati. He was denounced as not being religious enough, and his certificate was taken away.

In 1926, almost all the chalutzim who had made aliyah came back. This had a very bad effect on people, and the Zionist organizations ceased to exist.

In 1927, the Zionist organization was again revived through Abraham Kronenberg, Leibl Zilberlicht, Moishe Lichtenfeld, Baruch Wermut, Moishe Boim, Nuteh Kleinmintz, Hersh Ritzer, Yakov Shtempel, Beinish Adler, Yakov Edelsein, Abraham Shtol, and others. The head was Aharon Berman.

[Page 90]

The Zionist organization began an extensive operation. They attracted a large part of the Bilgoraj youth, and created a library which was widely used by the Jewish youth. They began again the work with the Zionist funds, and Bilgoraj was once again visited by Zionist speakers.

In 1928, two parties were formed out of the Zionist organization, Beitar and HeChalutz.

Beitar in Bilgoraj

A lot of the youth of the city grouped together in the two parties. They instituted Hebrew classes for both parties together.

[Page 91]

Even when both parties occupied the same place, there was no inter-party animosity in Bilgoraj.

Later, Beitar, headed by Abraham Kronenberg, and HeChalutz, headed by Abraham Shtol, rented separate locations, and both parties, along with Mizrachi, worked for the Zionist fund raising societies.

HeChalutz in Bilgoraj

Beitar, which had its premises on the Zamosc road, was always marching through the Bilgoraj streets, where the whole city, even the Christians, received them happily. Every year, during Polish Independence Day, they were invited to join the parade.

[Page 92]

A combined drama club of Beitar and Hechalutz was formed under the direction of Eliyahu Groisman and the following people: Abraham Kronenberg, Rechl Korenblit, Rochl Geist, Yakov Edelstein, Yakov Shtempel, Hersh Ritzer, Nuteh and Yosef Kleinmintz, Yakov Hodes, Minke Shur, Breine Renner, Yehudit Bromberg, and Yehuda Tauber. The first piece that was performed with great success was "*Shalom Bayit.*" The drama circle periodically gave performances that were received with great enjoyment.

The drama circle developed a good reputation in the surrounding area where they used to travel putting on plays. The same year, Mizrachi in Bilgoraj founded a Yavneh cheder, which continued to grow, bringing in more children, and offering higher classes, to such an extent that they had to rent a special place for the cheder, and employ a lot of teaching personnel of well qualified teachers, headed by Hillel Janower.

The Yavneh cheder in Bilgoraj

The departure of the KK"L representative in Bilgoraj

[Page 93]

In 1933 the dedicated and praiseworthy representative of KK"L in Bilgoraj, Feivel Lerman, departed.

Later, the position was taken by Abraham Kronenberg, the Zionist fund agencies got bigger, and extensive work for Keren Hayesod was undertaken.

With time, Beitar and Hechalutz revived Zionist aspirations among Bilgoraj youth, and when the drive for aliyah had grown strong, two companies of *hachshara*, one from Chalutz, and the second from Beitar.

[Page 94]

Like kibbutzniks they used to work in the Jewish sawmills, and for the city's businessmen.

The *hachshara* contingent from Beitar in Bilgoraj, "Pesach at the seder"

Bilgoraj showed that it worked for Zionism not only with words, but also with deeds. A strong aliyah from Chalutz began. Immigrating were Shimon Buchbinder, Yakov Shtempel, Hersh Ritzer, Israel Honigsfeld, and Binyamin Gershtenblit. From HeChalutz-HaMizrachi–Yakov Mordechai Shatz.

Because of the strained relationship between the Zionist organization and the revisionist party, Beitar did not receive any certificates.

Later when a new Zionist organization under Jabotinsky was created, Bilgoraj also created a "Brit Hatsohar" headed by the worthy Zionist, Yoineh Chaim Kronenberg.

[Page 95]

The Brit Hatsohar in Bilgoraj

Bilgoraj also had a Poalei Zion party, headed by Abraham Shtol, and Meir Bernblat. Both parties, the Brit Hatsohar, and Poalei-Zion attracted the older youth of Bilgoraj. They carried on their political Zionist activities with no enmity between the parties.

Mizrachi and Hechalutz-HaMizrachi in Bilgoraj, headed by the dedicated Mizrachi activists like: Itzchak Wirtzer, Hillel Janower, Chaim Mordechai Hirshenhorn, Leibel Milch, Feivel Lerman, Moishe Kornwortzel, and others, attracted the youth from religious homes. They instituted Hebrew courses and participated in all Zionist activities.

[Page 96]

In 1936, Yoineh Chaim Kronenberg left for Eretz-Israel.

The Zionist organizations in Bilgoraj existed like this until the outbreak of WWII, when Hitler's murderers destroyed everything and everyone.

Translator's footnote:

1. Keren Kayemet L'Israel. Jewish National Fund

The departure of Y. Ch. Kronenberg for Eretz Israel

[Page 97]

Agudat Israel in Bilgoraj

by Sh. Feller

Translated by Moses Milstein

With the emergence of the Agudat Israel movement in Poland after WWI, in 1918-20, Bilgoraj also founded an Agudat Israel party.

The party was headed by the most respected organizational leaders of the city, like: Levi Stern, Yakov Kanter, Yechezkel Teicher, Birach Hershman, Nuteh Fink, Nachum Wagner, Dovid Furer, Yakov Eliezer Goldbrenner, Yosef Rapaport, *hy"d*, and Harav Itzchak Huberman, and the writer of these lines who is now in Eretz Israel.

Agudat Israel was very active in various areas like, education, religion, and social issues.

Education

In the area of education, Agudat Israel established a cheder with the help of an American philanthropist, R' Moishe Frost, *z"l*, in which several hundred students studied. The first supervisor of the cheder was Mr. Alter Zuker of Dlugosiodlo who now lives in Bnei Brak, Israel.

The cheder was founded and run according to the instructions and the programs of all the other cheders and bet sefers that were created in Poland under the name of Yesodei HaTorah, with all modern facilities, and in accordance with the laws that were required by the Polish education ministry generally in matters to do with the school system.

[Page 98]

The committee for the cheder, "Zichron Yakov and Beit Moshe" in Bilgoraj

[Page 99]

In this cheder, the best pedagogical methods were always taught and studied.

According to the laws of the Polish school system, they also had to teach secular subjects in line with the public schools. So teachers from the government school came to teach the worldly subjects to the children.

The cheder was run by a committee headed by Harav Mordechai Rokeach, Levi Stern, and *hamavdil bchl"ch*, the writer of these lines, and others.

The cheder produced children steeped in Torah and piety, but also with a worldly education, many of whom are in Israel or America today.

Beit Yakov

In the area of schooling for girls, the Agudat Israel in Bilgoraj, established an exemplary Beit Yakov school with several hundred students, along the lines of the Beit Yakov schools that Agudat Israel created in all of Poland.

The founder and creator of the school was the writer of these lines with the help of the rav, *ztz"l*, and a committee of basically the above-mentioned committee of the cheder.

Shaineh Torenheit, *a"h*, was selected as a female teacher, pedagogue, and educator.

An excellent teacher, she brought the school to an appropriately high level. She was always organizing plays on religious themes, that would attract a large audience from the religious sectors.

She later married Baruch Stern, the son of Levi Stern, *z"l*, and settled in Bilgoraj, and ran the school until the war.

[Page 101]

A Beit Yakov performance in Bilgoraj

The Workers Movement in Bilgoraj

by A. Greener, B. Eichenblat

Translated by Moses Milstein

In 1905, Bilgoraj was part of Czarist Russia, and when the famous "strikes" were taking place all over the land, Bilgoraj was not left out.

Bilgoraj, which had a large number of sieve workers, young unmarried men, early on worked with the workers movement, which was then illegal, with the Bund. They used to organize various strikes and protests. The Russian police hunted for the leaders, but because Bilgoraj was close to Austria, they would cross the border illegally, and from there, flee to America. In this way, they avoided being sent to Siberia.

In 1926, the young workers were in a very bad situation. They had no opportunity to go to school, because by the age of 11 or 12, they had to start learning a trade–which then consisted of sieve work, tailor, or shoemaker–in order to earn enough for a piece of bread, because their parents could no longer support them. That was the situation in those days.

At that time, there was a certain Shimon Zilberlicht (Shimon Kashtan[1] he was called). He lived with his parents in very poor conditions. He too was forced, at a very young age, to learn a trade, and he apprenticed to a tailor. Later, when he had learned a little of the tailor trade, he realized he and his parents were in great need, and he decided to go to Warsaw where he thought he could live a better life materially.

[Page 102]

After living there for a while, he was drawn into the Polish Jewish revolutionary world, got a bit of an education, and returned to Bilgoraj.

In 1927, the first trade union in Bilgoraj was formed, and united all the workers of the city such as: shoemakers, tailors, domestic servants, bakers, brush association (sieve workers), and printers.

A drama club was formed of the following people: Hodis Bromberg, Perl Gerstenman, Rochl Leah Glicklech, Breine Eichenblat, Yakov Dorenbust, Yosef Schlechterman, Yakov Zimring, Orish Saltzberg, Eliyahu Dorfsman, (director), Berish Feder (prompter). Their first presentation, "The Bells of Siberia," and later, "Where are my Children," were a success. Huge audiences were attracted.

The trade union also conducted cultural work among the workers. They created a library, and brought knowledge to the Bilgoraj workers.

Various speakers used to come, and indeed, in 1930, when the union was located at Yakov Mermlstein's, a free-thinker came to give a lecture there.

When the religious Jews, who were at Minche-Maariv, heard about this speaker, they left the besmedreshim, and headed out for the trade union.

[Page 103]

It was quite a scene, and the lecture did not take place.

The Bilgoraj young workers became educated, and there was lots of activity. At the head were Shimon Zilberlicht, Yehoshua Shtark, Yosef Shirota, Yosef Ball, Shaindl Shtreichler, Yidl Sharf, Issar Kandl, Brombergs, and others.

In the meantime, the Polish police began to spy on every movement of the leadership. In spite of the disturbances, the drama club of the trade union put on, to great acclaim, *"The Romanian Wedding."*

Between the years 1932-1936, the Polish government was engaged in hunting down Communists, and fell upon the vestiges in Bilgoraj. Very many followers were arrested and sentenced to long years in jail. Some managed to escape, and later to cross over to Soviet Russia.

The police confiscated everything of the trade union, and the local was shut.

Even with all these arrests, Shimon Zilberlicht still managed to escape to Paris.

In 1936, a workers' party was again formed, "YAP." (Yiddisher Arbiter Partei), which began to put workers lives back in focus.

It did not last long. In 1938, the Polish authorities arrested the board of the YAP, held them under arrest for 14 days, and the local was closed.

No more workers movements were permitted in Bilgoraj.

[Page 105 (sic)]

This was how the workers movement existed in Bilgoraj. It brought light to the working masses, until the accursed Germans annihilated everything and everyone.

———

Translator's footnote:

1.   Chestnut

———

Cooperative Banks in Bilgoraj

by Sh. Feller

Translated by Moses Milstein

The emergence of the Polish state, proclaiming itself a democratic country, with the previous social orders, and socialist parties at the head of government for a long time, nurtured and valued the cooperative movement and cooperation in general.

Thanks to this, cooperative banks arose in every city and shtetl and served all classes of people with loans and the like.

Bilgoraj, which had a lot of sieve workers and merchants, was strongly in need of such bank institutions.

And in 1927, the Mizrachi association in Bilgoraj created the first "Payen-Bank,• which was later called "Bank-Udzalova.• Later, the "Bank-Spoldzielcy• was formed by people closer to the Agudat circle, and finally, the merchants in the city created the "Bank-Kupiecki.•

All three banks developed well, and served the city residents with loans and the like.

The Jewish banks were annihilated along with the community.

(From right to left) bottom row. Moishe Toitman, Shloime Zilbermintz, Shmuel Elyahu Groisman
(Second row seated) Itzchak Wirtzer, Yehoshua Pantser, Chaim Mordechai Hirshenhorn, Hillel Janower, Hersh Zilberberg, Feivel Lerman, Leibl Shneiderberg
(Third row, standing) Itzchak Meir Warshoviak, Yakov Tauber, Moishe Kornworzel, Shefsl Honigsfeld, Israel Roit, Yehoshua Fogel, Mordechai Loberblat, and Moishe Zisman

[Page 108]

Charitable Institutions in Bilgoraj

by Ch. Anger

Translated by Moses Milstein

Linat Hatzedek

In the city synagogue, to the right of the main entrance, there was a little shul where the young generation of shoemakers, smiths, wood-workers, butchers, netting, and horse traders, davened.

One Saturday in 1930, while the men were gathered there to pray, they discussed the situation of the poor tradesmen in Bilgoraj. What if someone fell ill, who was there to help him? So right then and there, they decided to establish a Linat Hatzedek. A committee was quickly formed with the following people: Chaim Anger, Aharon Leib Brenner, Chaim Eliyahu Anger, Pesach Sheinzinger, Zecharyahu Dornbust, and others.

The Linat Hatzedek quickly became popular in the city due to the help it unfailingly provided for the poor and sick. It negotiated large discounts from the city's doctors and pharmacists for patients referred by Linat Hatzedek. They purchased various medical appliances which they lent to patients for use in the home.

It became a well-regarded institution in the city, and continued to attract new members who paid a small monthly amount that allowed this very important institution to survive.

The Linat Hatzedek committee worked with devotion and heart and soul.

[Page 109]

There was not one celebration in town where Linat Hatzedek did not collect money. They also received support from the Bilgoraj committee in America which enabled them to continue to expand their work on behalf of the poor and ill.

Bikur Cholim

In 1934, for various reasons, a Bikur Cholim was established headed by the most prominent tradesmen of the city, such as: Levi Stern, Nuteh Kronenberg, Chaim Anger, Hershel Groisman, Chaim Mordechai Hirshenhorn, and Shloime Israel Shtall.

The Bikur Cholim carried on a strong and intensive work, giving help to any poor, sick person who came to them.

In 1937, Linat Hatzedek and Bikur Cholim united, and became a single institution dedicated to providing help for the needy sick.

The Linat Hatzedek v'Bikur Cholim was run by an amalgamated committee which continued to provide aid until the devastation.

Beit Lechem

In the last years before the war, the economic situation in Bilgoraj had deteriorated markedly so that many families could not provide for Shabbes.

Bilgoraj Jews who had always cared for the poor, established a Beit Lechem in 1934 headed by Yakov Shnitzer, Moishe Model, Chaim Anger, Dovid Zokman, Yekutiel Pest, Tevl Stempel, and others.

[Page 110]

Every Friday, the committee sent people to go from house to house gathering bread and challahs. Bilgoraj housewives would prepare beautiful, big challahs and happily give them to the collectors.

Later they would be distributed to the poor of the city.

There were also poor, reclusive Jews to whose homes the bread and challahs were sent for Shabbes.

Hachnasat Orchim

In Bilgoraj, as in all the cities of Poland, masses of poor people who wandered all over the country would arrive with no place to spend the night other than the hard benches of the besmedreshim.

Bilgoraj Jews could not merely look on at their plight, and so, in 1936, they established a Hachnasat Orchim where every arriving pauper was given a clean, spotless bed to sleep in, and a glass of tea.

These were the charitable institutions that existed in Bilgoraj until Hitler's murderers annihilated them all.

———————

[Page 111]

Drama Clubs in Bilgoraj

by Sh. Atzmon (Wirtzer) actor

Translated by Moses Milstein

Bilgoraj youth had always loved theater, and had a strong desire to put on plays.

Theater to them ranked higher than political partisanship. The ambition to perform united all spheres and classes.

A drama club was begun back during WWI, when the public kitchen and orphanage were operating, made up of the following people: Manik, Kubeh, and Esther Brafman, Perl and Golde Honigboim, Roize Shwerdsharf, Broche and Chaneh Grossman, Yakov Mermlstein, Shrentze Spiro, Hershke Goldbrenner, and others, under the direction of a certain Matchek from Zamosc. The first performance was "King Lear," from which all of the revenue went to the public kitchen and the orphanage.

In 1922, a drama club formed again of people with diverse backgrounds such as: Nissen Shlechterman, Gerstenman, Langburd, A. Y. Bramberg, Moishe Honigboim, Eliyahu Dorfman, Fessl Kandl, Pinchas Zimring, Chaim Oberhand, Zisman and Itzchak Meir Eilish, under the direction of Nissen Shlechterman. They gave frequent performances and all the revenue went to charitable goals.

Later, a drama club was formed by the Zionist organization with the following people: Nuteh Shwerdsharf, A. Bramberg, Y. M. Eilish, A. Weiss, Y. Bramberg, Chaim Oberhand, Esther Bromberg, and others. They put on a lot of plays, and the money went to K.K."L.

[Page 111]

The Zionist youth, the "Ze'evim," (Viltchukes), were keen and started a drama club with the following people: Yosef Shlechterman, Hodis Kornblit, Chantche Hodes, Rochl Yegerman, Neitche Honigboim, Ettl Bramberg, Necheh Bramberg, Feige Bin, Tsippe Kesselshmid, and others, under the direction of Nuteh Shwerdsharf. They put on shows which drew large audiences.

Photo inscription: Yiddish drama section in Bilgoraj 1922

[Page 113]

In 1927, the trade union formed a drama club with the following people: Hodis Bramberg, Perl Gerstenman, Rochl Leah Glicklech, Breine Eichenblat, Yakov Dorenbust, Yosef Shlechterman, Yakov Zimring, Urish Salzberg, Berish Feder, under the direction of Eliyahu Dorfman. They first put on, "*The Bells of Siberia.*"

In 1928, a joint Beitar and Hechalutz drama club was formed with the following people: Yakov Eidelstein, Yakov Stempl, Hersh Ritzer, Nuteh and Yosef Kleinmintz, Rochl Geist, Rechl Kornblit, Minke Shur, Breine Renner, Yehudis Bramberg, Yehuda Tauber, and Abraham Kronenberg under the direction of Eliyahu Grossman. The first performance, which was a great success, was "*Shalom Bayit.*"

The play, "*Shalom Bayit*"

From right to left (seated) Minke Shur, Braneh Renner, Rechl Kornblit, Abraham Kronenberg,
(Standing) Nuteh and Yosef Kleinmintz, Rochl Geist, Yakov Stempl, Yehude Tauber, Hersh Ritzer, Yakov Eidelstein, (Top) Eliyahu Grossman

[Page 114]

And Mizrachi in Bilgoraj also had a drama circle which put on religious plays.

Even the "Banot Yakov" in Bilgoraj used to present religious plays that were very popular.

And thus in Bilgoraj the chain of drama clubs stretched until the last minute before the *Chorbn*.

[Page 115]

Religious Zionism and its activities in Bilgoraj

by Tuvia Korenvurcel

Translated by Sara Mages

When we come to erect a literary monument to Jewish Bilgoraj with its institutions and people, who were wiped out of the world in such a tragic way by the Nazi oppressor, we must not accept the absence of a description, even an imperfect description, of the religious–Zionist part in it with its institutions and activities. The work, the deeds and the people, that the seal of Zionism was imprinted on them, were so integrated into the general life of our city that they actually formed an integral part of its public life.

There's no denying that the few lines that I – a former student of the "Yavne" School and one of the activists of the youth movement "*Hashomer Hadati*" ["The religious Guard"] in Bilgoraj – will express in my article will join a uniform and comprehensive picture that only people like the late, Yitzhak Wirzer *z"l*, who was one of the movement's leaders, could draw.

If my memory serves me correctly, a number of yeshiva students organized for the first time immediately after the First World War with the clear goal of becoming the foundation of the Mizrahi federation. A prayer *minyan* was formed, and shortly afterwards, "Yavne" School was founded. The beginning of the school was very sad: it was housed in one room and employed one teacher (Mr. Nahum Ber Gloz).

The establishment of a Hebrew school, whose language of instruction was Hebrew, and whose method of teaching adhered to the requirements of modern pedagogy, was a revolutionary step at that time, in a city like Bilgoraj which caused its organizers constant conflict from both outside and inside. In those days, most religious Jews in the city still did not understand the need for a modern religious school which would serve as a cover for new penetrating spirits whose tendency was to uproot traditional Jewish content. On the other hand, some residents looked at this new creature with open envy (to put it mildly), knowing that the establishment of "Yavne" School would prevent, once and for all, the establishment of a modern, non–religious school, in Bilgoraj.

And, indeed, no other school was established in Bilgoraj until the outbreak of the last war.

[Page 116]

"Yavne" School, the first school in the city, went through many stages before it reached its pre–war state of about 350 students, and the highest level of education. As mentioned, the school started with one teacher and one room at the home of the member, Yehoshua Panzer, *z"l*. It then moved to the home of Mr. Yakov Yehoshua Zilberzweig where it already occupied two rooms. Later, it resided in an entire building on the Third of May Street. The methods of teaching, and also the number of graduating classes, gave the school a huge impact in the city, and the number students in the school increased from year to year. Finally, it is worth mentioning the school's first founders: my esteemed father, Mr. Moshe Korenvurcel, may he live long, Leibel Milech, *hy"d*, who was among the founders of Mizrachi in Bilgoraj, Yona Haim Kronenberg who was a school activist until his immigration to Israel in 1936, Yitzchak Wirzer, *z"l*, Yitzchak Meir Warsoviak, *hy"d*, and also the first teacher, Mr. Nahum Dov Zchochity (Gloz). The last teachers were: Mr. Korman and Goldenberg (whose traces were lost in the war), and my esteemed father who joined the teaching staff in the last years. Haim Mordechai Hirshhorn, *hy"d*, the representative of *Keren Kayemet LeYisrael* [JNF] in our city, also joined the activists of the school and Mizrachi.

Mizrachi occupied a prominent place in all the Zionist activities that were held in our city. Mizrachi and its branches, the youth organizations, took first place in raising donations for *Keren Kayemet LeYisrael*. Mizrachi's influence, as one of the major parties in the Zionist camp, was also evident in the municipal elections, in community elections, and in the elections to the Zionist Congress. Mizrachi's representatives in the community were supported by all the Zionist parties in the city.

In 1935, with the increase in the possibility of immigration for craftsmen, a branch of The Center for Religious Craftsmen, which was affiliated with Mizrachi, was founded in our city. It was headed by the member, Daniel Beglbeiter, who is here with us.

And now a few words about the Mizrachi's youth movements, and they are: the federation of "*Tzeirei Ha'Mizrachi*" ["The Young Mizrachi"], "*Hechalutz Ha'Mizrachi*" ["The Mizrachi Pioneers"] and *Bruriah*, which concentrated the best of the older youth who originated from the Beit HaMidrash. Not only did they not abandon their previous education, but they also strengthened it by incorporating the doctrine of Zionism. And these two: the aspiration and action for Zion, with a traditional religious lifestyle, served as a guideline and a goal and purpose for their lives. We will only mention here two or three names. Moshe Shmuel Peil, Yehusua Maimon, Shlomo Magrem, *hy"d*, and long may he live, Gedalyahu Meiman who is now in America.

[Page 117]

With regard to the youngest branch, "*Hashomer Hadati*," I remember that in 1928, when I was eight years old, I was already a member of it. This movement, or its correct name, "*Ken Hashomer Hadati*," in Bilgoraj, developed a multidimensional educational activity among the Jewish youth in Bilgoraj, not only for those who received their education at "Yavne" School. Apart from Hebrew lessons, which also took place in "*Tzeirei Ha'Mizrachi*" and "*Hechalutz Ha'Mizrachi*," the youth were also given instruction in religion, and Zionism, pioneering, and personal fulfilment. There were many different and unusual educational methods used by "*Hashomer Hadati*" for the achievement of these goals. One of them was the "Summer Colonies." In the national "summer colony" for instructors of "*Hashomer Hadati*" in Nowy Targ, in the last summer before the war, the following representatives participated from the ken [branch] in Bilgoraj: my beloved friend Gershon Anger, *z"l*, Chaya Goldberg, *z"l*, (granddaughter of Shmuel Blender), and, may he live long, the writer of these lines.

"Yavne" School

That summer, two weeks before the outbreak of the war, a glorious celebration was held in Bilgoraj to mark the completion of the Torah scroll of *minyan* Mizrahi, whose writing took several years.

[Page 118]

The celebration was attended by a member of the movement's national leadership of "*Hashomer Hadati*," the member Yitzchak Meir Shenkar, *hy"d*. His appearance in a two–hour speech at the municipal synagogue in the presence of the Rabbi of Bilgoraj, the great rabbi R' Mordechai Rokeach, *z"l*, fascinated and excited the crowd which filled the synagogue to capacity. He captivated the public with the force and fluency of his speech, his rhetorical talent, his extensive knowledge of Judaism, and the enthusiasm he created in his listeners. As mentioned, the rabbi, *z"l*, was also among his listeners, and as a sign of admiration, he approached him at the end of the speech, and shook his hand in front of everyone. In those days, and under the same circumstances, it was an extraordinary step on the part of the rabbi, and added to the public's admiration for the speech and the speaker. The city of Bilgoraj had not seen such an occasion in a long time. (My last words will also serve as a memorial to the great soul of the aforementioned members who were also murdered by the accursed murderers).

When we now summon the memory of the city, Bilgoraj, with its Jews and their deeds, and we picture this festive and lofty occasion, the last one before the outbreak of the war, it will help us to understand what we had, and what is no more.

[Page 120]

Memories

The Knocker

by Shloime Weinberg

Translated by Moses Milstein

I was not born in Bilgoraj, although my father was from there. He himself was present at this event that occurred about 70 years ago.

There was a small house on Lubliner street where R' Lipeh Shochet lived. In that same house, up until the war, also lived Ben Zion Eilbert (Yechezkel Leml's son–in–law) who was the proofreader in R' Nuteh Kronenberg's printing shop.

One evening, when R' Lipeh Shochet was at the *besmedresh* for *minche–maariv*, his wife heard a knock at the window of their house. She thought to herself that it was probably a woman who, not wanting to enter the house, was knocking at the window so someone should come outside. But when she went outside, she was startled to see that there was no one there. She thought maybe the neighbor woman had knocked and left, or some child was playing a joke, so she went back inside.

No sooner had she entered the house, than she heard the same knocking on the same window. So she went outside again to see who was knocking, but again there was no one there. This happened a few more times until she became really frightened. She went to the *besmedresh*, called out her husband, R' Lipeh Shochet, and told him the whole story. She wanted him to know that the knocking was upsetting her.

R' Lipeh Shochet was a smart man, a great scholar, and he laughed at the story. He told his wife it was probably some kid playing a joke on her, and running away when she went outside. She obeyed her husband and went back home.

But, upon entering the house, she was stunned to hear the knocking again at the same window. In the meantime, R' Lipeh Shochet returned from the *besmedresh*. On hearing the knocking, he told his wife to stay indoors while he went out, and she would see that the knocking would stop.

[Page 121]

But he saw no one at the window, and he was astounded that the knocking could still be heard. He came to the conclusion that this was not an ordinary thing, and a great fear fell on him.

At that time, R' Nuteleh Berliner was the rav in Bilgoraj. R' Nuteh went to see him and told him what had happened. The rav immediately went over and heard the same knocking. So the rav ordered that a minyan should be gathered there every day for *minche–maariv*. (Because there was no noise during the day). But it did not help.

Every evening, the whole town would assemble there to witness the strange knocking. When someone yelled out it should knock louder, the knocking became stronger.

At this time, Y. L. Peretz was living in Zamosc, and R' Yakov Reifman was in Shebreshin[1]. When they first heard about this, they laughed it off. But when they began to hear the story of this mysterious knocking from a great many people, they both went to Bilgoraj. They searched all the places the noise could be coming from, but could find no clues. And this went on for a long time, people coming from all over the region to see this mysterious thing.

One day, R' Lipeh Shochet went to visit his rebbe (if I'm not mistaken it was *Haadmor* R' Abraham Hamalach). R' Lipeh Shochet told him about the knocking. The rebbe gave him some amulets, and the knocking stopped. And what caused this knocking is still a mystery to this day.

———

Translator's footnote:

1.   Szczebrzeszin

———

[Page 122]

The Horrible Murder in Bilgoraj

by Yehudeh Leifman

Translated by Moses Milstein

I, Yehudeh Leifman of Bilgoraj, (in Bilgoraj I was called Yudeh the singer's) am here to describe a horrible tragedy that happened in Bilgoraj to the Brandwein family 55 years ago.

There was a neighborhood in Bilgoraj called "the sands." It was on the road that led to the mill that then belonged to R' Leibtshe Worman, a big philanthropist. The mill was later bought by Hershele Sheinwald. Cossacks were billeted there.

In 1900, when Bilgoraj belonged to Russia, R' Yekel Brandwein was living in "the sands." He also had a food provision store there. He was the son–in–law of R' Yoneh Chaim Kronenberg.

R' Yekel had a family of four souls: He; his wife, Esther, R' Yoneh Chaim's daughter; a baby one year old; and a three years old boy, Shmuel Eliahu.

It happened Tishe–Bov….When people were on their way to the mill, they noticed that R' Yekel Brandwein's shutters were closed. Since it was already 10 o'clock, people began to fear that something had happened, and they called for the police.

When the police arrived, they broke open the door, and entered the house, and were confronted with a horrible scene.

[Page 123]

R' Yekel was lying dead near the door. The baby in its crib had been strangled. They found his wife, Esther, lying in bed unconscious, her face, her lips, her whole body lacerated. With great effort, they managed to revive her. Little Shmuel Eliyahu was nowhere to be seen.

As a large crowd was gathering, little Shmuel Eliahu crawled out of the clothes closet looking scared to death. Wailing loudly, he told them that during the night, three Cossacks broke in, and killed his father with an iron bar. They asked him how he had got into the closet, and he told them that an old Jew had come and put him in the closet, and warned him not to leave the closet until the next morning, and he told him he was his grandfather, Yoneh Chaim.

After little Shmuel Eliahu had calmed down, he told them that he would be able to identify the three Cossacks who killed his father.

When the colonel was informed, he immediately ordered the entire regiment of Cossacks to appear in formation. The colonel took Shmuel Eliahu, and together they walked through each row. Finally, little Shmuel Eliahu pointed to three Cossacks and said that these were the three who killed his father.

In order to be sure that little Shmuel Eliahu had not made a mistake, the colonel ordered the regiment to change its positions. They went through the ranks again, and for the second time, little Shmuel Eliahu identified the same three Cossacks.

[Page 124]

The three Cossacks were immediately arrested. The trial took place the following day. The three were sentenced to 18 years in prison.

That same year, Czar Nikolai went on a tour of his estate in Tomaszow–Lubelski. Along the way, travelling on his estate, the widow Esther's brother, Nuteh Kronenberg, submitted a plea to the Czar.

After a while, the widow Esther received a letter from the czarina containing 5 gold rubles. It was the czarina's duty to deal with welfare matters. She wrote that there had been many tragic occurrences that year, and that the treasury was empty.

———

[Page 125]

The Wedding in the Bilgoraj Cemetery

by A. Katari

Translated by Moses Milstein

During the First World War, Cholera raged through Bilgoraj, and people fell like flies. Every day so many people died that the *chevreh kedishe*[1] could not keep up with the burials.

The rebbe, old, and gray–haired, was constantly immersed in his books, searching for a remedy to stop the cholera. They tried writing; "There is no one here," in large letters, on every door, in order to fool the angel of death. When nothing seemed to be helping, the community decided to try the well–known remedy–celebrating a wedding in the cemetery.

In no time, the women charity workers, Gitl Moishe Itzi's, at the head, began preparations for the marriage of Mattl the Mute[2], who was getting on in years, and Yechezkeleh Viotch, the water–carrier.

They went around gathering clothing for the bride and groom. People gave their best. What wouldn't you do in order to halt the terrible plague?

On a given evening, in the small street behind the Rudniker *shtibl* where Mattl the Mute lived, the *machetunim* appeared, dressed in their finest, and with candles in their hands, led the bride and groom to the *chuppah*.

Yechezkeleh the groom went along happily in his fine clothes.

[Page 126]

The crowd grew from minute to minute. The cholera raging in town was forgotten for the time being. Old women with black shawls on their heads wailed continuously, considering the wedding not only a big mitzvah, but also a good remedy for an end to the plague.

At the cemetery, there was complete quiet. The *chuppah* was raised, the bride was led under it, the groom was made to circle seven times, and was placed next to the bride.

The rebbe took the ring, gave it to Yechezkel, and made him repeat word for word, "*Harei at mekudeshet li b'taba'at zo kedat Moshe v'Israel.*"[3]

Yechezkel had trouble with the "*Harei et*", and was so confused that he was unaware that a glass had been placed under his foot. He brought his foot down hard on the glass, and from everyone's mouth burst, "Mazel Tov! Mazel Tov!"

Leaving the *chuppah*, Gitl Moishe Itzi's danced with the *koiletch*, and the cemetery emptied out.

After the wedding, the plague gradually disappeared. Mattl the Mute continued to live in her hovel behind the Rudniker *shtibl*, Yechezkeleh continued to carry water for the tradesmen, and to live in the city poorhouse.

––––––––––

Translator's footnotes:

    1.   Jewish burial society
    2.   Die Shtumme Mattl
    3.   With this ring, you are consecrated to me according to the laws of Moses and Israel.

––––––––––

[Page 127]

Dream

by Shmuel Ben Artzi (Han)

Translated by Sara Mages

In memory of Bilgoraj my hometown

Tonight I was in my hometown
In a landscape that is dear to my heart in its glory. –
In my childhood well a reflection is still trembling,
My father's house is still standing.

The chestnut trees are already blazing red
Such is the nature of autumn in Poland.
My brother and I walk slowly as before,
We carry thatch for our *sukkah*.

The wind chases a cloud in the sky,
This evening the rain will not dare to come.
Soon we will be home
And we will quickly adorn our sukkah as prescribed.

We approached the house; - gentiles in our nest!
In vain I was looking for the Sukkah of Peace.
My brother left me his burden – and he is gone!
Alone there I cried to the end of the dream.

————

[Page 128]

At the Markets

by Rechl Kronenberg

Translated by Moses Milstein

The markets, which took place in all the surrounding communities, were the major source of income for the small merchants and tradesmen in Bilgoraj.

Throughout the week, Bilgoraj shoemakers, old–clothes tailors, hat makers, notions sellers, would travel around to the various markets: Monday, in Frampol; Tuesday, in Tarnogrod; Wednesday, in Jozefow; and Thursday, in Bilgoraj itself.

Before daylight, the market goers had their packs of merchandise, and tables ready, and waited for the peasant carts that were headed for the market.

Up until a few years before the Second World War, the roads that led to Tarnograd, Frampol, and Jozefow, were unpaved. On many occasions, the heavily laden wagons became stuck in the mud. The passengers had to get off the wagons, and walk through the deep mud, and more than one lost his shoes.

Worse yet, a wagon loaded with merchandise and people sometimes fell into the mud and overturned. Their screams could be heard for miles. It was painful to see them gathering their belongings in the muck.

The worst was the return trip late at night.

[Page 129]

The dark roads that snaked through the dense forest were frightening. It was not uncommon for bandits to ambush the wagons, and steal the entire income earned from the day's sale of merchandise.

Such an event did, in fact, occur in 1922. Two horse traders, Chaim Blutman, and Leibish Gerstenman were returning from the market in Majdan–Kojbaszewski when they were befallen by bandits. Having both been soldiers, they threw themselves on the bandits. After a hard struggle, they were both shot.

In spite of the danger, people continued, week in and week out, in the heat of summer, or the cold of winter, to travel to the markets in order to make a living.

————

[Page 130]

A Visit to my Shtetl, Bilgoraj

by M. Rapaport (Australia)

Translated by Moses Milstein

I can never forget my shteteleh, Bilgoraj, and her dear Jews who I remember with such reverence. Many were goodhearted people, who would readily sacrifice themselves for other Jews and for Yiddishkeit.

It is worth remembering Jews like R' Levi Stern, *a"h*, who was beloved and revered by everyone. He was not a rich man. He was a baker, a strong man who worked very hard. When he wasn't working, he was studying, or helping the poor and the sick. He was the *gabai* in the Rudniker shtibl, *gabai* in the *chevreh keddishe*[1], *dozor*[2] in the Jewish community, chairman of *Bikur Cholim*[3]. He was a *machnes oirech*,[4] a generous contributor to charity, and saw to it that others gave too.

During the war, after Bilgoraj was destroyed by fire, he went to Tarnogrod and baked bread in secret, helping the poor and the hungry.

In the month of Elul, 1942, he and hundreds of others from Bilgoraj and Tarnogrod were taken to Belzec and murdered in the gas chambers.

His son, Isrulke, who was a big scholar, was shot in Puszcza on the way to Belzec when he got off the truck to relieve himself.

[Page 131]

As the Jews were being driven through Bilgoraj, Levi, the strong one, jumped off the truck and with a mournful tone cried, "*Yidden*, where are they taking us?"

It is worth remembering a man like my uncle, Abraham Harman, a big philanthropist and *machnes oirech*. He had a special book for *gemiles chesed*[5]. If someone had to marry off somebody, or was in difficult straits, and came to him, he turned no one away. He died in Tarnogrod a short time after the aktion. He was buried in the Bilgoraj cemetery as per his request in his will.

It is also worth remembering such noble people, scholars, goodhearted Jews, like Nuteh Kronenberg; my uncle, Yosele, and my father, Shmuel Eliahu Rapaport; Hersh Weissman; Henoch Hochman; Isrulke Stern; Hersh Yechazkel Harman; Avrumele Hochman; Shmultche Shreiber; Motl Harman, and others. It is hard to list all these dear people who perished at the hands of the German murderers.

Soon after liberation, before Rosh Hashanah, I came to Lublin with the Polish army. The day after Rosh Hashanah, I went to Bilgoraj on foot. There was no train yet.

Arriving in the city, I felt its gloom pervade me. I was born in Bilgoraj, and lived there until the war. I walked around in the middle of the day, and hardly recognized a thing. Lubelski street, the large square where the shul was, the big *besmedresh*, the small *besmedresh*, the bath house, the slaughterhouse, the Zichron Yakov cheder, the old cemetery, the old rabbi's house, the new house of the Belzer rabbi's son, R'Mordechai, the Trisker shtibl, the Rudniker shtibl.–everything was one vast empty square where no living soul was to be seen.

[Page 132]

The streets, paved with tombstones bearing Jewish writing, filled me with fear. It looked like one big graveyard.

I went into a store to get a bit of butter. I stood there in shock as I watched the grocer wrap the butter in paper, in pages from the Vilna Talmud. I remembered how hard it was for a Jew to be able to afford a Vilna Talmud, for example, for his son–in–law's studies. It seemed to me I could hear the ringing melody of "*amar Abaye v'Rava.*" I threw the butter away when I left, and put the precious words in my pocket.

The new cemetery was a wasteland, the trees chopped down, the tombstones toppled, the walls demolished. The cemetery by Laizer Kigel was unrecognizable. Barracks had been erected there, and a paved road ran through it.

My erstwhile brothers–in–law survived the war in an attic over a pig sty at a certain Skako of the Boyars. They were Baruch Wermut, and Hersh Silberfein and a daughter; and Benny Hochman, and a son. Moishe Boim died in the bunker.

This is what became of my shteteleh Bilgoraj after the great destruction. I left with tears in my eyes, the echoes of *yitkadal v'yitkaddash* ringing in my ears.

———

Translator's footnotes:

1. Burial society
2. Member of synagogue council
3. Visiting the sick
4. Person who regularly invites the poor to his home
5. Society providing interest free loans

———

[Page 133]

Churban Bilgoraj

by I. D. Mittlepunkt

Translated by Moses Milstein

Va'yehie, and it came to pass, in the days of the
dark twilight,

In Hitler's era of death factories, concentration camps, bayonets,
When the enemy's wrath began more terribly
to roar, to seethe
And Bilgoraj was struck too, there are
no more Jews there.

With their last strength and breath,
To the clouded sky, high…high…
A prayer was torn from Jewish hearts,

"*Ya'aleh tachanuneinu*" from Yom Kippur night, and "Gates of Heaven open"
on *Neilah*.

The heartrending words, interrupted,
The devil of slaughter, burning, shooting,
Fire, rifle and sword,
Draped in black—mother earth…

Gone are the besmedreshim, *shtiblach*,
Organisations, unions, gone is Jewish splendor,
Shadows of Jewish destruction float in the air,
Over which the devil's dance is celebrated.

You won't see our beloved *amcho*[1]
On the bridge street, the Jewish sieve building,
You see other people going by—
Uninvited heirs of Jewish blood, need, and pain…

And the forest? Which echoed with
Joy, laughter and Yiddish sounds,
Shabbatim, yom Toivim and years of happiness,
No Jewish feet stride there now, there are
no more Jews…

And the little besmedresh'l,
Where our *amcho* got in a little *borchu*, a chapter of *t'hilim*
Heard a good word from *yalkut, midrash* and other holy texts
Everything is gone…no memory, no monument, no graves…

There is no more beloved idyll,
Of Jewish porters, decent, broad-shouldered men,
Who used to sit in the besmedresh at a table off to the side,
Or comfortably chatted behind the city hall.

In Bilgoraj there are no more *Sorelach, Motelach*,
The beloved boys and girls,
In little cloth *kapotkelach*[2]
And in checked little dresses…

And no longer are there children walking winter nights,
With lanterns from the cheders,
A horrible power,
Hurled them away somewhere…no tombstones, no graves…

Future generations will someday read,
A sorrowful tale of death factories, bayonets,
barbed wire,
Bilgoraj will also be remembered,
A Jewish city destroyed…

Translator's footnotes:

1. Our Jewish people
2. Long black coats

———

[Page 136]

A Jewish Teacher in Bilgoraj

by Y. Hodess

Translated by Sara Mages

My town, Bilgoraj.

As was the fate of tens of thousands of Jews, in every place the Nazi's boot stepped on, so was the fate of the Jews of my town, Bilgoraj. The enemy plotted to erase the name and the memory of the Jews, their towns and villages, but they did not succeed.

The surviving Jews, from every village and town, gather to establish a memorial to the extinct towns and the exterminated Jews. We, the Jews of Bilgoraj, will also raise the memory of our town, the memory of its Jews and its landscape.

We will re–weave the canvas of bustling Jewish life in the Diaspora of Poland and for this chapter, the chapter of Bilgoraj, and I also want to weave in my thread.

* *

I was born in 1915, at the height of the First World War, to my parents Mordechai and Leah Hodess – merchants in Bilgoraj. Four days after my birth, the war arrived at the border of our town, and I was taken by cart to Lublin – until the hostilities ended.

When I grew up, I began my studies at the general state school in Bilgoraj. It was a public school, for Jews and gentiles, and boys and girls attended it together. Most of the students were Jews, and so were most of the town's residents. Out of twelve thousand residents, the number of Jews reached 65%. Such a ratio, between gentiles and Jews, also existed at school.

I finished seven grades at this school, and contrary to what was customary at the time, I chose the teaching profession for myself. Since there was no teachers' seminary in Bilgoraj I was forced to leave my home. Without my parents' knowledge, I made my way by bicycle, a distance of fifty kilometers, to the city of Szczebrzeszyn where I was accepted at the teachers' seminary.

Those days were the days of the "*Numerus Clausus*" law[1]. It was not easy for a Jew to be admitted to a Polish school for higher education and therefore, even after I was accepted – my life was not easy within the institution's walls.

[Page 137]

Also, the subjects I chose for myself were not very typical for a Jew from a town in the Diaspora: nature and geography. As mentioned, my life in that institution was not easy, and at the end of two years of study I was caught "in a serious offense" – smoking a cigarette in secret – and was transferred to Lesna–Podlaska near Biala. There, I continued my studies for another three years, and in 1934 I finished my studies, and received a graduation certificate. That year, I returned home to Bilgoraj and was accepted to teach at the same school I had attended as a child. As was customary, I had to teach a trial year without pay, but I received a partial pay for my work.

I was the only Jewish teacher in the general state school, the rest of the teachers were gentiles. This fact gave me special roles. In addition to teaching, I had to serve as an instructor, I had to protect and encourage the Jewish students who were often persecuted by gentile teachers who were not completely free from the anti–Semitic complex. I had to serve as a deciding factor between the teachers' pressure on one hand, and the Jewish students' complaints on the other.

In addition to the two special subjects that I taught, geography and nature, I was instructed to teach the Jewish students the history of the Jewish people. I took advantage of the opportunity that we were Jews among Jews, and taught the history of Zionism. I told them about Eretz Yisrael and its construction, and to my joy the seed I had sown bore fruit. Of course, I also devoted time to the teaching of general Jewish history that, in any case, was integrated with the aspiration of the Jews for a homeland in Eretz Yisrael.

The close contact with the Jewish youth in the town, the sight of the terrible poverty in which they lived, their poverty and their distress, gave me another role: a broad action to raise funds and other help, to allow a minimum portion of food for the children, and some warm clothing.

I organized the few rich people in the town, and we did our best to improve the nutrition and clothing of the children who were, for the most part, in appalling poverty.

[Page 138]

In this manner, I taught at school until the eve of the outbreak of the Second World War. Anti–Semitism, which received a lot of encouragement across the border, had begun long before the outbreak of the war. My situation at school was very difficult in this last year, and I was offered a move to a Jewish school in Otwock near Warsaw. Before I started the new school year in my new place, I left for a regular school vacation. But it was no longer possible to start teaching: the first German bombs fell on Polish soil even before the start of the school year – the Second World War had begun. My fate was no different from the fate of hundreds of thousands of other Jews persecuted by the Nazi predators. But our town holds no special place in this story. The fate of a Jew born by chance in Bilgoraj was like the fate of a Jew born elsewhere throughout Poland.

*

A large and extensive Jewry was destroyed, but despite the suffering, killing and persecutions, the Jews shook themselves from their disaster and created, right after the great disaster, their wonderful creation – the State of Israel.

Among the founders of the country, its builders and defenders, it is also possible to meet those Jewish children, the students of the general school in Bilgoraj. The seed sown then bears fruit, and this serves a source of encouragement and consolation. The people of Bilgoraj in Eretz Yisrael erect a monument in memory of the town of Bilgoraj and its Jews.

Translator's footnote:

1.   Laws limiting the number of Jewish students allowed to attend an educational institution

———

[Page 139]

The Bilgoraj Feldsher[1]

by A. Kronenberg (Katari)

Translated by Moses Milstein

Up until WWI, there was only one doctor in Bilgoraj. He was called Sawicki. Jews rarely went to see him, because not everyone had the means to use a doctor.

In those days almost everybody used various folk cures and remedies.

When someone fell sick, the first thing they tried was "*opleshen koilen.*" They took a cup of hot water, and threw it on the burning coals. If the coals fell down, it was a sign that the patient was the victim of an evil eye. So they quickly called for a boy, gave him the name of the sick person, and his mother's name, and sent him to Sholom Hershele's or Itzi Meir Melamed who were specialists in exorcising the evil eye.

After exorcising the evil eye, they paid close attention to see if the patient yawned. If he yawned, it was a sign that the he had been affected by the evil eye, and that the exorcism had helped.

If the patient did not get better, they interrogated the kid to see if maybe he had not forgotten the victim's name, or mixed it up, which would then be the reason the treatment hadn't worked.

[Page 140]

In the case of someone who was paralyzed, word was immediately sent to Sarah Mordechai Yosef's. She would pour water on the victim's head, and interpret the signs of what had frightened him.

If someone had a rash, Sarah would take a bundle of flax, light it, and heat the rash while reciting various incantations, continuously repeating, "Black rash, into the fields with you, into the fields." After, she would take a handkerchief, smear honey on it, and apply it to the rash.

When a serious sickness struck, and the folk remedies hadn't helped, they sent for Shloime Roife the feldsher.

Three brass trays hung at the feldsher's door. (That was the sign). In truth, a feldsher then did not have a medical degree. Shloime Roife had served in the Russian army as an orderly, and after his service, he became a feldsher. He wore a black top hat, had a pointy beard, and was the only Jew in town who wore a short jacket. Women would whisper that he washed with scented soap, and ate tomatoes, which were then considered *treyf* in Bigoraj.

When he attended the sick, he was greeted with great respect, and attention given to his every word. He asked the patient where it hurt, checked his pulse, opened the little bag he used to carry with him, chose several instruments, examined the throat, and prescribed aspirin. (They could not, and were not allowed, to write prescriptions).

[Page 141]

He could administer "*gehakte bankes*," "*piafkes*," paint the throat, or make "*klizmes*." If someone had a toothache, he went to Shloime Roife. He would seat him on a stool, grab the tooth, and before he had a chance to yell, the tooth would be out.

He was the only barber in town.

In later years, his son would accompany him, and then take over the business through inheritance.

Translator's footnote:

   1.   Unlicensed medical practitioner

[Page 142 - Hebrew] [Page 280 - Yiddish]

If You Ever Want to Know

by I. H. Kronenberg

Translated by Sara Mages

Jew, if you ever want to know,
The history of your people and their
sufferings,
Don't turn to books
And don't listen to lectures.
Go to the fields of Europe and the forests of
Poland!
Listen to the trembling grass
And hear the secret conversation of the
trees.
And you will understand: in every rose a
mother's heart flutters,
In the green-veined leaves, a sister's blood is
flowing.
And the dew droplets – are the tears of a
child,
And know! These are your parents and
relatives.
Who watered the Polish soil with their blood
And their oppressors fertilized it with the
ashes of their bones,
Our ancestors became dust from its dust,
And it – to flesh from their flesh,
Our children's blood fertilized it, and it
conceived and raised a bud and a flower.
Mother Earth adorned herself with flowers,

And covered the grave of Able her son,
And as a victor stands Cain the "farmer,"
Who saturated his land with our blood,
And in his place, we, who were homeless
like Able, the "wanderers and exiled,"
without being given a foothold–

[Page 143]

The Passion for Eretz Israel

by Itzchak Rapaport

Translated by Moses Milstein

During the First World War, when Bilgoraj was occupied by Austria, the Bilgoraj youth joined the ranks of the *chalutzim* movement. The *Hechalutz* was created which imbued the youth with Zionism.

Later, after the establishment of the Polish government, at the start of the fourth aliyah, Bilgoraj sent its first pioneers. The memory of the celebration that reigned in the city at every departure for Eretz Israel is still fresh. Almost the whole city went to see them off at the kolejka (little train). The singing of *Hatikvah* and *Tachzeknah* carried through the whole city, and breathed life into the youth.

Even later, when aliyah was banned, Bilgoraj young people took part in the illegal aliyah, disregarding the difficulties encountered along the way. And in 1939, I had the honor to be one of the pioneers in the illegal aliyah. Even though I had a good home, I decided to dedicate my future to our land.

I will always remember the words of my father, z"l, "If you really want to join the "*Bilu*"[1] (*Beit Yakov Lchu V'nelcha*) may it also be "in God's light." Be a Jew. Remember "*K'mo sh'adam rotzeh lalechet, molichin otto.*" My old grandfather, R' Moishe Goldberg, z"l, also encouraged me with the words, " '*Kumi tz'i mi'toch ha'hafeicha, rav lach shevet b'emek ha'bacha, v'hu yachamol alayich chemla.*[2]' with God's help, you will surmount all the hardships."

[Page 144]

With such encouragement and faith, at the end of July 1939, I said goodbye to my parents and relatives, and left on the illegal immigration carrying only a small pack containing a change of clothing, a blanket and other trifles. I left Bilgoraj promptly at 12:30 at night. It is hard to imagine the feelings that overcame me then, tearing myself away from my beloved shtetl Bilgoraj where I was born and raised. But I was proud that I was going off to help build our sacred land.

In Zwierzyniec, I waited endlessly for the Lemberg–Warsaw train. Once on the train, I instantly sensed a different atmosphere. Every car was filled with young smiling faces. They asked me where I was from, and how many were travelling in our group. I settled myself in a compartment with others, and we quickly became like old friends.

When day was dawning, and the birds were beginning to chirp, Hebrew songs broke out spontaneously from every window. Upon arrival in Lublin, the whole company was concentrated in two train cars. We sang and danced the hora with youthful enthusiasm the whole way, the echoes carrying for miles around.

In Warsaw, we were taken straight away to a place prepared for us at the academic house in Praga.

[Page 145]

The academic house looked like a large train station. People were packing and readying things, writing, or just plain talking. Everyone was wondering, when will we be going? Three days passed as we waited in Warsaw.

One day, we received an order that we had 30 minutes to get ready for the train. There was a big commotion. Every group leader mustered his people. Naturally, there were many people missing. A search was organized, and before things were under control, the commander of the transport arrived and gave an order, and within 10 minutes 1500 people were arranged in military formation ready to march to the train station. After singing the Betar hymn, we left for the Gedania train station.

There was a huge crowd come to see off the travellers at the train station. The train was decorated in blue– white banners, and slogans. The whole leadership of Betar in Poland was in attendance, with Menachem Begin at the head. We entered the train cars in a pre–established order, and the whistle sounded. Singing Hatikvah, we left Warsaw on the way to the land we had long yearned for.

We had passed through several stations, when we received a big surprise. Menachem Begin appeared with the late Stawski, z"l. They handed a passport to each of us containing: the exit visas, and transit visas through Romania and Turkey to the territorial waters of Eretz Israel.

[Page 146]

We held the passports in our hands, and prayed that we would be worthy, that we would arrive safely. Hour by hour, we were distancing ourselves from our old home, and getting closer to our dream, Eretz Israel.

After a day of travelling by train, we arrived at the Polish border city, Sniatyn. We were billeted in the Jewish theater. It was run like a military camp with strict discipline.

In Sniatyn, we were told that for various reasons, we would have to spend several days here. Unfortunately, we spent several weeks there, and in the end, we were forced to go back. It turned out that the English government had found out about the large transport. They sent a secret message to the Romanian government demanding that the transport not be allowed through. Since the political situation was already tense, the Romanian government did not want to disturb relations with England over a few Jews who wanted to throw off the 2000 year old diaspora.

After 4 weeks in Sniatyn, Menachem Begin and Eri Jabotinsky[3], and others appeared. They gave a lecture on Eretz Israel, and informed us that, unfortunately, we could not proceed further. The Romanian government refused to let us pass through. We had to temporarily go back. There will come a time when we will be able to continue, we were told. In the meantime, if there were any who could get through Romania to Constantinople illegally, they would immediately be placed on board the ship still waiting for us.

[Page 147]

Groups quickly formed. Several dozen *chaverim* crossed the border, and in a few weeks landed on the shores of Netanya. The majority, including myself, opted for returning.

Back home, the first mobilization took place. The German murderers invaded Poland. Within a few days, our beloved shtetl Bilgoraj was burned down, and the destruction of our unforgettable city was underway.

By chance, some Jews left for Russia. I was lucky to be one of those. After living through various experiences, years in jails and camps, and after a span of seven years, I was finally able to walk on the soil of our long–awaited land.

———

Translator's footnotes:

1.   Settlement movement
2.   Arise and flee from the midst of the chaos, Long have you sat in the valley of tears, And He will grant mercy, mercy upon you.
3.   Son of Zev Jabotinsky

———

[Page 148]

I Loved You, Bilgoraj

by I. H. Kronenberg

Translated by Sara Mages

I loved you, Bilgoraj,
I always loved you, for your Jews:
Your merchants, your porters and your
workshops workers,
For the people of the "*shtiblekh*" and those
who come to your *Batei Midrash*,
For the alleys of "Bridge" Street that have
always been buzzing with your children.

I love the beauty of your plains and your
mountains,
The meadow pasture and the water of your
"springs."
The walk in the evenings and bathing in your
rivers,
The dew mists that cover your meadows,
The redness of the sun rising over your
forests.

I loved you for the beauty of your scenery,
And always hated you for your "Cains"
Who helped the murderess when they
slaughtered your Jews,
Laughed at the women who were dragged
through your streets naked,
And at the babies who rolled like pillows in
your streets.

Daughter of my nation! Foreign landscapes
and foreign land nurtured you,
Therefore you fertilized its soil with the
ashes of your bones.
Oppressed and foreign you were in the
Diaspora,
That's why many were your haters in the
whole world.

> Every house - a refuge for your murderers,
> Every place - ready to your crematorium
> And the bodies of the murdered in all your
> cemeteries.
>
> Happy is the eye that sees your return to your
> homeland
> And the building of your country, your birth-
> place.

––––––––––

[Page 149]

The Nest of Need

by Shmuel Baron

Translated by Moses Milstein

The courtyard belonging to Moishe Berl (Moishe Shtok) was angular, but not quadrangular. It was longer than it was wide, like a box with no top. The low, densely packed houses filled three sides. The fourth side was wide open, the gutter with its wooden bridge at the entrance separating the yard from the street which sloped steeply from Motl Itzik Hersh's house, past the new cheder, shul yard, and the old cemetery down to the river and the bridge. That's why the street was called the "Bridge."

Above the courtyard, exactly opposite the street, the terrain began to rise uphill, resembling an old person's rounded back carrying on it the ancient, multi-branched pear tree which shaded the closely packed houses, and did not allow any sunshine or warmth to penetrate.

To the right of the pear tree, two narrow lanes, like blood arteries, seemed almost to draw the houses closer together. They climbed up to the top where they united, dividing into two new directions, one to the Trisker *shtibl* and the shul yard, and the other through Zelig Merzel and the plum trees to the market.

Before Pesach, when the frozen ground began to warm up, and the accumulated ice to melt, the two narrow lanes released their contents, and the yard was flooded with water and whatever waste people emptied out of the houses, and everything swam downhill, flooding the yard and the houses before emptying into the gutter from both sides of the wooden bridge, and finally, the river.

[Page 150]

Slowly, the remaining mud began to dry, and vast clouds of flies that had been feeding on the debris carried by the water, waylaid every passerby, settled on the windows and the walls, forcing themselves into houses, and their buzzing, along with the noise of children, created a symphony of joy for the coming spring.

The days of winter passed. The sun rose high above Moishe Berl's courtyard. A new life awakened, the pre-Pesach days symbolizing days of redemption and renewal. The little square threw off the biting cold and frost. The mud was gone. A lighter, silvery dust gleamed in the sun's rays which crept into houses through the cracks where children reflected the rays onto the walls with broken bits of mirrors, and played "*feigelach.*"

The neighbors in the little courtyard prepared for the coming holiday. Mothers and daughters washed clothes in big round washtubs. The smell of soap and soda permeated the entire yard. From time to time, a dark gray skein of sudsy water from the emptied tubs flowed by. After this, the mothers and daughters carried the laundry and washboards to the river to rinse and beat it on the rocks.

[Page 151]

The happy sound of the washboards, mixed with joy and laughter, filled the surroundings until the evenings, until the sun went down behind the tops of the *tsmentash* trees.

Returning wet, the women again filled the little courtyard with long lines of ropes knotted together around trees and walls, and the whiteness of the hanging laundry gleamed in the light of the moon that illuminated the yard like a giant lantern.

Dawns came and evenings went. New worries and concerns arose; how to bring Pesach into the home.

In those pre-yom-tov days, everyone was forced to reckon with their poverty. The old carved commodes and cupboards opened their arms to reveal the destitution, the worn-out robes with torn elbows, pants, and undergarments. They were once nice, worn with joy at first. Many of them recalled the distant past, the first steps to a new life (the wedding).

Years went by, people aging prematurely. Children were brought into the world, partners in need and poverty. Pale little faces, yearning for good fortune, the warmth of life. How do these children greet the holiday? With tattered, outgrown suits, worn-out shoes with the color gone from the tops, white at the toes (nothing to polish them with), hats with torn peaks. How can you bring these sweet children along to shul? Sadness gripped the hearts of the parents.

The women may spend the whole year in the poverty of their homes, Shabbes with their Yiddish *chumash*, but yom-tov?

[Page 152]

How can a Jewish woman not go to shul? But how can she do it? Worn out, oft-patched skirts, threadbare shawls. The last earrings and candlesticks already pawned to get through the winter. No shoes, the wig dating from the wedding still not combed out.

The young girls look on with envy at the better off girls promenading on the street in their new dresses and shoes, bows in their hair.

These are the thoughts which arise looking at this poverty, black clouds shrouding the beautiful world–where, how, to make do?

There were cases where the appearance of the mailman saved our neighbors from desperation. An uncle, an aunt, or any relative in far-off America remembered his debt, and punctually repaid it. Then the situation changed completely. There was rejoicing in the home. The faces of the parents and children, like after a terrible storm, lightened up, and joyful shouts, and sometimes a little cursing filled the house.

Try this on, my child, stand straight. A houseful of stuff acquired–shoes, pants, caps, socks, and little *tallit katans*. Also a robe for father. The girls, since they don't go to shul, are left out.

This is how the erev yom-tov fever began. Mother and daughter took to patching the bed sheets, mending clothes, whitewashing the walls and ceilings yellowed by smoke. After the whitewashing, the floors were scraped with knives revealing the wax-yellow, washed boards.

[Page 153]

Clothes are aired out after a whole year. Windows, and window panes were washed. In the corners, white dazzling sheets hold matzos that were baked cooperatively. Smaller jobs remained like hanging the lamp with its chains–refurbished after a year of dirt, and fly specks, with a gold powder–so that it sparkled, and a new wick installed. Fresh straw was put into the beds that had been cleaned with boiling water, and curtains were hung over the windows.

Pine logs crackled merrily in the stove where the pans were heated, and later smeared with lime. The rooms took on a wonderful aromatic warmth. Yom-tov is on the threshold, Pesach is here.

Pesach passed with its eight carefree days. The courtyard returned to its daily cares and worries. The long, hot summer days arrived. Children from the courtyard went out to gather blue lilacs whose smell tickled their noses, and whose beauty charmed the young shining eyes.

The old pear tree in the courtyard began to come back to life, its crown decorated with white-violet buds. The buzzing of the bees around the opening buds was like a musical drone accompanying the work.

After a short time, the blossom petals began to fall en masse creating a snowfall around the tree. Its crown was soon festooned with small green leaves. It was a sign of its rebirth, growing taller and broader, more stately and prouder, the nakedness of its branches bejeweled with new fresh growth as if it had just burst through the soil.

[Page 154]

It changed from day to day. The leaves became bigger, wider, dark green, and between them like beads, the tiny pears. Even below, around its old trunk, the stones and roots uncovered from the ground, dried out, light green young grass grew in a semicircle on the side where the sun's warmth could reach.

The lives in the houses also changed, and took on a summer aspect. The old, small, boarded up windows were opened wide, throwing off the lime packing which had been nailed and glued around the windows in winter to keep the cold out.

The tall oven reaching up to the ceiling, and the wide stove with six burners, two doors and a grate in the middle got to rest. We no longer snuggled against it, reviving ourselves with its warmth. The broad bench that stood before the length of the oven, was orphaned, abandoned, like its neighbors.

Just once a week, Fridays, the little door was opened. A small red fire of crackling spruce lit the darkness of the kitchen depths, carrying itself into the cracks in the old bricks, into the air.

[Page 155]

This kingdom belonged to her majesty all week. The "feet" stood on tin pans. Near the soot covered feet, the mothers stood and blew their breath on the glowing coals and wood. A *Shtchaf*[1] borscht that the children had picked in the meadow was cooking in tall pots, a soup to dunk bread in, or a few dumplings with potatoes, when they came home for lunch from cheder. Dumplings and beans were cooked for supper when the men returned from Minche-Maariv. If God had bestowed a good day, in the evening dark, you could smell a stew of veal and buckwheat kasheh. After such a meal, the men would take a nap. The neighboring women would sit outside on the benches and thresholds of their houses, and talk about things they had heard, about good Jews, and demons.

Most of the time, the evening ended with gossip about one neighbor from another, what she herself had seen, what another had heard. In the morning, they went to investigate, and all the stories popped like soap bubbles. They quarreled, became angry with each other, would not look at each other until either a *simcheh*, or God forbid, a tragedy occurred, and they would make up, shed tears…for someone's misfortune, or rejoice for another's happiness.

The youngsters ran around the courtyard barefoot, sometimes with bloody toes, playing hide-and-seek.

[Page 156]

Their high-pitched voices rang through the whole courtyard until they became tired and they fell on their beds with feet blackened by dirt and dust. The older ones undressed the younger ones, and everyone went to bed in the dirty shirts they had worn all day.

After a hard day's work, the young people returned from the river in the evening, after having washed their young bodies delighting in the clean cold water. In the dimness of the courtyard they were as swallowed up, everyone to his own house, eating quickly. Some were tired and went to sleep in order to rest their tired limbs for the following workday. Some attended organizations that were noisy and lively until late at night.

Others sat in the red shine of a night lamp, reading a book that gripped their youthful imagination, and took them into the lives of the characters, feeling and reliving the story until a weariness came on them, and their eyelids began to close. A young deep sleep overtook them, and separated them from the day.

The courtyard became quieter and quieter. The last lights from the night lamps in the windows went out. The last shutters were shut with a squeak from their rusty hinges. A deep darkness enveloped everything in its night-arms, until dawn, until the first cock-crow.

Thursday, market day, has passed. For whoever has bought what they need, prepared for Shabbes, for the week, there is only Friday left, the last day of the week.

[Page 157]

Friday has arrived in the courtyard. Not as usual, not like other days. At first cock-crow, when the night surrendered its kingdom to the daytime, when the first red-streaked rays appeared low in the east, the courtyard residents began to awaken. The shutters opened with a noisy crash. A cold early-morning wind rushed in through the open window that was immediately shut for fear the children should not, God forbid, get sick. The stale night air in the house condensed on the windows like fog. The red fire of the fireplace, looked like a hanging spark against the emerging day.

The morning brightness continued to flood into the dimness of the house. The call of the cuckoos sitting in the pear tree woke the residents as if to morning prayer.

Housewives wake up, the daughters after them. The father, after putting on his taliss and *tfillin* chops wood for the stove. The housewives remove the pillows from the kneading troughs where the dough for the coming week has been rising, and begin to knead. The girls knead the dough for the challahs and poppy seed cookies. The oven is already burning with a red flame of pine that spreads over the half-round vault of the oven, and is carried out the little doors to the chimney.

Page 158]

Outside, the courtyard gives the impression of a giant industrial center, with dozens of chimneys from which thick clouds of smoke rise to the sky. A cozy warmth fills the homes. The children have gotten up, washed, said the *broches*, and made their way to cheder–bringing along some fresh *paplinkes*.

But the Friday fullness and happiness did not reign everywhere. This could even be seen from the outside. You just had to look at the chimney to see for whom the coming Shabbes would not be a happy one. In those houses, people did not get up so early. The doors and windows were shut. The children went to cheder hungry and worried that they had no money for tuition, afraid the teacher would send them back home. These homeowners, like guilty people, left the house early, as if afraid they would miss something.

At lunchtime, these housewives heated the stoves, placed pots of water into the chafing dishes so that it would look like something was cooking so that if a neighbor came in, ostensibly to ask something, she would not detect what the situation was in the house. Unfortunately, this rarely worked, because many neighbors used the same ruse.

This is how guarded they were; this is how they were apprehensive at every creak of the door. If he were lucky, the homeowner, at noon, could maybe borrow a few Zlotys, or pawn something, even at two or three o'clock, and the housewives and their assistants, like robots, would come to life.

[Page 159]

Immediately, bread, challah, herring, and candles appeared; beans, rice or kasheh began cooking.

First thing they did was eat. The mood changed. The rooms were swept, cleaned, the children washed with the tubs of water. They even lit and blessed the candles like everyone else.

All the fathers came straight home from davening with a "*guten* Shabbes," as they entered the house. The candles were cheerfully burning, Shabbes-like. Soon a fervent "*Shalom aleichem, malachei hasharet, malachei elion*" could be heard, every word like a flame ignited…and soon, "*Eyshes chayel mi yimtsah.*" She, the *eyshes chayal* of a poor Yiddish household, sat like after a hard-fought victory, exhausted, worn out. Her chest softly rising with each breath. A tear gathered at the corner of her eyes, as she listened to the songs of praise from her husband for the *eyshes chayel*. It is forbidden to be sad on Shabbes. A good Shabbes, a worse Shabes. It's all Shabbes. If there is no fish, herring is also food. And, in fact, between the herring and the dumplings with beans, a few songs, "*Menucha v'simcha, or l'yehudim, yom shabaton, yom mechmadim.*" the children sing along, and the poorness of the table is forgotten.

And this is how time passed, day-by-day, week-by-week. The hot summer sun burned the skin of the thin courtyard residents who, in their free moments, sought rest in the shade by the river among the bushes and trees.

Mostly, it was the young and the children who could take the time to rest.

[Page 160]

The older ones could not afford the luxury due to the demands of need and time, and which responsible adult goes swimming with youngsters in the middle of the day? The adult men would go down to the river in the evening, quickly dunk themselves a few times in the water, and go off to Minche-Maariv their beards and *payess* dripping with water.

The days were bearable, but the nights were tiresome. The cramped houses mostly consisted of one room with a vestibule, the large kitchen and the stove with its hearth taking up a third of the room, with no creature comforts.

A thick, choking air hung in the homes, and served as food, and reproduction for various insects.

Before the night lamp was extinguished, the black, irritating flies with their coarse legs, and biting mouths, chewed on the flesh of the sleeping children. Hundreds of brown long-mustached cockroaches assaulted the oven, the kitchen crannies, and the mantelpiece like a swarm of locusts.

The children, pressed together, sleeping head to foot in bunk beds, or in bedding laid out on the boards of the bunks, tossing in bed, were awakened, shouting, "They're biting, *mameh*, they're biting me." When mother lit the night lamp, clouds of red-bellied, blood- sated bed bugs began to run over the bedding into their crevices. As soon as it was dark, the vast plague returned to bite and suck the anemic children again, until exhausted, they fell into a deep sleep, shielding them from the pain.

[Page 161]

In the morning, the children awoke with red, bitten, and scratched, bloody bodies, with red, swollen lips or eyes.

Summer with its hot days can be felt to be coming to an end. The wheat fields around the city had been harvested. The peasants have tied the cut wheat into sheaves, and carried them in wagons piled high, to the farms, only the cut straw, like yellow wire ends, left sticking out of the black earth.

A cold, biting, autumn wind began to blow in the evenings, tearing the remaining yellowed leaves from the chestnut trees and orchards. And the old pear tree in the courtyard also changed its appearance, its little green pears long ago dislodged by kids throwing stones. They covered the fruit with straw to make into *lezhilkes*. Bees no longer buzzed around its crown. The cuckoo did not sing its early morning song. It looked pitiable, like an old man abandoned by his children.

From time to time a black crow alighted on its branches, holding tightly with its sharp claws. Stretching its black-feathered neck, its mouth opened in a noisy shout, until the kids aimed a stone at it, and it flew away.

The courtyard cats also played among its branches, leaping from one branch to another.

[Page 162]

Or a hungry horse with his old yellowed teeth gnawed on the bark down to the wood. The courtyard was enveloped in gloomy sadness.

Rosh Hashanah passed, and Yom Kippur followed quickly. The courtyard residents' faces changed, took on a worried and careworn appearance, wrapped in fear of the coming judgment day. They trembled at every movement; even their own shadows frightened them.

Erev Yom Kippur, before the fast, when the men returned from Minche, the atmosphere in the houses was tense. The table was hurriedly set for the pre-fasting meal. One urged the other to eat faster, so that, God forbid, they would not be late for Kol Nidrei. The little kids cleared the table, drank seven gulps of water–a remedy so that the coming thirst should not be too onerous–the girls washed the dishes, and mother placed the candles in the candlesticks.

Time was suspended. A holy stillness enveloped the houses. People rose to the highest heights of piety. In those moments, they examined their souls, themselves entirely, as if they no longer belonged to themselves.

When mother let her hands fall, and uncovered her face, and tore her red, tear-filled eyes from the burning candles, a heart-rending cry from the whole family pierced the walls, doors, and windows, going from house to house, from room to room, floods of tears washing over the heads of the little children.

[Page 163]

Warm paternal and maternal hands hugged the little lambs, and blessed and pleaded with the creator not to, God forbid, separate them, orphan them, shame them, gladden their enemies, or humiliate them.

The weeping at the blessing of the children rent the heavens. The bleeding, woe-filled, hearts of the parents opened a year's worth of wounds. It appeared to them that just in these moments–in the holy moments–they were in a position to plead for everything good for their babies, for their suffering, hungry children. They wept, fainted, spasmed, shedding tears, and trembling for their souls. Finally, the father wiped his red eyes with his handkerchief that he kept in the bosom of his *kitl*.[2] Passing by the mother, he murmured, "It's time. Enough, old woman. We will leave now." The door opened, the father kissed the mezuzah, and behind him, the children and the mother carried the *talissim*, and the machzors.

A red sun had set. A cold evening beset the courtyard. The road from the courtyard to the besmedresh was paved with tears and prayers, and neighbors encountered along the way greeted each other amid tears.

The sun had already set below the horizon. From under the light clouds, twinkling stars appeared and graced our little world with light. There, in the shuls, shtiblach and besmedreshim, Jews stood in taliss and kitl, between tall wax *yizkor* candles lit for holy, departed souls, and with godly holiness, sang Kol Nidrei along with the chazzan.

[Page 164]

The heartfelt melody brought everyone together in brotherhood, young and old, near and far. Even the Christians gathered in the vestibule by the door to experience the holiness, the still Yom Kippur night, the holy yom-tov.

Sukkot, the autumn holiday also passed. Cold biting winds howled in from the meadows to the courtyard, blowing through the holes left when the putty fell away from the window panes, and through the rotten shingles on the roof, into the attic, whistling through the ceiling, and frightening the children.

Dawn was grey and cold. The roofs were coated with a silvery white frost. The mud froze into stony lumps. And in the gutters, an icy film formed over the scum thrown there in the dawn by the houses' wastewater, and children on their way to cheder happily slid on the ice on the soles of their shoes.

The low winter sun cast its weak rays, and around ten or eleven o'clock the roofs began to thaw and weep, and large gleaming water drops formed small turbid pools of water. The homeowners, in the morning, used them to make a yellow, sticky lime, and stuffed all the holes with hemp, and glued it with lime above, and closed off any opening where the cold could get in. The work went on until evening, until fingertips felt the biting cold. When it began to feel like needles piercing the nail beds, work was stopped, warm breath blown on fingers, and quickly into the house.

[Page 165]

The entire household would be found around the stove. Mother sat in front of the open door of the stove warming her knees and hands, rubbing them together. From time to time, a cloud of smoke puffed out, blown by the wind coming down the chimney. The wet branches smoldered, a dirty fluid coming out of their tips.

The dim interiors of the houses darkened deeper. A tongue of red flame from the open oven door reflected onto the adjacent wall. The father washed his hands, and began to daven Minche. In the meantime, the young kids had roasted rounds of potatoes, eating them hot, burning their lips and tongue.

After Minche-Maariv, they lit the night lamp, and ate supper. On the window panes, as if unnoticed, the frost began to create flowers and leaves. As they grew, they began to resemble velvet, fluffier and whiter. The cold began to be felt in the poorly heated houses. Outside, hanging from the edge of the roofs, long, pointy, icicles like spears, formed. The courtyard went to sleep, escaping from hard reality, until the first cockcrow, until dawn revealed a new world. Winter in its full rebirth, a white, dazzling deep snowfall covered everything like a white carpet and penetrated everywhere. The sounds of distant bells hanging around the necks of horses pulling the first sleighs, carried to the courtyard, for whom the first clean snowfall brought joy and delight.

[Page 166]

Our courtyard was deadened, locked, as if torn away from life, shutters closed, frozen windows. When the door opened, we quickly ran through it so as not to let any cold in. Quiet as a cemetery. Above the courtyard, where thin clouds of light-blue smoke from the chimneys of the low, huddled houses were carried high, only the old pear tree stood. On its branches, instead of the small pears and leaves, lay fluffy bunches of white snow.

This was Moishe Shtok's courtyard, the nest of need.

This is how people lived here, and thanked God. Born here, grown up here, and with great effort and sweat, earned a living. They lived in a confined narrow world, through time and generations, until Hitler annihilated everyone, and everything.

Translator's footnotes:

    1.   A kind of broad-leafed plant
    2.   Long, white coat worn on certain solemn holidays.

[Page 167]

The First Days With the Germans

by David Brik

Translated by Moses Milstein

When I think of how our beloved shtetl, Bilgoraj used to look, and what became of it, the blood curdles in my veins.

It was a city with such precious institutions: the Yesodei Hatorah cheder, a yeshiva with more than a hundred children maintained for free by the city.

The Chasidic Jews, with rav R' Mordechai Rokeach, *z"l*. The Rudniker shtibl and its dear Jews; the Harmans; R' Levi Stern, and others. The Gerer shtibl with such wonderful Jews like Nachum Wagner, and his children; Aaron Weinberg; Chanoch Rotenberg; Chanoch Leichter; Isreal'ke Weinberg, and others. Studious Jews, charity contributors ready to help any needy Jew in the city.

When I fled Bilgoraj, I met the Rosh Yeshiva of Bilgoraj, R' Yakov Eliezer Goldbrenner, in Sieniawa. He was greatly affected by the devastation. The *kol hatorah* that you could hear in Bilgoraj every hour of the day and night was silenced.

*

As soon as the German murderers entered Bilgoraj, they instilled fear among the Jews by seizing people for forced labor, and beating them mercilessly.

One night, they detained people for work, me among them.

[Page 168]

An SS man made us form into rows and marched us in military fashion to the courtyard of the *starostva*[1].

There I encountered other Jews, some young and some elderly. They were carrying garbage in their bare hands that others were sweeping in the yard. The Germans were chasing them around ordering them to go faster. It looked demonic. I too grabbed some garbage and began running back and forth.

They made us run with our garbage through a gauntlet of SS murderers, who kicked us viciously, and laughed uproariously.

I managed to sneak through so they didn't get me. But an SS man shouted out, pointing at m–this dog hasn't got his yet. He came at me with wild aggression and kicked me in the belly so hard that I suffered from it for 5 months.

Later, they took me and Yakov Zweck away, gave us small axes, and with those we were expected to chop up a heavy oak cupboard.

The SS men were going in and out, while we sat there in great fear. Suddenly one of them came over and says, "Are you aware, *Yude*, that all Jews must be shot?" Yekl Tzwek began to plead with them, that he had a wife and children. The German responded with a laugh, "That doesn't matter. The women and children will also go *kaput*."

I could not imagine that this could be true, but, unfortunately, history proved that they could annihilate 6 million Jews.

[Page 169]

Melamdim and Cheders

[Page 170]

According to Russian law, every melamed had to have permission to run a cheder. Not every melamed in the city had such a permit.

The melamdim with a license, for the cost of a few rubles, were informed several days in advance if the school inspector from Lublin would be coming for a visit to Bilgoraj.

In haste, and with the help of the students, floors were washed and scraped with knives and files. The picture of the Kaiser and the *doska* (blackboard) were brought down from the attic and wiped clean of the dust that had lain on them from one visit to the next.

The melamed and the students together studied the "*Bozhe tsara chroni*"[1] in Yiddish letters—the melamed himself did not know any Russian.

When the inspector arrived, the melamed and the children chanted the words which were unintelligible, and the inspector left.

Translator's footnote:

1.   God save the tsar.

[Page 171]

Leibish Melamed

by A. Karmi

Translated by Moses Milstein

When little boys reached the age of three, their mothers would take them to the *dardeke melamed*[1] who lived in the market near the butcher shops.

His son, Moishele Belfer (assistant) took the child, placed him with the others, and handed out candies.

R' Leibish was an old Jew of average weight, with a white beard where there were still some black hairs remaining that glistened in the sun, and a pair of glasses tied together with two strings riding on his nose. He sat at the head of the table, a pointer made of bone in his hand, and around him, on both sides of the table, sat the children. He taught with a loud, clear voice, and a beautiful, ringing *nigun*. This is how a little boy says, *aleph*, this is how a little boy says *beis*, punctuated by a jab from the bony pointer when they failed to repeat the *aleph-beis*.

In the second part of the house, the oven burned like in hell. Its burning flames reflected off the blackened walls where his wife (the rebbetsin) baked special sugar cookies for nursing children. She also used to bake cookies in various shapes, and paint them with different colors.

She would pick a child and get him to cut out the cookie forms—birds, dogs, and other things. Later, she would bake them, and her daughter Leah would take them and sell them to the stores.

[Page 172]

His son, Moishele, used to pick up the children and bring them to cheder, and afterwards, take them home. When a woman in town gave birth to a boy, they would inform Moishele, and he would bring his *zecher kvitlach* for *Shmireh*, and he would stick them up in the house. Every evening, he would assemble the whole cheder, and march them off in rows to read the *Kriat Shema*.

Upon entering, Moishele would shout loudly, "*A guten ovnt*" to the baby, mazel tov, and all the children did the same after him.

After the Kriat Shema was read, Moishele distributed cookies or candies to the kids, and again shouted, "*A gute nacht*" to the baby, and all the kids repeated after him. He celebrated the eight days like this, until the *brit milah*.

At night, Moishele used to go and study davening with girls, or he delivered wedding invitations. Sukkes, he used to go around with an *etrog* to the women for them to bless. Simchat Torah he used to sell flags to the little children. Purim he would deliver *shalach moness* from one household to another. And in spite of all this, he remained a big pauper.

Translator's footnote:

1. Teacher of young children.

[Page 173]

Yekl Melamed

by A. Kronenberg

Translated by Moses Milstein

R' Yekl Melamed was a tall, very thin, man who used to go around in a long smock down to his ankles. He was a very modest man. He looked like a forty year old, with his dark grey beard, but was in his seventies. He was a *dardeke melamed*[1] , but of a higher class. He taught *halb-traf*[2], and *gantz-traf*[3] (*nikud*). He lived for many years in Chanina's house with the big courtyard where the children liked to play.

The children liked to be taught by him. He had no whip or pointer. He would teach by simply pleading with them, "*Nu, kinderlach*! Everyone say already*, kometz alef o, kometz beis bo,* " and the children actually repeated after him with their ringing little voices.

He had a special method. In a short time, he taught the children to read Hebrew fluently.

Yekl Melamed would also accompany the children to *Kriat Shema*, but quietly and modestly.

After his wife died, he moved in with his employers, the parents of the children he taught.

Translator's footnotes:

1. Teacher of young children
2. Reading letter by letter.
3. Reading by syllables.

[Page 174]

Itseleh Melamed

by A. Karmi

Translated by Moses Milstein

He was a short man, with a nice, stately looking beard. He lived opposite the besmedresh. He conducted his teaching in a somewhat modern manner, teaching in classrooms. He would stride around the classroom, his switch under his arm, and teach *chumash* and Rashi with a ringing melody. *Vayomer*, he said, *Adonai*, God, *el*, to, *Moishe*, one of them was called Moishe, and so on.

He made sure that the children repeated after him. Whoever did not repeat accurately received the switch.

The children liked to attend his school, because he did very little teaching. He was the only bookseller in town where you could buy a siddur, a *slichah*, a *Kinah*, a Yiddish *chumash*, and all kinds of fiction.

Every day, he spread out his entire stock in the big besmedresh for all the *minyans* while the davening went on. Erev Rosh Hashanah and Yom Kippur was a hectic time for him. He took the older students to help him, and they considered it a big honor.

His wife (the rebbetsin) was a short, very thin woman, who brought milk from the villages to sell to the Jews in the city. Even with all this, he struggled to make a living.

[Page 175]

Itzi-Mayer Melamed

by A. Katari

Translated by Moses Milstein

He was a short man, with a broad, half-grey beard, and a heavily creased forehead. His face was yellow as wax. He would cough a lot, suffering from asthma for years. He drank several glasses of water a day adding a tablespoon of soda, making a *brocheh, shehakl*. Afterwards, he would stroke his beard as if he had just a good glass of spirits.

R' Itzi-Mayer was a Gemara teacher. He taught the children *chumash* with Rashi, and a little bit of *Siftei Chakhamim*[1]. He would also teach a chapter of *sfarbeh* (24, nun"khof), which was not an easy thing then for Bilgoraj Jews. He was a good interpreter.

He lived in a small house by the Klotz's for many years. The huge oven and the kitchen took up half the room. The other room, reached by going up two stairs, was the bedroom for his family of 9 people.

He conducted the cheder in the kitchen at a long table that ran from one end of the room to the other, and his 30 students sat along the sides. At the head sat the rebbe with his switch under his arm, always angry.

The rebbetsin (Basheleh) was an *eyshet chayal*. She would sometimes go after the rebbe and his students for not bringing any tuition money, or Rosh Hashanah money, cursing with a variety of curses.

[Page 176]

She would bang on the table. The rebbe could not abide this, and he would blurt out, "*Yiddeneh*, enough already."

Smoke and steam together were always coming out of the kitchen where the rebbetsin was occupied with making lunch.

In summer, when they used to leave the cheder for lunch, the boys would run down to the river for a swim, meanwhile sneaking into an orchard and picking apples or pears, someone always returning without his hat, or with torn pants, trying to fool the rebbe with all kinds of excuses. The rebbe, of course, understood, and introduced them to the switch. Every evening one cheder battled with another. More than one housewife complained that the boys scattered her firewood.

On Friday, you had to know the *chumash* off by heart. Those who brought tuition went first and were let off easy. For these boys, the rebbe, on Saturday evening, after a chapter of Mishnah, would go listen to them read at the parent's house, handing out all kinds of compliments. Kids who hadn't brought tuition, became the victims.

Purim, the boys did whatever they could to beg their parents for *shalach moness*[2] for the teacher. The lucky ones ran to the cheder, and delivered their *shalach moness*. The rebbe and rebbetsin were waiting seated at the table. She took note of which of the students failed to bring any, and these boys suffered the rest of the year for it.

Translator's footnotes:

1. Commentaries on Rashi
2. Purim custom of bringing gifts of food to friends and family.

[Page 177]

R' Todieh Melamed

by H. Wallach

Translated by Moses Milstein

R' Todieh, the Gemara teacher, lived on the Lubelsky street, up a set of high stairs. He was a tall man with a white beard and long, curled payess. He had a wide, creased, scholarly, forehead. He wore white pants and white socks, He was a pious and observant Jew.

He always walked around in a *taliss kotn* with long *tsitsis* reaching almost to the ground. He spoke with a Lithuanian dialect.

When davening, he made all kinds of grimaces, banged his fists on the wall, jumped up in the air almost touching the balcony, and in order to be certain that he had not left out a single word, he spoke each word several times.

He never wanted a big cheder. He used to teach Gemara with *tosafot*[1], and other *meforshim*[2]. Whenever he encountered a difficult passage with his students, he would search all the commentaries. He searched until he came up with the right explanation. Then he would wipe his brow with the sleeve of his white robe, and with a happy expression say to his students, "Nu, we got through it."

During the war between Poland and the Bolsheviks, a couple of Polish soldiers went by his window. Hearing shouting, they entered his house. R' Todieh was standing davening, his fists clenched. The soldiers, thinking he was yelling at them, were going to arrest him.

[Page 178]

But after things were explained to them, they let him go.

R' Todieh used to make wine. He supplied the city with kosher wine for Shabbes and for Kiddush.

Before the holidays, R' Todieh and his children would be up all night making wine.

Anyone who wanted good kosher wine, would buy it from R' Todieh.

————

Translator's footnotes:

       1.   Annotations to the Talmud
       2.   Exegetes

<u>People</u>

[Page 181]

R' Shmuel Eliyahu Shwerdsharf

by Shmuel Honigboim, Y. Ch. Kronenberg

Translated by Moses Milstein

One of the most illustrious people of that time, known for his good deeds, was without a doubt, R' Shmuel Eliyahu Shwerdsharf.

He originated from Lublin, the son of R' Eliezer, the author of the book, "*Damesek Eliezer*" on the Passover Hagadah, and other essays, and a grandson of R' Duberish Heilpern, who was known as the "Lubliner *Magid*." His wife, Esther, was the daughter of R' Yechezkel Tumim-Weinberg of Bilgoraj, the son of R' Leibish Zavochvoster, who was the brother of the Leipniker rebbe, R' Baruch, the author of the book *Baruch Tem*, and *Ateret Chachamim*, whose son-in-law was R' Chaim Halberstam of Tsanz, the renowned Tsanzer rebbe. The wife of R' Yechezkel Meir was the daughter of the Bolgoraj rebbe, R' Itzchak Natan Nute Berliner, a son of the Berlin rebbe who was known as R' Hesheleh Berliner.

Aside from his illustrious lineage he was himself a paragon of virtue, a wise man, and a scholar. He was a wealthy man with an estate in Sokolewke, and he knew how to use his wealth, and helped anyone in need.

He was an acquaintance of the Russian minister, Platanow, who had several estates in the Bilgoraj area, and mixed in the highest circles including the court of the czar where he was presented to the Russian czar Alexander II who bestowed on him a diamond ring.

Exploiting his status, he was always ready to help any Jew who found himself in trouble.

He had two sons: R' Moishe Zvi, whose wife, Miriam Frime's was the daughter of R' Itsheleh Levi of Cracow. R' David Tevl whose wife, the well-known Gnendeleh was the daughter of R' Yakov Asknenazi of Memel who was the cousin of the Lubliner rebbe R' Yehoshua Heshl Ashkenazi. The oldest daughter, Gitl, was the wife of the well-known Bilgoraj scholar, R' Yonah Chaim Kronenberg. The daughter, Freideh, was the wife of the long-serving head of the *kehila*, and activist, R' Itzchak Yishayeh Harman, who was called Itzik R' Motl's. The daughter, Chantche, was the wife of R' Abraham Chaim, the son of R' Michl Michelson of Pioterkov. She was the mother of the Plonsker rebbe, Zvi Yechezkel. The daughter, Zlateh, was the wife of Wolf Lvov, the son of R' Yakov Lvov of Komerneh, a grandson of the author of the book, "*Yishiot Yakov*." The daughter, Neitshe, was the wife of R' Itzchak Garfinkle, the son of the renowned Chasid and rich man, R' Klaman Leib of Pulaw.

R' Shmuel Eliyahu was a big philanthropist. He built the small besmedresh with his own money. As mentioned above, he was an important man. When the city synagogue was being built, he invited the governor of Lublin province to lay the first stone. When the governor failed to arrive at the scheduled time, R' Shmuel ordered them to start building without him. The governor arrived later, and seeing the building already in progress, he was not pleased. R' Shmuel quickly interceded, and said to the governor that the walls of the shul are not the most important thing,

[Page 183]

but instead it is the construction of the *balemer*, that was important, and it is for this that they were awaiting him. They handed him a silver trowel, and he laid the first stone.

———————

Itzik R' Motl's

by Yakov Herman

Translated by Moses Milstein

R' Itzchak Yeshiahu Herman, who was called Itzik R' Motl's, was short with a white, stately beard, a broad, scholarly forehead, and deep-set black eyes and bushy eyebrows. He was the son-in-law of R' Shmuel Eliyahu Shwerdsharf.

From early on, he devoted himself to *kahal* causes and was the head of the kahal in Bigoraj for many years. There was no benevolent cause in the city that R' Itzik was not involved with, and for that reason the whole city called him "Uncle Itzik."

R' Itzik was held in high esteem by Bilgoraj Jews. He was a very intelligent man, and people used to come for him for advice.

When he died he was eulogized in the city shul, and a procession was held in which almost all Bilgoraj Jews accompanied him to his eternal rest, and bewailed the great loss.

[Page 184]

R' Yakov Shleicher, *zt"l*

by HaRav R' Yitzchak HaCohen Hoberman

Translated by Sara Mages

R' Yakov zt"l Shleicher was called by all R' Yankele Michel–Milners. He was a little taller than medium height, had a large and bright forehead, bright eyes, big *payot* and a long and broad beard. His description attests to a great scholar whose wisdom illuminates his face. Despite his life of poverty, his clothes were clean, and a stain was not found on them.

When I first entered Beit HaMidrash he was still studying all day standing. He arrived before dawn. The rain did not stop him in the summer and winter, the snow and frost in the winter, and the sun did not burn him in the summer. He studied without letup. He was a distinguished scholar, and most of the days I knew him he studied *Gemara*, *Poskim* and *Teshuvot* with *Shitah Mekubetzet*[1].

The greater wonder, he did not have one unnecessary word in the long explanation of the Rashbam [RAbbi SHmuel Ben Meir] on Baba Batra, and it was also necessary to use *Shitah Mekubetzet*. He also explained the genius' words at full length without an unnecessary word.

He stood by the first window in the northern corner of the Beit HaMidrash and studied in a pleasant voice. At first I thought that he was standing there by the entrance, on the northwest side, so as not to confuse and disturb the worshipers who ascended east and south. Later, I saw him washing his hands several times, in the middle of his studies, in the sink next to him in the west corner as annotated in *Shulchan Aruch* – "he who touches his head should wash his hands." While reading a deep matter, he forgot and rubbed his head and beard, as is the custom of those who read. I thought that's why he was standing next to the sink. Later, when I saw him during prayer, when he ascended to the head of the table in accordance with the law that a person should always enter through two doorways in the synagogue and then pray, I agreed that his standing there was due to the magnitude of his humility. It was not significant to him that he was not worthy to ascend to the east, for he felt the sanctity of the house of God and "*Ma Norah HaMakom ha'zeh*" [how full of awe is this place].

At the end of his life, he became very weak and had to study while sitting. His place was next to the Holy Ark on a bench attached to the *Bimah*. We never found him sleeping or talking. We did not dare ask him what we did not understand in our studies, since we knew that every moment was precious and sacred to him.

My teacher, the great rabbi, R' Yakov Mordechai, *zt"l*, talked to him at length on *Divrei Torah*[2] and praised his clever explanations. He was a scholar and his teaching was his art. The worshipers of the Beit HaMidrash, the big and the small, provided almost all his needs, and at the end of his life also the worshipers of the Hassidic synagogues in Rudnik and Trisk.

When he passed away, my teacher, HaRav R' Yakov Mordechai, gave him a long eulogy, and all the people accompanied him with great weeping.

He had two sons, Yitzchak David who lived in Frampol, and Eliyahu who lived in the village of Gized. Both, *hy"d*, were murdered in the Holocaust by the Nazis, may their names be blotted out.

––––––––

Translator's footnotes:

1.   *Shita Mekubetzet* is a collection of glosses on the Talmud. Within the work are many passages of Talmudic commentary that are not found anywhere else.
2.   *Divrei Torah* is a talk on topics relating to a *parsha* (section) of the Torah, typically the weekly Torah portion.

––––––––

[Page 186]

R' Shneur Zalman Goldberg

by HaRav R' Yitzchak HaCohen Hoberman

Translated by Sara Mages

R' Shneur Zalman Goldberg was a distinguished scholar. He was knowledgeable in most of the six orders of the Mishnah, and knew the Bible by heart. He wrote the books: "*Sede Tvuot*" [Field of Grains, Innovations and Annotations on the Torah], "*Shoshanei Pe'er*" commentary to the Torah, "*Havatzelet HaSharon*" and pleasant poems with the approval of *Av Beit Din* [chief of the court] of Lomza.

R' Shneur Zalman was born in Homyel [Gomel] in Russia, and came to Bilgoraj for family reasons. All day, and most of the night, he stood in the southeast corner of Beit HaMidrash HaGadol his face to the wall and his lips whispering. He studied orally or prayed, and it is worth noting that despite his great poverty he was always happy, and a song was always in his mouth. He had pleasant movements in the order of prayer. In *Seder Ha'Avodah* [service] for Yom Kippur he stripped off his street clothes and put on white garments, and in *piyuut* "*Unthanneh Toqeph*", when he started to say the words, "A man's origin is from dust," in the movements he composed for them, even someone who was hurrying to leave for some reason could not do so because he was like nailed to the place by the magnitude of the sweetness.

All his days he tried to study in the Beit HaMidrash with the young men. They studied the Gemara and he listened and explained the matter to them orally. The teaching of the Holy Torah was like a second nature for him.

Despite his poverty he bought books for the Beit HaMidrash and tried to convince people to buy books and donate them to Beit HaMidrash.

He also received all his provisions from the worshipers of Beit HaMidrash HaGadol and Beit HaMidrash HaKatan.

[Page 187]

R' Mordechai Yosef Schatz,
his memory will live in the next world

by HaRav R' Yitzchak HaCohen Hoberman

Translated by Sara Mages

All day, and most of the night, he sat in the Beit HaMidrash on the bench next to the table in the southwest corner close to the bookcases.

Most of his days, he engaged in the study of *Gemara*, *Poskim* and *Teshuvot*, and at the end of his life, studied a lot of Rambam [Moshe ben Maimon]. According to the Holy Gaon of Buchach, may his virtue stand us in good stead! he was a great expert on the book "*Tevu'ot Shor*" [laws of *kashrut* and ritual slaughtering]. He also engaged in the Kabbalah and Hassidut and prayed in the style and intent of ARIZaL [Rabbi Yitzchak Luria z"l]. He wrote two books, "*Mei Meonot*" about the Torah, and "*Beracha Meshuleshet*" on the holidays. Both books were burned in a fire at the arrival of the Nazis, may their names be blotted out.

At first, when he was strong, he organized evening classes and studied *Mishnayot* and *Ein Yaakov* with simple homeowners, craftsmen and several simple tailors. He recognized those, like Yehusua Schnieder and Shelomo Eliyahu Szpiajzen, who had great knowledge and good understanding in the study of a page of Gemara.

If he heard of a breach in religion, he voiced his concern in the Beit HaMidrash and went to the rabbi and shouted. He did not rest until the matter was corrected.

He had a son, R' Yeshayahu *hy"d*, who was shot to death by the Nazis, may their names be blotted out.

He also received most of his provisions from the worshipers of Beit HaMidrash HaGadol, and Beit HaMidrash HaKatan.

[Pages 188-189]

HaRav Pinchas Mendel Singer *zt"l*

by HaRav R' Yitzchak HaCohen Hoberman

Translated by Sara Mages

HaRav HaGaon R' Pinchas, who was called Pinchas Mendel, was the son–in–law of my teacher, the righteous rabbi, R' Yakov Mordechai, may his virtue stand us in good stead! He was a native of Tomaszów Lubelski. His father was the great rabbi, R' Shmuel, a teacher of righteousness in Tomaszów. His lineage goes back to the light of the Jewish people, the true *posek*, Shach [Shabbatai ben Meir HaCohen], author of "*Siftei Kohen*" ["Lips of the Priest" on *Shulchan Aruch*] as explained on the title page of his book, "*Magadim Hadashim*," on the Talmudic tractate "*Avodah Zarah*" [foreign worship].

His mother was a famous righteous woman who walked all day with a small *tallit* over her clothes. On the Holy Sabbath she gathered all the young women and studied with them the laws they needed to know, and when she finished, before she went home, she asked them to testify that they did not speak slander and gossip.

At a young age, as was the custom then, he married the daughter of HaRav HaGaon, R' Yakov Mordechai Zilberman, *zt"l*. He was appointed Rabbi of Leoncin, a small town near Warsaw. There, he wrote his book "*Magadim Hadashim*" about the Talmudic tractate "*Avodah Zarah*," and was willingly accepted among the learners.

Since this town was unable to provide his livelihood, he moved and settled in Warsaw, on Krochmalna Street. Soon he became famous for his wisdom and honest rulings, and many flocked to him from all around for *Din Torah* [arbitration].

It's interesting to relate the following fact: Once, the women of the same neighborhood washed their undergarments and hung them in the attic under the roof. Once, a woman stole a lot of her neighbor's nightshirts, and they began to quarrel. In the end, they came before him for *Din Torah*. First of all, he ordered them to bring all the undergarments to his home. He ordered the Rebbetzin to take some of their own beautiful nightshirts, and mix them in the same package. The next day, when they came to hear the verdict, he told one of them to go and take from the package all those that were hers. She went and chose hers. Then, he mixed them again and ordered her friend to do the same. Since she wanted to steal from her friend, and since she did not know which nightshirts belonged to her friend and which to the rabbi, he realized that she wanted to steal. Then, against her will, she admitted that she had failed in a sin.

This clever verdict was also published in the Polish press.

After the outbreak of the First World War, and after his father–in–law passed away in Lublin, he came and settled in Bilgoraj. He engaged in Torah all day, but his livelihood was very meagre. From there, he was accepted as Rabbi of Stary Dzików in Galicia. There, he wrote his second book, "*Avnei Zikaron*" on *Masechet Berahot*.

He had three sons, Yehoshua[1] who was a famous writer in the United States, Yitzchak[2] who is now a famous writer there, and Moshe who managed the rabbinate in Dzików after his passing.[3]

At the outbreak of the Second World War he was exiled to Siberia and died there.

––––––––––

Translator's footnotes:

1. Israel Yehoshua Singer
2. Isaac Bashevis Singer. Nobel laureate in literature
3. He also had a daughter, Esther Kreitman, who was a published writer as well.

[Page 190]

Figures

by Isaac Bashevis Singer

This article is excerpted from the story, "*Nayeh Chaverim*", in Isaac Bashevis Singer's book, "*Mein Tatten's Beis-Din Shtub*", chapter 59, p. 347.

https://www.yiddishbookcenter.org/collections/yiddish-books/spb-nybc206234/singer-isaac-bashevis-mayn-tatn-s-beys-din-shtub

The English edition of the Yiddish book is entitled, "*In my Father's Court.*"

[Page 196]

Gnendele

by Perl Honigboim

Translated by Moses Milstein

Genedele was the daughter-in-law of R' Shmuel Eliyahu Shwerdsharf. She came from Germany, was a very educated woman, and very pious. When she was young, she was very rich. She devoted her whole life to good deeds, which is why everyone in town called her Aunt Gnendele.

There was not one poor bride who Gnendele did not care about, and see that she got married.

She spent all day cooking soups and carrying them to the sick, even when she was in advanced years. She could be seen even in the coldest weather going around with her basket full of jars of jam, *vagodnik*, and *vishnik*, for a treat for the ailing

Early on Friday, she would make sure the poor were provided with challahs. She knew every poor person and their situation.

Life on this earth is a passage, she would say. The important thing is to prepare for the next world. Whenever she felt a little ill, she would take a laxative, wash herself, so that the *chevra kedisha* women would have little work to do on her, and she used to say, "Nu, kinder, you can go and tell them…I'm ready."

She was able to write Hebrew fluently, which was a rarity in those days. The letters she used to write often to her son-in-law, Hersh Yechezkel Michelson, the erstwhile Plonsker rebbe, (later among the renowned Warsaw rabbis) were full of flowery phrases and examples of a cultured style, and were published in books.

[Page 197]

Her letter, "*Die Din Torah*," was very interesting and was published in the book, "*Pinot HaBayit*," by her son-in-law, Zvi Yechezkel, in which she requests that as soon as he hears of her death, he should say kaddish, and in that vein, she writes: "I am certain I will get through the first fire."

Not a day passed without a number of local poor people, or visitors, eating at her table. Near the time of her death, she stipulated that a piece of the table where so many paupers ate, accompany her. Her request was fulfilled.

The entire city came to her funeral. The stores were closed. The rabbis eulogized her. The Kreshever rebbe's eulogy made a strong impression. He said she was truly an *eyshes chayal* as it is written: "*Kafa prasha l'ani*." When she was wealthy, she gave on her own. *V'Yadia shalacha l'evion*. Later, she made sure that others gave. Everyone mourned, especially the poor, the great loss of Gnendele of Bilgoraj.

———

[Page 198]

Blimele

by Shoshana Lerman

Translated by Moses Milstein

Blimele was the head of the women's *chevra kedisha*[1]. Nothing could be done without her. She occupied herself with *mitzves* every day, taking care of poor brides, and the sick. Her main duty was visiting all the sick in the city, and bringing them something to eat.

Even during the coldest, rainiest days, you could see her walking–wearing her winter shawl–with slow steps to visit the sick. When she was asked why she went out in the rain, she answered that the sick person was at the moment lying there alone, and therefore she went to greater pains.

When WWII broke out, she fled to her son, Itzi, in Lutsk, and there she was killed, along with her whole family, in 1943, by the German murderers.

———

Translator's footnote:

    1.   Burial society

———

[Page 199]

Gitl Moishe-Itzi's

by Rivke Goldstein

Translated by Moses Milstein

Gitl Moishe-Itzi's occupied herself with *mitzves*. She knew who all the poor in the city were, who needed a bit of soup, a little compote, where there was an orphan bride who wanted to get married, which poor person needed a hat, a pair of pants. Everything depended on her

Friday evening, a wet snow was falling outside, it was dark and slippery, but by *babbe* Gitele it was warm and bright, clean throughout. Uncle Itzi returned from davening, said *sholem aleichem*, and filled the cup for kiddush. He waited for grandmother to come for the kiddush, but she was preparing something in a basket, and groaning. When the uncle gave me a sign, I understood that I had to call her to the table. The uncle did the kiddush, and grandmother, with tears in her eyes said, amen. She did not sit down to eat, but said: "Chinkele has not sent for any food today. I have to bring the food to her.

[Page 200]

I will not eat before I have done this." I then said to my grandmother that if she hasn't come today, it's probably because she doesn't need to.

Grandmother grabbed me, and gave me a package, and she carried a basket of food. We went out on the slippery street. Chinkele lived near the bridge. The dark stairs were lit by a small Shabbes light. Old Chinkele was lying hungry in bed, the daughter-in-law on the other side. Barefoot children were wandering around the house. Though she was blind she recognized us and called out happily, "Gitlele, blessed may you be!" Grandmother laid out the challahs, wine and fish. I left the house in tears. Grandmother was happy, and said to me, " Come my child. Now that the hungry have enough food, we can go and eat."

The children used to shout at Gad, "Compania!" Gad used to tear his clothes, and would come to Gitl's window, naked. Gitl never got tired of this, and gave him new clothes and food to eat.

Shaindl Flam used to come often and sit in Gitl's kitchen. A Warsaw merchant used to come and eat in Gitl's guesthouse. When he saw Shaindl, he said, "It's not pleasant for me to eat when this woman is in your kitchen." Gitl replied, "You can go and eat anywhere you like. I don't need you. They–pointing at Gad, Shaindl and others–they need me, and I live for them." But Hitler, may his name be erased, did not care about good deeds…She perished along with her son, Shmuel-Eliyahu, and his family in Mizocz.

[Page 201]

Chinkele

Translated by Moses Milstein

The cemetery was her salon. She felt more at home there than someone in his house.

As soon as she got up in the morning, her first visit was to the cemetery, even though it was far outside the city, and there she would spend almost the whole day. She knew every grave, and who was buried there, even those of long ago, and she remembered everyone's yorzeit. Anytime someone got sick, they ran to Chinkele she should go to the cemetery to pray for the sick person for which she received some money.

Years ago, she was a rebbetsin teaching the girls how to daven.

In later years, she became blind and was helped by her only son, Abraham Chaim'l, who led her to the cemetery every day.

Whenever someone came to the cemetery for a yorzeit, they would call for Chinkele right away. She led them straight to the grave, knocked on the tombstone, and called out, "Sarah, Sarah, your daughter, Perl, is here."

And even when she became blind, she led everyone to the right grave same as before.

————

[Page 202]

The Man of Faith

Translated by Moses Milstein

There was a man in Bilgoraj who was called R' Itzchak'l "*Ki L'Olam Chasdo*." They called him so, because he was very pious, and while davening "Kie L'Olam Chasdo, he would make all kinds of gestures. He was a tailor, with a pointy, half-blonde, elongated beard, with straight, long *payess*. He was cross-eyed. He wore a tall, velvet hat with needles stuck all over it, the brim turned to the side, a torn, faded, cloth smock, and two torn shoes. He was always cheerful and full of faith.

He was a "specialist" tailor. If someone brought him a torn piece of clothing to repair or to alter, and he was asked, "R' Itzchak'l, can we make something of this?" he would reply, " Don't ask, don't ask, ay, ay, ay, old merchandise, better than today's new stuff. I'll make you a *kapote*, you'll see."

If someone complained about the work, he would get angry–look who's an expert. He would take a hunk of chalk out of his pocket, put it in his mouth, spit on his hand, clap on one side then the other and say, "Prima result. Could not have turned out better."

He was the tailor at R' Abraham, the rich man of the town. He was content with him, and was also a frequent guest of his on Shabbes.

He was a poor man with several children, and lived in a lane off the bridge street in a low, half sunken house, with one small window. The walls always seeped water, the roof was so decrepit that you could see the sky through it. The house was always so full of smoke coming from the cooking that one person couldn't see the other. The floor was wet and broken.

[Page 203]

The children lay in bed covered in dirty, torn bedding, hungry, freezing. There was never enough food in the house to satisfy the hunger, not even in the golden times when he was overwhelmed with work.

His only possession was his rusty old sewing machine that squeaked like an ungreased wagon. When he had no work, he recited psalms at the top of his voice, and paced throughout the small house, back and forth, stirring up a wind.

His wife was modest and quiet. She made do with what she had. She did not have any great ambitions. She used to sit half the night by the little kerosene lamp plucking feathers. When the children cried, "Mameh, bread!" she would go over to him, "Itzchak, what will we do?" He would reply, "We have to have faith."

Itzchak'l was very pious. He made all kinds of grimaces and gestures while davening. For "*Modim*" he used to bend over with so much energy that anyone standing next to him was almost bowled over. At the end of *Shemone Esrei*, he was always short of room. At "*Aleinu*," he used to spit so that anyone near him got spattered.

He never used to hurry his davening. After davening, he used to recite a few chapters of psalms. He used to say, what you can fit in, you have.

When he worked for a whole week and still had nothing for Shabbes, he did not lose his faith. He rose early on Friday morning, davened, put on his *gartel*, and went begging door to door.

[Page 204]

When he finished, he came home happy, and spoke to the wall (he did not look at women), "Nu, you see *Yiddene*, that you have to have faith." He gave her the money, and she took to preparing for Shabbes.

Itzchak'l then went to the mikvah, and from there to the besmedresh to recite *Shir Hashirim*. After davening, he often used to go eat at R' Abraham's, at a nice, bright, set table, and sing along with them the "Shalom Aleichem."

In his house, small Shabbes candles burned. There was bread and herring on the table, and Itzchak'l sang Shalom Aleichem with fervor, the little ones helping out. Between courses, he sang a few *zmires* until the little ones became tired and fell asleep.

When there was little work for him to do, he again did not lose his faith. He took his household, and moved to Goraj, his birthplace, and where his "rebbi," Motele, lived.

And when Itzchak'l had no work at all, he retained his faith. He divorced his wife, and stayed in the besmedresh.

Erev Pesach, when a little work became available, he got married to the same woman. He did this several times, divorcing and marrying the same woman, and never lost his faith.

[Page 205]

Bilgoraj Community Activists

Biłgoraj Community Activists

by Sh. P

Translated by Jerrold Landau

Reb Levi Stern, z"l

He was a tradesman, a baker by trade, a scholar, a very faithful communal affairs worker, and a zealot for Judaism, who dedicated himself to Jewish affairs. He participated in all the institutions for Torah and benevolent deeds, in all the societies, and in philanthropic institutions such as *Linat Tzedek* [for providing lodging for poor wayfarers], *Bikur Cholim* [society for tending to the sick], *Chevra Kadisha* [burial society], and Beit Lechem [provision of bread to the poor]. He gave of his energies with a full heart. In short, he was an early organizational activist, an influential Jew who stood up for his views, a Hassid, and a proper blend of Hassidism, activism, and zealotry. He was a good husband, a man of stature, an energetic man who could impose fear, possessing a balanced temperament, a man who was able to use his energies in a manner appropriate to the situation, the place, and the time.

He was called Levi Bracha's. Who in Biłgoraj did not know Levi Bracha's? He led the Rudniker *Shtibel*. Nobody would raise a hand or a leg were it not for him.

Woe over those who are lost but not forgotten.

Reb Yisrael Moshe-Itzis, z"l

He was a Trisker Hassid, and head of the *Chevra Kadisha*, always pursuing mitzvot, working in charitable and benevolent endeavors. There were times, acknowedged by the Jews of Biłgoraj, when he literally put himself in danger to save a fellow Jew. He was a man of stately countenance, a community activist of an earlier generation.

Reb Netanel Shier, z"l

He was a sieve and wine merchant, a Gerrer Hassid, and a very wealthy man, who loved charity and benevolence. He led a proper Jewish religious home. He knew how to make use of his wealth. He took sons-in-law from the finest Hassidic, scholarly homes, such as: Shimon Warszawiak, Chanoch Rotenberg, and Itamar Feferman.

[Page 206]

His sons were Chanoch Shier, Mendel Shier, and Yitzchak Meir Shier.

He was responsible for a generation of pious, Hassidic people.

Reb Avraham Harman, z"l

He was one of the finest Jews that Biłgoraj possessed. He was wealthy, and gave charity and performed benevolent deeds in a generous fashion. He fled from honor, not wanting and not allowing attention to be drawn toward himself.

On the contrary, he was shy, humble man. He dedicated his time to Torah. He made sure to run a strongly religious home.

He worshipped in the Rudniker Shtibel. He was always at his place in the corner. He did not take on any trusteeship, and did not promote his opinions. Nevertheless, his entire presence evoked honor. Regarding such individuals, one says: "Woe regarding those who are lost but are not forgotten."

Reb Eliezer Buchbinder, called Reb Eliezer Mohel, z"l

He was the son of Reb Moshe Buchbinder of blessed memory, with whom the writer of these lines had the merit of studying. He was a scholarly Jew, who spent days and nights with Torah. He benefited from the fruit of his own labor.

His son Reb Eliezer was a great Torah scholar. He was a *mohel* [ritual circumciser] in this city, without expectation of remuneration. He categorically refused anyone who wished to reward him, for he wanted to obtain the mitzvah in a pure fashion. He was involved in business, having a grocery story from which he earned his livelihood. Finally, he studied with young men.

He was one of the prominent Jews of Torah and Hassidism in Biłgoraj. Our generation is now bereft of such people – and that is unfortunate!

* * *

Biłgoraj had many scholarly Jews who were G-d fearing and wholesome. There were merchants and tradesmen among them. They did not know of politics. They were dear Jews with warm hearts. We will note only a few of them here, such as Reb Aharon Waeiberg, Yechezkel Teicher, David Furer, Tebl Stempel, Moshe Model, Yekutiel Fest, Yaakov Goldbard, Shamai Adler, Hillel Janower, and others.

[Page 207]

Who remembers the Jews as they appeared on the Sabbath in their festive clothes, with their bright faces, entering the Jewish homes on Friday night or on festivals – the warmth, the genuine Jewish family life, the "your children are like olive saplings around your table"[1], the harmony between parents and child, the guests at the beautiful Sabbath or festival table.

There were social organizations that concerned themselves with their poor fellow man, providing them with everything. Whenever a poor Jew found himself in dire need, our dear tradesman stopped their work, and provided help for anyone.

Woe over those that are lost and are not forgotten!

Yona Akerman

Who from Bilgoraj does not remember Yona Akerman? He was honored by all circles and strata – Hassidim, householders, merchants, and artisans. Every one of them knew that Yona Akerman was the symbol of honesty, without airs, sycophantism, and politics. He attained the highest positions in almost all the official capacities of Bilgoraj, such as: representative in the communal council, representative in the city council, etc. His goodwill was evident in all of them. He was truly someone who did not chase honors, but honor pursued him. Simplicity and modesty were his way, despite his intelligence, tall stature, and knowledge of languages. He did just about everything with no expectation of reward.

He lived simply and modestly, in an ordinary manner. His profession was to write claims. He would give advice in all matters, mainly gratis. He literally hated rewards. Gentiles also recognized his traits, benefited from his advice, and honored him very much.

He did not benefit from the world. He lived like an ascetic, always suffering and never speaking out. He was the patron of the entire Akerman family. He took care of everyone, setting them up, even though he himself was satisfied with the minimum.

[Page 208]

He was one of the first ideological Zionists. He lived with and got along with everyone. He worshipped with Hassidim, and everyone honored him.

During the war, he travelled through Russia and endured a great deal of suffering. His refined character could not withstand the tribulations. He died alone in deep Russia. Thus did he live and thus did he die…

May his soul be bound in the bonds of eternal life.

Shochtim[2] in Biłgoraj Before the Holocaust

Reb Eliezer Shochet, z"l

He was the type of honorable Jew seen of old, a great Torah scholar and a Hassid. He was good to his fellow man, and occupied himself faithfully in communal affairs. He had all the fine traits that are required for a *shochet*. He was honored by the Jewish people of Biłgoraj. He worked with great faithfulness and wholesomeness. He was killed in the great destruction. Woe!

Reb Zev (Velvel) Shochet, z"l

He was taken on as a shochet in Biłgoraj while still a young man. He was G-d fearing, wholesome, and a great scholar. As the son of wealthy Jews, he spent his young years in Yeshivas, and learned a great deal. He worshipped and socialized in the company of tradespeople., and studied Talmud with them. Later, he also became a *mohel*[3]. He did everything in a wholesome fashion for the sake of the mitzva.

Reb Yontshe Kantor, z"l

He was a young man, a Sokolower Hassid, and a merchant, who became a *shochet* in his later years. He was a scholar, G-d fearing, an activist for the Aguda *cheder*, to which he gave of his energies for education. He was involved in the *cheder* and Beis Yaakov in Biłgoraj. In fact, he took part in almost all the institutions. He earned his livelihood from the toil of his hands. He was beloved by his fellow, and greeted everyone politely. He had a good temperament, with all the traits mentioned by the sages. Who can give us a replacement!

Translator's footnotes:

1. Psalms 128:3
2. Ritual slaughterers
3. Person who performs circumcision

[Page 209]

Everything Vanished Like a Dream

by Simche Shatz

Translated by Moses Milstein

Whenever I find myself in solitude, a picture from 17 years ago, when I was a child of 13, comes to me.

As in a dream, I see the leaning house and its shingle roof, near the city power plant, the windows looking out to the garden full of green trees and leaves, the fragrant *matchiekes* calling to you and casting a spell just like a lover her love. The whole garden resembles a green velvet carpet from which various flowers in different colors sprout.

The windows are open all night long, the delicious fragrances filling hearts with joy and hope.

In the evening, when the sun goes down, it is a pleasure to sit in the garden surrounded by trees.

Old and young stream to the power plant's garden. Beautiful songs sung by Jewish youth elicit joy and pleasure in the listeners, and the hearty voices cut through the stillness of the night.

And Jews lived like this and were happy until the cruel days of the Holocaust arrived.

It was the end of August, a nice summer day, kids playing at Pinye Tsimring's place, catching butterflies, playing football. It is a pleasure, birds are singing, people are happy on this summer day, neighbors are sitting in the courtyard warming themselves in the sun, so lighthearted you want to sing along with the birds.

In a corner of the courtyard a young girl is sitting embroidering a kerchief, and singing a song to herself about a young tailor who loved a pretty girl.

[Page 210]

It seems as if the pleasant singing is coming from far away, becoming weaker and weaker until no sound is heard and then with one voice you hear others shouting, "Bravo!" She becomes embarrassed, reddens, and runs into the house.

The courtyard becomes strangely still, the dogs barking as if they sensed something bad. I am sawing wood with my brother when suddenly someone cries, "Fire!" I scamper up to the roof of the house, and I see huge clouds of smoke billowing from the bridge street. People begin to speculate, one says it's certainly the bathhouse, another says it's the Boyars, the peasant community. Jews are standing around venturing guesses, but soon they see a large fire on the other side of the city, the Zamosc road, the Bagner road. There is fire on all sides now.

A panic ensues. Everyone carries bedding and other things to the lawns near Hershele's mill. The fire grows bigger, swallowing house after house, street after street. Streets disappear like: Rinek, Kosciusko, Zamosc, Bagner, Third of May, Shul Street, Pilsudski. The flames destroy the "big" synagogue, the besmedresh, the cheder, the yeshiva, city hall, the butcher stalls, the city cinema. The Kosciusko street down to the "sands" miraculously survives. The burned-out Jews go to neighbors, acquaintances, and family.

And thus, Jewish possessions and property, the result of hundreds of years of toil and effort, disappeared with the smoke.

[Page 211]

Personalities

Translated by Moses Milstein

[Page 211]

Chaim Bruder

In his youth, he worked as a barber in Izbice. Even though he had a lot of problems there, the town remained beloved by him to his dying day.

His sole desire was to travel to Izbice, or to Russia where a brother lived. "A nice city, Russia," he used to say. These were the two "cities" he loved, and talked about constantly.

Later, Chaim returned to the city of his birth, and worked for his uncle as a barber, and helped out playing at weddings. He livened up every wedding he attended. Half the city stood under the windows. More than once, in the middle of the wedding, he would grab his fiddle, and disappear out a back door.

The biggest insults were the shouts of "Chaim Bruder, *mamzer*."

When his uncle died, he stayed with his aunt, Malkeh. His favorite dish was hot bobeh.

Once, he asked his aunt to bake him a bobeh. When some guys heard that Malkeh was baking a bobeh for Chaim, they poured castor oil, in the bobeh.

[Page 212]

Chaim really enjoyed the bubeh, and kept saying–what a rich bobeh. Come nighttime, he almost died. From that point on, he didn't want to hear anymore about bobehs.

At the age of 60, he decided to get married. He thought no one knew about his wedding, and he had no idea what was in store for him. When the klezmorim who Chaim played with heard about the wedding, they all got together with their instruments, and hid near his house.

Chaim got up at dawn and prepared for the wedding. When he left the house, and got up on the carriage, the klezmorim appeared on the street, one in front with a flag, and they began to play. Soon the whole city was there, and they all accompanied Chaim to the outskirts of town.

Chaim's house was dearer to him than his life. He was afraid to have electricity in the house, because electricity can make the house shake.

When Poland instituted *urbanistik*, and required picket fences around every house, Chaim became very sad. He thought that even the roof had to be made of pickets, and how was he to keep the rain out in that case?

When he got old, he lost his sight. He would often sigh, and when he was asked–R' Chaim, why are you sighing? He would answer–If I had known I would lose my vision, I would have gone to see my brother in Russia.

Near the time of his death, Chaim expressed his greatest sorrow, that he could not see his house at least once before he died.

Yechezkeleh

He was forever young and happy. Years ago, when he was asked, Yechezkel, how old are you? He would always answer, 35 years old. And to the end of his days, he was never older than 35.

He was even happy when, during WWI, as the cholera was raging through the city, they married Yechezkel to a deaf woman in the cemetery as a remedy.

There was not a wedding in town where Yechezkel was not invited and regaled the crowd with his dancing and singing during which he recounted his entire lineage. Yechezkeleh Viotch–that's me. Meirleh Botch–my father. Chanahleh Du–my mother. Leibeleh Showolski–my uncle, and in this way he recited all his family.

He also remembered well every march played to the chupah 40 years earlier, and for whom.

[Page 214]

Godl

by H. Feigenboim

Translated by Moses Milstein

In his younger days, Godl was a *zipper*.[1] He worked hard for his daily bread. He was never the brightest.

When the Poland-Bolshevik war broke out, Godl was drafted into the Polish army and sent to serve in Szczecin.

A short time later, he was brought back mentally ill. He would run around town in torn clothes performing military exercises, screaming the whole time, "Company." From time to time he would stop, hit himself in the face, and continue on.

He could only remember one thing. There was no one in town whose name he didn't know. If someone was pointed out to him, and he was asked for the name, he would jump up and down, and give the name.

Translator's footnote:

    1.   Someone who worked in the sieve industry

[Page 215]

Shimon'le

When he was young, he was a women's tailor, which meant delivering the finished garments with his master.

He refused to allow his tenants to close the shutters. I'm the boss, he used to say, and he would shut them.

Later, he joined the household of the city rabbi. He was ready to sacrifice himself for the rebbe and the rebbetzin. His most grateful expression was, " Rebbe, you are a great guy." His mother's death made him angry at her. He said, "Good for you. You refused to eat, now you lie there."

Later, he cut off his friendship with the rebbe and rebbetzin. He left them and became a water carrier.

But the reason for his quarrel with the rebbe and the rebbetzin remains a mystery.

[Page 216]

Avremele

Avremele was a person of average size, with a black, broad beard. He lived with his parents in a village near Bilgoraj, He used to go around town talking to himself. He used to pick up papers from the ground and stuff them in his bosom.

When WWI broke out, his mother, who was very pious, died during the cholera epidemic that raged in the Lublin area. She could not be buried in the city, so they buried her in the forest. At that time, his father left the village and came to the city.

After the war, his mother was exhumed, and it was said that her body was still fresh. The peasants there used to say that there was a light shining from her grave when they passed by at night.

Avremele was arrested by the gendarmerie, when Bilgoraj was occupied by Austria, and placed in chains in the belief he was a spy, because of the wads of papers he carried around. However, when things were explained to them, he was let go.

His favorite dish was hot potatoes. That's why he was called, "*Avremele, Heisse Poples.*"

After his father's death, he lived in the besmedresh doing odd jobs for people, and receiving food in return.

[Page 219]

The Destruction

War Breaks out

by Shmuel Bron

Translated by Moses Milstein

The last sunny days of August were truly sparkling and beautiful. From time to time, an angry, autumn wind appeared ruffling the yellowed leaves of the chestnut trees. But it quickly disappeared, as if it had never been, and again the sun appeared with its barely perceptible warmth like a pat, a caress, like a whispered good–bye. As if it wanted to chase away the gloom with its last rays, to remove the frowns from worried faces, refresh them, warm them, and gird them for the future.

The world isn't ending yet, Jews argued. It's just saber rattling. Neither the Poles nor the Germans are so eager to go to war. The old days are over. We no longer lived in an era of "positional" battles, where soldiers rot in trenches, lousy, like hairy apes, waiting for years for the auspicious moment, for the bayonet charge, for the triumphant taking of a position.

Today is a different time. Today, steel birds fly in the skies, and blow up the earth. Giant, mobile fortresses, their killing necks protruding, spit lead and fire. They can destroy worlds. And the most horrible of all–gas. Both countries have it. Suffocating gases, burning gases, gases that cause the body to melt away. But the birds don't have to crawl through barbed wire.

[Page 220]

They can fly over the highest mountains. Each side faces the same dangers, and so it won't come to war.

What's the fight about anyway? Is it about boots? (Referring to the Danzig gulf). They'll work it out between themselves. Furthermore, Poland is not alone. It has alliances, and its own army. As Rydz–Smigli used to say, "We won't give them a button!"

So the Jews speculated, consoled themselves, and fended off the terrible specter of war. Jewish fathers and mothers had sons spread throughout the Polish army. There were Jews who had already served, fathers of young children, who had to be ready at any moment to be called up, further contributing to the reluctance to believe it was really going to happen.

The last days of the month went by quickly. Clouds formed in the sky, and the last birds, flying in formation, left our region on their way to warmer places. We tried to suppress the unsettling feelings, but they grew stronger.

Young and old stood in Todros Lang's store, and in other places, and listened carefully to the scathing speeches on the radio from the Polish authorities, with their slogans, "We will not yield an inch of our land!" confident that should war break out, Poland would be the winner. People listened with a mixture of fever and cold, anxiety and denial. After the speeches, and the war anthem (yeshtsieh folsko nieh zginenla), everyone left for their homes, neighbor to neighbor, to discuss what was heard.

[Page 221]

It wasn't just fear of war that troubled Jews. There was another worry that caused them to tremble–their Christian neighbors. On the eve of the outbreak of the great storm, they, the great patriots, went around arrogantly, with smug faces, saying, "Let war come and we will give the Jews what they deserve. (Your grandfather Pilsudski is long dead.)" By this, they made it known that we had lost our last protector. They were just waiting for the right moment when they would be free to riot among the Jews.

And it was, indeed, the looks in those gleeful faces that depressed us and chased away the last hope that war would be avoided.

That last Thursday, August 1939, we clearly felt that we were on the eve of something, but of what, no one knew.

The city seemed to be anticipating some great event. Business in the market was sluggish, without its usual energy, in spite of the fact that the proprietors had bought more than usual to be ready for any situation. Why this was so, no one could say. It was only a feeling that drove them, a feeling, if it could be articulated, that there was a snake's nest somewhere at the edge of civilized mankind, and there the devil waited with a watch in his hand for the birth of the unfortunate first of September, 1939, so that he could open the gates of hell. A hell that human imagination could not conceive.

[Page 222]

On Friday, September 1, 1939, at 4:00 am, the first bombers awakened the Polish people, erstwhile friends of Hitler's Germany, and announced that the war had begun.

With the break of day, the news spread with lightening speed across the entire country, and reached Bilgoraj as well.

Gloom and depression beset everyone. Muffled wailing and weeping in the homes. Mothers ran to the synagogues, to the cemetery, to pray fervently to ward off the imminent danger, to pray for their children to be saved, for the fire to pass them by.

People became sadder still when Kosibucki, the town crier, went through town, banging his drum, and read out the mobilization orders, and orders from the local city council with respect to the outbreak of war.

The mustachioed Pole looked very serious. He read each word slowly, with care, sharply accenting the words. The Polish army, wanted to be seen as the vanguard of the country, and to join with those who will, in the coming hours, be in her service. His earnestness remained even after he ended his reading. None of the usual jokes or puns came out of his mouth. He quickly turned on his heels and left for another part of the city.

[Page 223]

There, he beat his drum again, and again another group gathered around him.

But they gathered not just around Kosibucki. Masses of people were glued to the billboards that had been erected everywhere. Reading the mobilization orders, everyone felt condemned, lost. The frightened eyes of mothers and fathers searched for some way to save their sons who could, at any moment, be lost.

War! War atmosphere in the homes, in the street, in shul, in *besmedresh*. No more work, no business, no *cheder*. Everything paralyzed, as if suddenly struck dead. Except here and there, a door opens, a young man steals quickly out, a little pack in his hands, and looks back several times. In the shadow of the doorway, stand transfixed fathers and mothers, younger sisters and brothers, their eyes wet, their arms outstretched as if they had lost their dearest possession. Another would vanish the same way, all headed in the same direction–to the kolejka (little train) which gathered up all the youths, and took them away to a nameless future.

The tension was even greater in the evening when the sun had gone down below the horizon. Daylight disappeared as if a light had been extinguished leaving a black darkness. The whole city looked like a large velvet cloth, the streets unlit, the windows covered, the shutters closed, so that, God forbid, no light should escape from them, so that when the enemy flies over, they will not recognize the city.

[Page 224]

The city was locked up tight in the depressing gloom. The only things moving were the pair of night watchmen slinking around to guard the telephone poles against saboteurs.

Several days after the outbreak of war, the city was engulfed by a wave of Jewish refugees. They were mostly from Tarnow, and the Cracow environs. They arrived exhausted, drained, having lost their homes, their worldly goods, their blood and sweat from generations of hard work, all gone. They described the speed at which Hitler's hordes advanced breaking through all the Polish army's defenses. Entire regiments surrendered to the Germans, clearing the way for the German hordes.

Hearing the news from the refugees sent a shudder through everyone. It was clear that all the protective barriers were failing. People felt helpless. In the meantime, food had become scarce in the city. The locals still had resources, because everyone had prepared something. The situation of the refugees was worse. In spite of the help they received, they stood in long lines at the bakery for bread. As to their other needs, every household shared with them, like with family. They cooked for them, found them beds. There was practically no house without refugees. Concern for their plight affected everyone.

[Page 225]

These were the first signs of war, the first scenes of exile and suffering.

Wednesday, September 6. As Bilgoraj Jews were working with shovels digging defense trenches, not far from the kolejka, they suddenly heard the loud noise of airplanes. They were flying so high that it was hard to identify them, until a piercing whistling from the falling bombs rent the air, and the detonations from the explosions could be heard, and we knew that they were bombarding us.

The city siren started howling after it had all ended. No Jews were harmed. People stampeded to find a safer place. The streets emptied out. People disappeared to their hiding places, their hearts racing with fear of another attack. So we lay until the siren sounded the all–clear.

Thursday, during the day, was calm. There was no market. People were still reeling from the effects of the previous day's bombardment. We felt that the war was now also beginning in Bilgoraj.

Friday September 8 did not look as it usually did. The men got ready for shabbes, but without the usual joy and enthusiasm. Their movements were restrained, quiet, without noise, in order not to disturb the Sabbath. Everything was done quickly in order to finish as early as possible.

Ten o'clock in the morning, menacing loud noises were again heard over the city. A squadron of German bombers appeared in the clear skies of Bilgoraj.

[Page 226]

Soon explosions followed, one after the other. A wild stampede ensued. People were running without knowing where, falling, getting up and running further. Women fainted, had fits. Children trembled with fear. People waited in indescribable panic and fear until the sound of the airplanes retreated, until the danger, for the moment, had passed.

Dozens of bombs had fallen in various places in the city: Itzchak Wertzer's house was entirely destroyed. Two bombs fell in Nuteh Kronenberg's garden, and destroyed his entire property. Not one window remained whole.

On the other side of the street, in Nathan'le Maimon's garden, neighbors who had hidden among the fruit trees were fired on by the circling airplanes sowing death from their machine guns.

Sunday, September 10. A *podporutznik*, and a sergeant in the Polish army, were riding the kolejka from Zwierzyniec to Bilgoraj. While sitting in the train compartment they overheard a discussion, in bad Polish, on the other side, and the name, Miller, mentioned. The two soldiers were from Bilgoraj. One, Skawerzak's son, knew Miller, the patriot, who used to make speeches on Polish national days. The two travelers struck them as suspicious, so they decided to follow them.

[Page 227]

Not long after, they disembarked and went off in the direction of the forest where Miller lived.

The two soldiers succeeded in getting into the yard. To their astonishment, they discovered that they were dealing with a widespread spy ring, with Miller at the head.

One of the two soldiers went to inform the city police. Within minutes, the courtyard was surrounded. The police commissar, accompanied by policemen, broke into the cellar under Miller's house, and discovered the whole gang gathered around the radio transmitter they had installed there.

On Monday, September 7, at 10:00 o'clock in the morning, the whole gang was shot at the trenches behind the jail. The inmates relayed the last words of the German spy, "Hitler, Hitler, we work for you." To the police commissar he had said, "You may shoot me, but in half an hour from now, Bilgoraj will be annihilated." And so it came to pass.

This was the start of the war in Bilgoraj, the beginning of the terrible end.

———

[Page 228]

The Fire

by Sh. Atzmon (Wirtzer)

Translated by Moses Milstein

Certain events occur in people's lives that can never be forgotten. For me, when I was still very young, it was the outbreak of the war and "the Bilgoraj fire."

Monday, September 11, 1939 was a beautiful, sunny, autumn day. I was playing with other children in the yard. We were interrupted by the wailing of the city siren, and the ringing bells. Bilgoraj was on fire!

Terrifying tongues of flame quickly engulfed the Jewish neighborhood by the bridge street. The bathhouse was on fire! It all happened at exactly the time the Nazi spy, Miller, had mockingly predicted. The fire was regarded as an act of vengeance for his execution.

We could not figure out where the fire was coming from. The flames had already reached the bridge street, the marsh street, Szewsky street, Pilsudski street. Spreading along Kosciuszko street, the fire enveloped the market. People were running around in a daze among the flames. Bilgoraj is in flames, Bilgoraj is burning! The first thought was to rescue people from the houses. Bedding, clothes, furniture, dishes, lay trodden underfoot, and were later consumed in the frightful heat of the blaze. The wooden telephone poles ignited and fell burning.

[Page 229]

People stood in shock, wringing their hands as they watched as all their possessions, the work of years, went up in smoke. There was not even anything to fight the fire with. The firemen had left at the start of the war, taking the equipment with them.

Masses of people. Women and small children, carrying what they had rescued from the fire wrapped in white sheets, were leaving the city. They ran through the meadows to the river, or along Gosh Street to the fields.

My father, *z"l*, asked my mother to take the children, and follow the others to the river. He went back to the city, with others, to save whatever they could. Amid the panic, and the crying of children, women were shouting, "*Gevalt, es brent, Bilgoraj brent!*"

When we looked around, we were confronted with a frightful scene. The entire city was one black cloud of smoke. Giant flames, towering to the sky, devoured one house after the other. In the space of an hour, the entire city was aflame, a torch of Jewish worldly goods.

When them men got to the *shul–hof*, flames were shooting out of the windows. Without hesitation, they went in to the burning *besmedreshes* to save the Torahs. They emerged, half–dead, filthy, clothes and beards burned, carrying a soot–covered Sefer Torah.

[Page 230]

The Polish underworld took advantage of the fire. They broke into Todros Lang's store, and began to steal the merchandise. Police arrived on the scene quickly, and shot one of the robbers.

While the fire was consuming the whole city, the loud rumble of bombers was heard overhead, followed by the sight of a squadron of airplanes dropping incendiary bombs. The fires raged with a terrifying roar. Having done their work on the city, the planes began to circle the riverbanks over the burned, confused, Jewish refugees.

An indescribable, wild stampede ensued. People began to jump into the river. Women, clutching frightened children, fell on the ground to protect them. The planes descended very low, and opened fire on the terrified Jews.

People began to rush madly to the little grove of woods near Sheinwald's mill.

It was deadly quiet among the trees. Children lay shivering from the cold wrapped in things that had been saved from the fire, their only complaint,"Where is father?"

Night fell. The air was full of stifling smoke. The city looked like a glowing lantern. A cold dew covered everything. From time to time, a loud groan could be heard. The great disaster was on everyone's mind. A few hours ago, they had been leaders of households. Now, they were homeless.

[Page 231]

As night fell, we saw a group of men approaching, and among them, I recognized my father.

I will never forget the way my father looked. Completely blackened, his clothes burnt, his hair in disarray, he was carrying something wrapped in a half–burned *taliss*. We started shouting,"Father," and he came over to us. When he got closer, we saw that he was carrying the"new" sefer–torah that the Mizrachi organization had sponsored, and had paraded with great ceremony to the Yavne cheder.

He told us that he and other men were helping rescue efforts at Itzchak Meir Warshaviak's, when cries were heard that the fire had enveloped the *koszcelne* (Shewski) street. He remembered that the rescued Sefer Torah was lying in a house there. He quickly ran over.

When he got there, he saw that the roof was on fire, and black smoke was billowing out the windows. He wasted little time, and entered through a side window. The room was already on fire. He grabbed the Sefer Torah and left the burning room.

The way back was much harder. The whole neighborhood was engulfed in flames. There was simply no way to get through. But thanks to the fact that his hat and the *taliss* were soaked with water, he succeeded in breaking through the flames, and returning safely to us.

People spent the entire night out on the meadows, and shivered with cold.

[Page 232]

My father kept consoling himself that the Sefer–Torah had been saved.

In the morning, as soon as the sun crept above the horizon, the wailing began: "Yidden, we are all burned up, all burned up! A punishment from God!"

They awakened the children, who had slept all night wrapped in whatever was rescued, packed up, and set off for the city, some to their burnt–down house, some to a relative, and others to an acquaintance whose house was still intact.

A sorrowful train of people carrying packs on their backs. Jews, who in the space of one day, had lost everything, burnt out, left without a roof over their heads, and no way to make a living…

Arriving in the city, we were gripped by fear. It looked like a volcano had erupted. A layer of white ash covered the smoking, still burning embers. Walking was difficult. Streets were unrecognizable. All of the Jewish community's worldly goods lay trampled underfoot. The city was one great ruin.

[Page 233]

Bilgoraj After the Fire

by A. Kronenberg

Translated by Moses Milstein

The day after the fire, people wandered through the ruins looking for anything that might be useful. They dragged out half–burned sacks of flour, sugar, and other things.

People slowly began to make arrangements for themselves. Some went to acquaintances, some to relatives, and some rented rooms from a Christian whose house was still standing. They soon turned their minds to pragmatic questions. They gathered stones, lumber, bricks to begin building a roof over their heads. One of the first was Yoel Baker (Weiss). By the third day after the fire, he had already fixed up his burned bakery, and had begun to bake bread.

Wednesday September 13, 1939. The Polish military was retreating. To our great misfortune, the general staff sought safety in Bilgoraj and was quartered in the *shule* building. Soon a squadron of planes appeared and began bombing the city from all sides. A wild stampede took place. People ran around crazed, not knowing where to hide. Having done their devilish work, the airplanes left.

When people had calmed down a little, they went out into the streets to see what damage had been done. They learned that the first three victims fell near Sharf's mill and were: Israel Sharf, {blank space} Sharf, and Hersh Yechezkel Harman who was badly wounded in the head, and died two days later.

[Page 234]

Thursday, September 14. The city was full of Polish soldiers retreating in great disorder. The Jews, still reeling from yesterday's bombardment, left their homes and fled to the nearby forests. The retreating Polish army exploited this event. They broke into Jewish houses, and took everything. When the Jews returned exhausted, hungry, they found an empty house.

Friday September 15. A light rain was falling. Jews got together, neighbor to neighbor, in order to daven with a minyan. They waited with anticipation for nightfall. They argued that it wasn't possible to bomb in the dark. Then suddenly, the roar of heavy bombers was heard, rending the air. A squadron of bombers appeared, and began to bomb the city. Several bombs landed and destroyed three houses and the people in them. In Yehoshua Klezmer (Zeifer)'s house, 30 people perished, men, women, and children.

As soon as the airplanes had left, a big crowd assembled, and was confronted with a horrible spectacle. Logs, stones, and bricks were mixed together with human arms and legs. The wailing and crying were heart–rending.

The crowd gathered there began to drag the dead from beneath the ruins. They brought out: Shmai Adler and his wife; Bertshe Stolar (Yegergarn) and his daughter; Mendl Erlich and his wife, (he survived); Devora Hiter (Sheinsinger), and a daughter; Yehoshua Seifer and his children.

[Page 235]

Removing the dead from under the rubble went on until late in the night. Terrible, heartbreaking scenes took place when people recognized their relatives. The wailing could be heard all through the city.

The dead were gathered together and brought to the house of the city–rabbi, which had not burned down, so that they could be buried in the Jewish cemetery after the holidays. People got together and davened in a minyan. But the holiday atmosphere had vanished. The chazzan ended, "*Tichla shana v'kileloteha, tachel shana u' birchoteha*[1]" with deep emotion. The participants left quietly, each to his family waiting impatiently.

Saturday, September 16. A fierce battle was fought over Bilgoraj. The Polish army deployed in the middle of the city with heavy machine guns trying to prevent the German advance troops from cutting off the Polish army retreat. Heavy German artillery continuously pounded, the whistling of the shells cutting through the air right over our heads.

A shell fell on one of the remaining houses in the shul street. The house began to burn, and quickly enveloped the rabbi's house where the dead were lying.

[Page 236]

In minutes, the house was consumed. We could not remove the dead, and all of them were incinerated there.

That afternoon, the Polish army left the city. A city militia was quickly established that patrolled the streets, and protected the city from attacks and looting. A deadly silence reigned in the city. The streets–dark, unlit. The only sounds were from the night watchmen patrolling the streets.

The Jews sat in their houses listening intently for any movement in the city. They spent the whole night as if glued to the cracks in the shutters, and peered out looking for any movement. A multitude of anxious thoughts worried their minds. What will tomorrow bring?

Sunday, September 17, 1939. At eight in the morning, the first Germans appeared riding motorcycles. They made a circuit around the market. Soon armored jeeps appeared with four Germans in each, and trucks, foot soldiers, tanks, and other personnel. The city quickly filled with Nazi troops.

German officers could be heard giving orders. The shouting, which penetrated through the shutters into the Jewish houses, caused fear in the hearts of the listeners. We soon saw whose hands we had fallen into…

[Page 237]

The real suffering of the Jews quickly began. Non–Jewish hooligans went around town pointing out–"here, Jude"–the houses where Jews lived. At every house you heard the same, "Aufmachen!"

Armed German soldiers arrived, and the robbing began. The best things they kept for themselves. The less valuable things they gave to the Polish hooligans who followed them around, and helped them in their thieving.

Every day, Jews were forced into labor. The work consisted of filling the craters made by the bombs. While they worked, they would be beaten with the butts of the German rifles. After a day like this, they returned home beaten, and bloody. The German murderers broke into Lipeh Wagshol's wholesale store and took his merchandise. The Polish population promptly gathered around the Germans, who then distributed some of the things. It was shameful to see how our Polish neighbors plundered Jewish possessions. Every day at daybreak they would break into the Jewish residences. They would drive the half–dressed Jews out to work with blows from their rifles. The German murderers derived a special pleasure from seizing doctors, engineers, or others of the intelligentsia for labor. They gave them the hardest, foulest work to do, like cleaning the latrines with their bare hands, and after that, they beat them horribly.

September 22. The whole day, they went around seizing Jews for various brutal tasks. When night fell the Jews shut themselves in their houses, lit the Yom Kippur candles, and with sad, quiet tears, began to chant Kol Nidrei.

[Page 238]

With that, the Germans began to break into house after house, robbing and murderously beating.

While we were sitting, confined in our house, around the body of our brother, Baruch, who had died Erev Yom Kippur at four o'clock, we heard a loud pounding on the door that led to Koszcziuszki Street. We pretended not to hear it. When the banging became more forceful, and we realized that they were going to break down the door, I went over to the door, and innocently asked, "Who's there?" Then I heard the murderous command, "Aufmachen!"

As soon as I opened the door, two Germans burst in, revolvers in hand. We were all struck with deadly fear. They gave me a hard shove so that I fell hitting my head on the edge of the table. My parents protested loudly that there was a dead person lying here. They uncovered the dead body, and ordered my father to take a candle, and go with them to the first floor. The said they were looking for bread. They searched for a while, then left.

The First Victims

People slowly got used to the situation. They resigned themselves to it with the thought, "What can we do?" In the meantime, the Germans broke into Hershele Sheinwald's mill. A line of Poles quickly formed, and the Germans began to distribute flour. When the Jews in town, who were already suffering from a lack of food, learned of this, they sent some young girls over to see if they could get a little flour.

[Page 239]

Food was already hard to find then.

A long line of Christians stood by the mill, among them the Jewish girls. The Germans were distributing flour. When the turn came for the line where Chelke (Yudashka's niece) was standing, the Poles pushed her out, calling her a Jew. Upon hearing this, the German pulled her out of the line, cold–bloodedly took out his revolver, and shot at her. He hit her in the leg. Pandemonium broke out among the Jewish girls. They ran back home terrified carrying the wounded Chelke. That same day, at noon, the Germans broke into Mordechai Shtulman's food store, stole the flour, and proceeded to distribute it to the Polish population that had quickly formed a line. No Jews were allowed. As the Germans were distributing the flour from Shtulman's store, Mordechai Lieber (who had worked for years as a porter at Shtulman's) came over to them, and begged for a little flour for his starving children. The German pulled out his revolver, and shot the porter in the belly. Why? For having the audacity to beg for some flour that the German murderers had stolen from a Jewish shop? Having done his murderous work, the German nonchalantly returned to distributing flour to the Christians.

Mortally wounded, they hurriedly carried Mordechai to the hospital, but he died in great agony on the way.

[Page 240]

After the two events, the Jews of Bilgoraj were gripped by terror. We began to see that the Germans were getting ready to exterminate the Jews.

No Jews were to be seen on the streets. People shut themselves up in their houses, afraid to go out in the light of day; there was no life to be seen.

Monday September 25. The day after the murder, the Germans again seized Jews for work details. No one hid anymore. We had seen what the murderers were capable of.

Rumors began to circulate that the Red Army was going to come in, but because of the dejected state the Jews were in, they were reluctant to believe it. But soon, some signs appeared that the Germans were departing. The army was slowly leaving town.

Wednesday, September 27. Erev Sukkot. The Jews, knowing the Germans were leaving, and afraid of a pogrom, locked themselves in their houses, and listened anxiously for any disturbance.

The Germans left the city at night. There was no one in charge the entire night. Nevertheless, the Jews felt a little happier. We were certain that the Red Army would now be coming.

Thursday, September 28. A Polish army detachment entered town. A firefight ensued with the last remaining German patrols, and a German soldier was badly wounded.

[Page 241]

Two Bilgoraj Jews, David Brenner, and Yehoshua Hof, happened to be passing by, and saw the soldier writhing with pain on the ground. They picked him up and carried him to the hospital.

After the shooting, a German armored vehicle with several soldiers arrived along the bridge street, and drove to the Jewish neighborhood. They seized several Jews, accusing them of firing on the German patrol.

They were deaf to any arguments. They were going to shoot the Jews. Suddenly a real miracle happened. The Polish soldiers reappeared. The Germans abandoned the Jewish captives, and took off after the Polish soldiers. When the Jews saw the Germans leaving they immediately fled. For the rest of the night, the Jews stayed locked up in their homes, alert for any disturbances.

Friday, September 29. At four am, the rumble of tanks was heard. The Jews sere seized with terror. Are the Germans returning? But it did not feel like it. All night long, an army streamed through without end.

People could not contain themselves. They sent out children to find out what was happening. They quickly returned with the news: the Red Army had arrived.

The news spread like lightening through the entire city. The Jews jubilantly went out into the streets shouting, "Yidden, we are saved!"

[Page 242]

Red flags were fluttering on all the state buildings. Jews breathed a little easier after the terrible ordeal with the Germans. A people's militia was quickly formed which restored order in the city.

The celebration was short lived, however. Rumors began to circulate that the Red Army was abandoning the city. Several Jews even asked the senior officers whether the rumors were true. Their answer was, "Wherever the Red Army sets foot, it will remain." This was of some consolation for the Jews.

Tuesday, October 3. It was becoming clear that the Red Army was leaving. Gloom settled in all the Jewish houses, and hope vanished. In the streets, circles of troubled Jews formed, asking the same question, "What should one do? Where should one go?"

At 9:00 am, a Russian commandant informed us that the Red Army was leaving the city, and that whoever wanted to was welcome to leave with them. Everyone would be provided with every opportunity.

An indescribable panic arose. Young and old, men and women with children, rushed to be ready for the withdrawal, which was to begin in the early afternoon.

A light rain was falling. There were people with packs on their backs, and women with small children seated on wagons. It is hard to describe the scene when the carriages began to move. The heavens were rent with the weeping from children parting from their parents, parents from children, men from women, women from men, while the rain kept falling more and more intensely.

[Page 243]

A large crowd had gathered at the kolejka which was taking people to Zwierzyniec. Parents were left standing in shock when the kolejka's whistle blew, separating them from their loved ones forever.

In spite of the heavy rain, wagons full of people kept coming all through the night to the train to Zwierzyniec. Afraid of what tomorrow would bring when the red Army was gone, Jews were leaving in mad panic.

To go, or not to go? No one had an answer to that question. People's minds wrestled with the question. Many still remembered the flight that had taken place in WWI, the wandering, the homelessness.

Wednesday, October 4. The talk in town is that the kolejka will be making its last trip. Pandemonium in the city. People who had resigned themselves to staying got caught up in the tide. They stopped everything, packed the necessities, and ran to the kolejka.

The kolejka was full. All the places were taken. It was deathly quiet except for some quiet weeping. The sad partings pierced the heart. Everyone's eyes were wet, tears flowing from a never–ending well.

The sounds of the whistle blowing, the locomotive's heavy panting, were mingled with the people's crying. The kolejka began to move, handkerchiefs waved from the windows.

[Page 244]

Fathers, mothers, relatives and friends stood watching as the departing train took their loved ones away on an uncertain journey.

This was, in fact, the last train. The Red Army loaded the locomotive and all the cars onto the big train, and left Zwierzyniec.

And, just like that, the Red Army occupation had come to an end. Jews were left in fear of the morrow, dreading the return of the murderous German army.

Saturday, October 7, 1939. The German Army has re–entered Bilgoraj. Their entry immediately spread fear among the Jewish population. There was not a single Jew to be seen on the street. That very day, the Germans ordered all Jewish men to present themselves for whatever work the German army required.

As if that weren't enough, they also demanded a large contribution from the Jewish community, and in order to be sure they got it, they took several prominent Jews hostage.

Discussions were of no use. The hostages were mercilessly beaten. The Jews had no option but to pay. The hostages were released thereafter. Yechezkel Kandel was so badly beaten, that he lay an invalid for months.

[Page 245]

After this business, the Jews could see what lay in store for them under the German occupation–their lives would be in constant danger.

People began to search for a way out. Some went to Tarnogrod, smuggled themselves over to Sziniawa which was then under Soviet control.

In the early days, the border was practically open, and many people did, in fact, cross over, and saved themselves. But the border was later closed, and crossing over became impossible. There was the danger of being shot, or ending up in a Russian jail.

And that is how a large part of Bilgoraj's Jews ended up in the murderous hands of the German executioner.

Several days later, the German murderers arrested David Brenner who had brought the wounded German soldier shot by the Polish patrol to the hospital. They accused him of shooting the German soldier.

In short order, Christian "witnesses" appeared to confirm the fabricated charges. Tears were of no help. Neither was the intervention of the city priest. The German savages sentenced the innocent, David Brenner, to death.

They tortured the innocent victim for several days. Finally, they led him out, barely alive, to the fields, and shot him.

After this horrible murder, many people, notwithstanding the danger of crossing the border, fled the city.

[Page 246]

From right to left: Meshulem Honigbaum (killed); Yakov Stempel's wife, Shimon Buchbinder, Raizl Stempel (lives in Israel); Leah'tshe Goldberg (killed); Levi Sheinwald, Baltche Greenfal, (lives in Israel); Nechemiah Lang (killed), Sholom Greenfal (lives in Israel)

Translator's footnote:

1.   May the year and its curses come to an end; may the year and its blessings begin.

[Page 248]

Survivors Testify

Bilgoraj Jews Under Occupation

by Israel Geist

Translated by Moses Milstein

A world of decrees began pouring down on the Jews whose intent was to single out and separate the Jews from the surrounding Polish population.

Towards the end of 1939, a Judenrat was established in Bilgoraj with the following people: Chaim Mordechai Hirshenhorn, chairman; Hillel Yanower; Itzchak Meir Warshaviak, Yechezkel Kandel, Yosef Rapaport, Shmuel Arbesfeld, Shimon Bin, Zelig Rosenberg, (director of the warehouse), and others.

Their job was to provide laborers for the German authorities for tasks such as road work, building a field hospital for the Wermacht on the "sands," or loading and unloading cement, gravel, coal, lumber and other things from the Zwierzyniec train.

The Judenrat, in collaboration with the German authorities, created a Jewish police with the following members: Yakov Taber, Moishe Bleichman, Moishe Panzerman, Sinai Shper, Balek Entberg, Moishe Shwanenfeld, Yakov Alender, and others. Their job was to deliver the workers for the Germans, and also, to help in the various deportations.

In April 1940, the Germans issued a decree requiring every Jew over the age of 14 to wear a patch on the right arm, with a blue Star of David, so that he could be identified by everyone as a Jew.

[Page 249]

People got used to the troubles, and the Judenrat continued to supply the Germans with Jewish workers.

Bilgoraj Jews in Labor Camps

Erev Shavuot, the Germman *kreizhauptman* (*starosta*[1]), informed the Judenrat that all men over the age of 17 must present themselves at the plaza opposite the *starostve*. Failure to do so would be met with strong punishment. Rumors circulated that from there, they were going to choose people to send to various labor camps.

That very day, a good portion of the Bilgoraj men showed up at the designated place. But some hid, and did not present themselves.

Then the Gestapo and the *kreizhauptman* showed up, and began to sort everyone into two rows. They began to select people, but no one knew which row would be sent away and which would stay. People tried to read the Gestapo's eyes. They ran in confusion from one row to the other, not knowing which one it was better to be in.

Finally, they chose a number of young, strong, men. The representatives of the Judenrat made a list of their names, and informed them that they were to be ready at the kolejka in the morning, bringing clothes and food for one day.

[Page 250]

The selected were: Geist Israel; Yeshiahu–Nuteh, Mordechai, and Shmuel Wagner; Shmuel Zisman; Ber Yanower; deaf Yankel; Betsalel, Michal and Meir Obligenhartz; Porcelen Pesach; Yosef and Leibl Kleinmintz; Baruch Wermut; Yoneh Shmirer, Hershel Solomon's son–in–law; Yosef Hirschenhorn; Shloime Zilberlicht; Trib Zelig (from

Tarnogrod); Moishe–Chane Shuldiner; Dudish Entberg, Shloime Dorenbust; Zvi, Moishe, and Itzchak Brilliantstein; David Berlinerman; Yitzchak and Leibish Widerpelz; Zelig Bergstein; Itzchak Gedacht; Michal Olive; Schlechterman Feivel; Berger Eliezer, and others.

The following day, the first day of Shavuot, the selected men showed up at the kolejka. The Bilgoraj Christians, and the train workers, stood around happily and watched.

We crowded into the cars and went to Zwierzyniec where we transferred to the big train. We were in a good mood the whole way, not knowing what awaited us.

It is of interest to note that, travelling with us was Mordechai Basevitz, from Majdan. He spent about 6 months in the camps and would eat no *treyf*, subsisting only on bread and water.

Towards evening we arrived in Werbkowice, which is between Hrubieszow and Tyszowce. There, we were greeted by the German guards composed of Volksdeutsche. They have a lot of dirty work on their consciences over what they did in the camps and at the *aktions*. They began to drive us on foot in the sand.

[Page 251]

Many stopped and dropped their packs in order to run faster and avoid being beaten.

We arrived at Turkowice where there were blocks of housing in a Christian orphanage. We were all taken to an empty building. We were told to find wood and straw in order to build plank beds for ourselves.

An SS officer arrived and introduced himself as the head of the camp. He appointed Nuteh Kleinmintz as chief Jew. His job was to provide the prisoners with food.

The next day, we ourselves fenced in the area with barbed wire. Armed Volksdeutsche were recruited to guard us. The same day, they drove us to work deepening and widening a channel to the Khuchva River which is near Tyszowce.

The work was terribly hard and dangerous. We worked barefoot, up to our waists in water full of leeches which attached themselves to our legs, and sucked our blood. The heat was unbearable, yet we were not given a drop of water to drink, and we had to drink from the contaminated river.

The engineers and supervisors, who were Christian orphans, treated us sadistically and beat us murderously.

At the same time, the Jews in Bilgoraj were demanding that the Judenrat provide information as to what was happening to those who were sent away. And, in fact, we did receive a visit from a representative of the Judenrat in Turkowice.

[Page 252]

Meanwhile, in Bilgoraj, a hunt was underway. Truckloads of SS arrived and began to seize Jews to transport to Belzec which is near Tomaszow–Lubelski, and where they were building military fortifications. Among the captured were my father, Hershel Geist, and my brother, Shloime. Work there dragged on until late into the winter. A small number were let go. The majority was taken to the rock quarry in Chrabrowka, near Cracow. After a long time there, they were freed, and came back to Bilgoraj on foot.

**From right to left: Esther Ritser, Chayah Spiro, Tileh
Harman, Rickl Spiro and Basheh Spiro (All were killed)**

[Page 253]

In the meantime, the camp was enlarged. A transport of Jews arrived form Tomaszow–Mazowiecki.

In the autumn of 1940, work was interrupted, and we were transferred to the river "Khuchva" to continue deepening it. The work had to be done before winter. Almost all of the Jews in the camp were from Warsaw and Lodz.

When winter came, the camp was dissolved, and the Jews released. Back in Bilgoraj, we were continuously pressed into hard labor in construction, loading, and chopping wood.

In April 1941, the first deportations took place in Bilgoraj. 800 Jews were exiled to Goraj, among them my uncle, Eliahu Goldberg, and his family. After a short while, they almost all slowly came back.

There was not one quiet day. Every day, motorized vehicles carrying SS came and captured Jews for all kinds of work. People hid, but the SS rooted them out of their homes, and gave them a good beating in addition.

A decree was issued prohibiting Jews from leaving the city. The first victim was Israel Plotz who had gone to a village to buy some potatoes for his starving family. On his way back with his meager provisions, he was spotted by the Germans and shot.

One day, the Gestapo called for Hillel Yanower, and Shimon Bin. They were held until late causing widespread concern, because it was unusual to be held so long. The thought that something bad was going to happen, worried the Jews in the city.

[Page 254]

That night, they were taken out to the forest and shot.

Hersh Zilberberg was chosen as Jewish elder.

The First Extermination *action* in Bilgoraj

May 1942. A rumor was going around that the Judenrat was ordered to provide a certain number of Jews for deportation to the Ukraine. People ran to the Judenrat begging to be kept off the list. There was a feeling that things were not as they seemed. There were rumors that the Jewish people were being exterminated. There were also rumors going around that whoever worked at a German *placowka*, could remain. So there were many who paid large amounts of money to secure a work place.

The Judenrat could offer no way out. It had to provide the identified contingent. They secretly made a list, and on the last day, they informed those on the list that they must present themselves at the kolejka with all their baggage. And everybody showed up. Among them, me and my whole family, Zisman wth his family, and others.

When the train cars arrived, and the whole crowd was assembled, all the foremen appeared and began to disembark their workers. My father went over to Shloime Shtender, and asked him to come down. His response was, "What do I need this whole business for? I'll go to the Ukraine, get a little piece of land, and work."

[Page 255]

All the workers who had been removed by the foremen immediatcly went to their workplaces. Their wives and children snuck away from the transports unnoticed.

As they began moving the crowd into the carriages, it became clear that it was going to be bad, that the Jews had been duped. Their belongings had been taken away.

A deathly stillness reigned in Bilgoraj after the first *action*, when hundreds of families were taken away. People who had no work places, tried with desperation to find one reckoning that they would stand a better chance of staying alive.

A while later, the SS arrived and began seizing Jews for transport to Majdanek. Among the captured were Itzchak–Meir Warshoviak, Ber Yanower, and even people who were in the Jewish police like: Bolek Entberg, Tuvieh Kandel, Moishe Bleichman, and others.

At the end of October, rumors circulated that another *aktion* was being readied, and that only tradesmen would remain in the ghetto.

The Judenrat, which was headed by Hersh Zilberberg, had prepared a list of 70 tradesmen that had to remain in the ghetto. The people were: Todros Lang, his two sons, and his wife; Isaac Renner with wife and family; Sholem Porcelen; Hershele Shulman's 4 sons; Hersh Torm (Kras's son–in–law); Pinchas Farshtendig and a son; David Laks (Moishe Shtrikendrier's son); Shloime Zilberlicht and his wife; David Bendler with his wife and children; Aaron Harnfeld; Beinish Adler and his wife; Abraham Yanower and his wife; Moishe Lichtenfeld; Moishe Boim; Fishl Kandel; a son of Chaim Hachner; Shmuel Zisman; Laizer Fruchtlender; Pesach (the Frampoler carpenter), and others.

People ran to the Judenrat begging to be put on the list of workers. The Judenrat made promises, though their hands were tied. In the end, the list stayed the same. There was pandemonium. Those whose names were not on the list gave their valuables to those who were on the list.

Sunday evening, November 1, 1942. The Judenrat announced that everyone on the list will, after tonight, have to move to the ghetto which consisted of the houses of Alezar Kandel, Yantche Kantor, and Hersh Panzerman, all on Third of May Street.

The city was in a dreadful frenzy. We could see the end coming. People on the list were already moving their last things into the ghetto.

The Germans purposely separated families. There were heart–breaking scenes of men parting from wives, parents from children. When night fell there was no sign of life. The Jews lay in their rooms in great fear of what the morning would bring.

A lot of people not on the list stole into the ghetto and hid in holes, in attics, in closets.

The Second Extermination *aktion* in Bilgoraj

November 2, at dawn, we heard shooting coming from all sides of the city. I ran out of the house along the entire length of Third of May Street, to the kolejka. There, I hid among the stacks of wood waiting to be onloaded.

I hid there for a while until I was found by some Christian workers. They threatened to call the Germans. I got out of there and ran through the fields. I ran into an open wheat barn. Inside, I came upon Mordechai Sharfman's two children, hiding there in great fear. I could not stay there; it was too exposed.

The shooting had been going on ceaselessly the entire time. I fled the barn. There were some newly built barracks {nochen skarb}. I pried open a window, and hid there until it got dark.

[Page 258]

I could hear the shooting around me the entire time. The German murderers were hunting Jews like wild dogs. I left the barracks, and went to Polowa, a Christian acquaintance. She told me that the German murderers went from house to house shooting. They herded together all the Jews to Berach Hirshman's, and from there they took them to the barracks built on the old cemetery near Laizer Mitzner.

As they were driving them through the city, they would shoot at them. Dead bodies covered the whole city, and the gutters ran with blood like a slaughterhouse.

At a wedding in Bilgoraj
Wolf Boim (lives in Brazil), Israel Honigsfeld (lives in Israel), all the rest (killed)

Since I had not said farewell to my parents, I decided to go surrender myself, and to suffer the same fate as everyone.

The entrance at the barracks was guarded by a German. He asked where I had been the whole day. I told him I had been working. He didn't believe me, but let me in anyway.

Once inside the barrack, I met my mother and sister. I also saw: Sholem Rofer; Yosef Moynes; Yoneh Rofer and his wife and children; Isaac Shper; Wolf Bendler; Ephraim Zimring and his family, and others. A large number had been killed trying to escape. My mother told me that my father had been shot that very day. She told me I was wrong to have surrendered myself when others were running away. Her words inspired me to live, and I resolved to get out of German hands at the first opportunity. But in the meantime, hunger and thirst gnawed at us.

The next day, November 3, in the afternoon, Lithuanian guards appeared, dressed in special black uniforms with German insignia.

[Page 259]

They assisted in the liquidation of the Jewish community.

We were all driven out of the barracks, and made to form rows near Shloime Israel's stable. Then we were driven on foot to the Zwierzyniec train. And thus began the death march of the remaining Jews of Bilgoraj.

The Lithuanians drove us along, while continuously shooting, and people kept falling, among them, my mother, *A"H*, on the Tarnogrod road.

People began to beg for water. They handed over their money to the Lithuanians in return for some water. Once the Lithuanians got the money, they shot the Jews saying," You're all going to be shot anyway. It's a pity to waste the water."

I made a pact with Wolf Bendler, and Isaac Shper to escape at the first opportunity. But we saw that escaping was impossible. First, the road was far from the forest. And second, whoever stepped out of line and tried to run, was immediately shot by the Lithuanians.

Along the way people kept falling helpless, among them Sholom Rofer, and Yosef Moynes. I carried them on my shoulders with my last bit of strength, as far as I could.

In the evening, when we were near Zwierzyniec, the Lithuanians stopped shooting into the crowd. When some peasant carts came by, they put the slowest ones on.

By the time we got closer to Zwierzyniec, it was good and dark. Coming to a fork in the road, I quietly moved away from the group, and took the road to the left.

[Page 260]

After about 100 meters, in the darkness I saw, a woman and a child walking. I was going to go past her, when I realized it was my cousin, Gitel Goldberg, and her little brother, Issachar–Ber. She had been hit by a bullet.

We wandered together without a destination, hungry and freezing. We came to a field, in the middle of which was a peasant wheat barn. We went in, lay down on the pile of refuse, and fell into a deep sleep.

When we awoke, it was already day. We went out and, looked around, and saw that we were in a village. We began to walk, and after only a few steps, we were grabbed by two peasants. They took our last few pennies, and tied us together with ropes. Tears, and pleas for mercy to let us live, were of no avail. They laughed, and said, "Ocekaliszcze is transport," and took us to the village jail.

In the afternoon, they took us to the train and handed us over to the German guards. They opened the gate, hit us with heavy blows, and threw us in with the rest.

At the assembly place, I saw my sister, Gitel, and my youngest brother, Abraham Moishe. My cousin, Chayah Goldberg, told me that they had run away yesterday too. They had wandered aimlessly around in the forest the whole night. They were caught by peasants, and taken to the assembly place. Among the escapees, was Chana Berlinerman (Kopl–Bayle–Gitel's daughter). She too was captured by some peasants, and on the way to the assembly place, the Germans shot her.

There were several thousand people assembled at the train. They were from Bilgoraj, Tarnogrod, Frampol, Goraj, Kraszew, and elsewhere. People lay in the dirt, wounded, exhausted, tortured by hunger and cold.

[Page 261]

On Wednesday November 4, 1942, empty freight cars arrived, and they began to load people into them. The German murderers stood, armed with batons, along the entire length of the train, beating people bloody as they jumped into the freight cars. When the first car was full, they sealed it, and went on to the second, and so on.

In the wagon I got into, children were crawling about on the floor, half–dead, and dead. The German murderers packed us in so tightly that the children were trampled underfoot.

While we were locked in the cars suffocating and thirsty, the Lithuanian guards appeared, opened the doors, and asked for money in exchange for water. People gave up everything in order to get a drop of water. At first, they did bring water, but later, they took the money and said, "In Belzec, you'll get water."

Pinchas Zimring had a sum of money with him, but rather than giving it to the Lithuanians, he hid it in the wagon.

We talked among ourselves, standing in the locked cars. Maybe they will take out the young strong men to work in German factories. As we are talking about this, the door of the car opened, and we heard the command, "All the men out." People got up in a daze, they thought they were going to be safe. But we quickly felt the blows of the Germans who were lined up along the length of the cars on which was written, "Belzec." We were packed in with adults, and the car was sealed.

[Page 262]

In the wagon, I again met Bilgoraj Jews, among them, Yosef Shmirer, Moishe Toitman, Isaac Shper, Wolf Bendler, and others. We decided to jump off the train.

I Jump Off the Train

As soon as the train began to move, Yosef Shirer began to daven minche–maariv. He said, there are people here who want to jump off the train. Let us daven the keddushah wth a minyan. Right after the keddushah, we discussed who would jump first. Only one person at a time could jump from the small opening we had made in the window. I could see that Bendler and Shper weren't keen on going first.

It didn't take me long to make up my mind. I grabbed onto the opening, they gave me a boost, and I went out feet first, and then the rest of my body followed. I was hanging on with my hands as the train rushed on. The guards on the roofs opened fire on me with machine guns. Going back in was impossible, nor did I want to. Better to fall under the wheels of the train than be burned in the gas chamber of Belzec. I let go. From the strong momentum, I was flattened against the wall of the car. I jumped down.

Once down, I pressed myself against the rails to shield me from the fierce volleys coming from the guards.

When the train was gone, I jumped up and began running to the nearby forest. I soon began to regret having jumped, seeing I was all alone, and my loved ones were going to their death. (Shper and Bendler had not jumped).

I was alone in the unfamiliar forest and I trembled at my own shadow.

[Page 263]

Lying alone in the forest at night, I noticed some movement in the distance. I buried my head deep into the earth, to become invisible.

I soon saw a man with a large moustache coming closer. The picture of a Christian. I thought I was lost. I lifted my head up slowly, and I noticed he was walking with a limp. It quickly became apparent he was a Jew. Shloime Feil (Asher Feil's son), had also jumped from the train. He was hit with a bullet in the foot.

We had a hard time together. There was nothing to bandage him with. I tore a piece of my underwear, and made a bandage.

**Chaya'le Greenboim, fell while serving as a nurse
in the Red Army**

He told me, that he jumped out of the train leaving his jacket and money behind. It was to be thrown out after him. He searched everywhere but couldn't find it. I had little money, but I gave him some.

[Page 264]

We decided to spend the night in the forest. When night fell, he was to go to the nearby farmers, and beg for some food. After walking a ways, we saw a light shining. He went in there. I waited for quite a while, and when I did not see him coming out, I thought I had lost another one. But he finally returned, and told me that he had eaten there, but that he had not brought anything for me. He explained, he didn't want to let them know he was not alone.

I visited a farmer, and begged for food. He said that someone of my kind had already been here, and that they had no more to give. On the way out, I noticed a pot of potatoes and took some and left.

I got back to Feil, and we went back to the forest to spend the night. In the morning, we found a peasant house with a well, and drank our fill. Then we went over to the window, and asked the old woman there where we were. She said we were near the highway, and to be careful, because there were always Germans on the road.

Shloime Feil tried to convince me to go with him to some Christians he knew near Frampol. There we would be able to survive the war. I didn't want to go along with this. I knew that in the Bilgoraj ghetto there were 70 Jewish workers, and maybe there was a way for me to get in with them.

The next day, Thursday November 5, we left for Bilgoraj through the forest, avoiding the roads which were full of Germans. There were always Poles too, looking for Jews to turn over to the Germans.

We stumbled around in the forest until Sunday November 8. We had no food; we ate plants that grew in the forest. We came to Parnasaw Mountain. The sides were bare of trees, and we were forced to travel on the open road. Here we separated. He took the road to Frampol, and I to Bilgoraj.

[Page 265]

Coming down from the mountain, I ran into two Poles on bicycles. They stopped me and asked me where I was going, accused me of escaping from the transport, and told me to go back.

I pleaded with them to let me go, but they insisted I return. One of them gave me a shove with the bicycle, and I fell. I immediately stood back up, and took off into the plowed fields.

After a while, I turned around to see if they were chasing me. I saw a car with Lithuanians coming. They stopped the car, and pointed to me to show them an escaping Jew. The Lithuanian gestured with his arm as if to say "Let him run. He's done for anyway."

When I got to the "Rapess" near Bilgoraj, I met Elimelech Weintraub in the forest. He had been wandering all alone the Bilgoraj forests. I proposed to him that we both try to get into the ghetto, but he did not want to. I never saw him again.

Sunday evening, I came into town, soaked from the rain, through Gosh lane. I snuck into a Jewish house, and changed my clothes. Then I went through Yechezkel Arbesfeld's street and onto Third of May Street. There I ran into Shmuel Zisman. I asked him to help me find a hiding place. He showed me a place near Sholem Rofer, in the attic of the icehouse. He promised me that he would help me with food.

I immediately went up to the attic. I found bedding there, barred the entrance and went to lie down and rest.

I lay in great fear, and couldn't fall asleep.

[Page 266]

Every movement of the straw in the attic frightened me.

As I lay there, I heard fierce shooting on the Third of May Street. I looked through a crack, and saw Polish police shooting at the empty plaza near the Zimrings. Several Jews had been hiding there. I heard them say in Polish, "Where did so many come from?" Gzibek, the policeman in Bilgoraj before the war was among them.

When hunger became unbearable, I would creep down before dawn to the Jewish houses, and gather together abandoned things like dried–up carrots, beets, onions, and potatoes, and I lived on this for a while.

I often stumbled on Jews hiding in various holes. Once I came on Pinches Zimring's two children, who were hidden in the house of their grandfather, Hersh Yosef Zimring.

One day, in the attic, I thought I heard footsteps. I slowly went to look out the crack and saw my aunt, Rucheleh (Eliahu Goldberg's wife). I called to her softly. She came over in great fear and told me that she, and her two children were hiding in the attic at Shloime candlemaker, (Bendler)'s children. There were 19 people there.

Lying sleepless at night, I heard the steps of a German patrol, passing by the cellar, and talking; "Here there no Jews. Here is our beer cellar." When they had passed by, I could breathe a little easier. They certainly didn't imagine there were Jews hiding above their beer cellar.

Saturday, November 14, 1942, very early, I heard the sounds of people running by. Through the crack, I saw my brother, Shloime. I yelled, "Shloime" He looked around, couldn't figure out where the voice was coming from, and kept running. I saw that he was running towards the ghetto. I immediately left and headed over to the ghetto. When I got there, the gate was shut. I called out to him, and he came and let me in. When I got in, we embraced. I told him where I was hiding. If he were to get kicked out of the ghetto, he knew where to go.

There was doctor in the ghetto, a German–Jewish refugee from Tarnogrod. He chased us, and others, out of the ghetto. In the attic of the icehouse, my brother told me that he had been hiding in a Mendl Hurwitz's bunker, in Eliezer Tayer's yard. There were over 70 people there, and he could not stay there. Together we blockaded the door so no one could get in. Our food stores were gone, and days of hunger began.

I decided to go down to the ghetto to see some people I knew, Abraham Yanower, and Moishe Lichtenfeld. Maybe they could help us with food.

I stole out of the attic at dawn. The German patrols were over, and the Polish population was still asleep, so it wasn't too dangerous to be out in the street.

In the ghetto, I went to Abraham Yanower. He immediately gave me a parcel of food. He asked me to take his youngest brother, Meir, with me to the attic. He was hiding in his room in the ghetto, and his life was in constant danger. He was trying to make him legal as quickly as possible, but it was extremely difficult.

I agreed with the plan, and early the following day, I took him up to the attic over the icehouse. The responsibility now fell on me to provide food for three people, and so I went to the ghetto every day for food.

[Page 268]

One Saturday, Meir wanted to visit his brother whom he badly missed. I could barely get him to wait until the afternoon. I wanted to watch the street through the cracks in the attic to see if there were any German patrols. In the evening, I carefully opened the door and let him go out in the street.

I saw him approach the gate, and knock. I felt something bad was happening there, and soon I heard several shots.

The next day, I discovered that when he got to the ghetto, the Gestapo were, by chance, also there. They took him and several others out to the fields, and shot them.

One night, after midnight, we heard footsteps in Eliezer Tayer's yard, and then shouts of , "Heraus!" We were riveted in place, scared to death, and at the same moment, we heard banging on the door of the attic and a yell, "Open up!" I immediately suspected it was someone from the bunker.

I carefully opened the door and let him in. It turned out, it was Abraham Hurvitz (Mendl Hurvitz's son) from the bunker. He used to bring them water from Sholem Rofer's well.

Suddenly there was a loud explosion. We heard someone running past our wall, the cries of, "Halt!" and shooting.

The next day, we learned that it had been Yotche Weintraub's son. He tried to take advantage of the darkness to run away. A few days later, he fell in the fields around Bilgoraj.

Abraham Hurwitz told us that there was a big store of food in the bunker, and we decided we would both go down to the bunker before dawn and get the food.

We did not sleep that night.

[Page 269]

At dawn, we stealthily left the attic, and got to Eliezer Tayer through Sholem Rofer's yard. A horrible scene confronted us. The whole yard was full of dead men, women, and children. It looked like a battlefield.

Abraham Hurwitz ran over, and grabbed the fur hat which had belonged to his father. He clasped it to his bosom, and weeping said, "This is all I have left from my whole family." Approaching the cellar, we found that everything was mixed together in blood and earth. There was torn paper money scattered on the ground, ripped up by the innocent victims, in their last moments, to deny it to the murderers.

We left the bunker heads hung low, despondent, in despair, knowing that the Germans, and their Polish accomplices went around, with axes and iron bars, liquidating one bunker after another, in return for 2 kilos of sugar.

The day following the slaughter, I overheard Szwiersz, the pig dealer, going by and saying, "Israel has fallen, for sure." He used to help me with food always.

We decided that we would go to the ghetto, and speak to Hersh Zilberberg, in order to get Abraham Hurwitz registered, so he could legally reside in the ghetto. Several days later, he succeeded in getting registered, and my brother and I were left alone with our hunger in the attic.

One day, Chaim Brandwein, (Yeshaye's son) came out of the forests to the ghetto. But he couldn't stay in the ghetto because of the daily Gestapo visits. Someone told him that we were hiding in the attic of the icehouse, and one night he came to us. Although we had little to eat from the ghetto, we shared what we had with him.

[Page 270]

The German guardian of the Jewish possessions–furniture, machinery, dishes–had piled them up against the wall of the icehouse where we were hiding. Our every movement put our lives in danger. The peasants came and bought up the goods of the murdered Bilgoraj Jews.

Once, when they had brought a load of furniture, I heard the peasants joyfully describing how when they had moved a cupboard away in Antschel Shur's house, they discovered a group of Jews, among them, David Zokman, Henoch Shier, and others. They took them to the cemetery, and shot them.

Lying in the attic, I saw through the gaps, the Gestapo Majewski, leading Nuteh Kronenberg, his wife, Rochel'tche, and his daughter. Exhausted, Nuteh fell down. The Gestapo shoved him with his foot a few times, and then shot him. A little further on, he shot his wife.

My grandfather, Shmuel Blander, had been hiding for several weeks, in the sheds which had remained on his property. One night, the gendarmes came and shot him in his bed.

My uncle, Eliyahu Goldberg, had been hiding for quite a while at the mechanic, Solski. The Germans found him, and shot him.

One day, at dawn, going through Yechazkel Kandel's to the ghetto, I came on a horrible sight. Dead, naked bodies lay spread throughout the yard.

[Page 271]

I later learned that the Germans, with the help of the Polish underworld, had discovered the best camouflaged bunker where the following were hiding: Yechezkel Kandel and his family, Abraham Taber with his son–in–law, and his family, Malke Kornblut and others.

Another horrible scene. I was lying in the attic when I heard a big commotion in the street. I looked through the cracks. I saw Germans, and the gangster, Kulasze, and peasants armed with axes, and iron bars. They went into the Bendler's yard. I did not move from the spot. I needed to see how this ended, because my aunt Rocheleh Goldberg and her children, and some other 19 people, were hiding there. I was glued to the wall. I heard boards breaking, and soon after, I saw them leading my aunt, and her children, and the others. They were all taken to the cemetery and shot.

Berl Shutz, and Itzchak Becher in the Bilgoraj forest

Chaim Brandwein told us that it was impossible to remain in the forest. The peasants lie in wait for any Jew. His entire group had been liquidated by the peasants. He was the sole survivor. We began to search for a way to get into the ghetto.

[Page 272]

On Sunday January 4, 1942 I went to the ghetto for the second time. I hid in a wood shed. Abraham Yanower was to tell me when Hersh Zilberberg was coming, so that I could talk to him.

Suddenly a commotion erupted in the ghetto. There was talk that they had found our hiding place in Sholem Rofer's attic. They led out my brother Shlomo, and Chaim Brandwein. Chaim Brandwein managed to escape. They took my brother to the cemetery and shot him

This was the end of the bunkers in Bilgoraj.

On hearing the news, I fell completely apart. I did not return to that place. I did not get to talk with Hersh Zilberberg. Abraham Yanower spoke with him, and he promised he would get it done. But in order to become legal in the ghetto, I had to have a photograph. So the next day, I shaved, and simply took a chance and went to the photographer who lived in Zimring's house. Back at the ghetto, I gave the photo to Hersh Zilberberg, and the next day I had my certificate as a worker in the Bilgoraj ghetto.

The Liquidation of the Ghetto

During the last days of my stay in the ghetto, there was talk that the Germans were preparing to liquidate the ghetto.

Friday, January 10, 1943, the Germans and the gendarmes surrounded the ghetto. Still in our beds, we heard banging on the shutters, "Get up! Control!" People said to each other, this is the end.

We got dressed, it was still dark outside, and everyone went outside to the yard.

[Page 273]

The Gestapo ordered everyone to form two groups: young men in one, and old men, women, and children in the other. When some daylight appeared, the young group was given an order to march out of the gate. The group was: Israel Geist, Shmuel Zisman, Abraham Yanower, Beinish Adler, Shloime Zilberlicht, Binim Shulman, Moishe Lichtenfeld, David Bendler, Aaron Hornfeld, Pinchas Farshtendig, Sholom Porcelen, Elizer Shochet's two sons, Abraham Hurwitz, David Laks, Berish Lang, Moishe Boim, and Fishl Kandel.

And in order to finish the work in progress, they left behind: Nachman Renner, Laizer Fruchtlender, and Nechamia Lang.

We later learned that Nachman Renner, and Laizer Fruchtlender had run away to the forest. Nechamia Lang had gone to a Christian acquaintance who was supposed to hide him. All his money was taken from him, and he was poisoned.

As we walked along, we heard shots being fired, and we knew that everyone left behind was being killed.

In the Bilgoraj jail, the Gestapo ordered us to hand over all our money and valuables. They left us a small amount. They told us we were being transferred to a camp. They tortured Fishl Kandel to get him to reveal where the Judenrat gold was.

People who had money threw it into the latrines to keep it out of the murderers' hands.

A tall man, a giant, dressed in a Gestapo uniform, by the name of Pinkowski, , came to see us in the jail. He asked us where our women and belongings were. We told him that everything had been left behind in the ghetto.

[Page 274]

He stopped the torture of Fishl Kandel, arguing that the money the Gestapo had left us should be given to him, and in return we would get food in the camp. He took two people with him to go to the ghetto for some blankets.

In the ghetto, we saw that everyone left behind was dead, their bodies lying spread across the yard. We took a few tattered blankets, and returned to the jail. In the evening, Pinkowski showed up in a truck and parked it in front of the gate.

He stood there, revolver in hand, and as each man was let out one at a time, he shot those who did not please him. Among the fallen: Pinchas Farshtendig, and David Laks.

Once seated in the truck, the murderer, Pinkowski, ordered that the boots should be removed from the dead. The last one in, Michal, a Frampoler, jumped down, but as he was too slow taking the boots off the dead for Pinkowki's liking, he shot him.

But the murderer was still not satisfied, and again ordered that the boots should be removed. So someone jumped quickly down, took off the boots, gave them to Pinkowski, and we drove off in the direction of Zamosc.

We arrived at our destination late at night. It was a horse stable where the inmates of the camp lived.

Driving and Riding school for SS Janowice

We opened the door and saw people lying in terrible conditions on the floor. An awful smell hit us.

There was a small place in the stable for a stove.

[Page 275]

He ordered them to make soup for us which we greedily ate. He made all the sick people give up their places for us, and moved them to the back of the stable.

We talked to the healthy Jews in the camp almost all of whom were from Zamosc. They were working on building a riding school for the SS. The architect was a Jew from Zamosc, Broinstein, and a Czech Jew, Basch.

One day, the murdered opened the stable door, and shot randomly into it. He hit Aaron Hornfeld, who died on the spot.

From time to time, the overseers had to provide people for execution.

And to such a contingent, as it was called, Eliezer Shochet's two sons, and Yakov Renner from Bilgoraj, were condemned.

As they were being driven to be shot, they jumped from the car, and came back to the camp and hid there. The Czech Jew, Basch, for a large sum of money, managed to convince the killer Pinkowski to let them stay.

There was Typhus in the camp and Bilgoraj Jews were affected as well. The sick were shot. Isaac Renner managed to avoid getting shot, but died of the disease several days later.

In May 1943, the Janowice camp was closed, and we were marched to another camp, Luftwaffe, and from there we were loaded onto trucks, packed in like herrings, guarded by armed SS. While underway, one of the trucks broke down, so they packed everyone into the other trucks. They took two people to help repair the truck, and afterwards, they shot them.

[Page 276]

Arriving at the gate, we saw a large sign that read, "Majdanek labor camp: Arbeit Macht Frei."

Driving through the gate, we saw half–dead people wearing prison clothing with stripes.

We were unloaded from the trucks and led to a barracks. We had to form a line, and pass by an SS man who called out, "Lay down all your money, gold, earrings, and rings." We had to take off all our clothes, raise our hands, and feet, open our mouths, to check whether we had hidden anything on our naked bodies. From there we went to a nearby barrack where they had the shower and the gas chamber.

We went into the showers in great fear, afraid of the deceptions we had already seen, afraid we were going to a gas chamber and not the showers.

There were barbers there who shaved our heads and everything. After we had washed, we were given the striped clothing, and wooden shoes.

There were benches in the blocs, but we were not permitted to sit on them.

After lunch we were driven out to the yard to perform exercises. Woe to him who could not keep up. I would rather have worked than do the "exercises" all day. And the next day I was, in fact, assigned to a work detail. It consisted of building a road in the camp with stones from destroyed Jewish houses in Lublin.

The work was this: Me and another prisoner had to fill a cart with gravel with our bare hands, and run with the cart to another spot. We were struggling to run in the wooden shoes, when I heard a cry from the overseer, "Bik dich!" I stopped still, not knowing what he meant. He called over an assistant, who grabbed my head and held it between his legs. The supervisor began hitting me with a club, and when I cried out, he hit me harder. I have the scars to this day.

After this bloody joke, they sent me back to work. After several days, I met Itzchak Meir Warshaviak, and Feivel Ziskraut (Rivkeleh Meir Greener's son).They were captured in 1942, and sent to Majdanek. Itzchak Meir Warshoviak looked very bad. He told me that he just got out of the hospital. His toes were frostbitten, but he was returning to the hospital, knowing that he would not leave there.

I also met there other Bilgoraj boys who had been caught with Warshaviak and sent to Majdanek. They were always ready to help other Bilgorajers in any way they could.

With the passage of time, we were witness to the abominable crimes of the German killers. They hung people in the middle of the square, and forced everyone to watch the executions.

There were people missing at roll call every day. They were searched for and found hanging by their bunks, and their bodies brought to the roll call.

One day during a hard rain, one person was missing. They made us stand in the rain for hours while they searched for him. After a lengthy search, they found him drowned in the latrine.

After a month, I heard rumors that they were going to ship the healthy people out to German factories. We thought, whatever it is, it's better than this hell.

Every day, after work, they returned carrying the bodies of those who had died under the murderous beatings.

[Page 278]

Then began a whole business with doctor exams, and lists. I ended up with the healthy.

From Majdanek, we walked for about half an hour on the road to Lublin. We arrived at the train where the freight cars were already waiting. We were loaded on, and the cars were sealed. After a tedious voyage, we arrived the next day at a station. The doors were opened, and we were ordered down.

Getting off the freight cars, we were confronted with a sign stating, "Hassag Skarzhisko." We were handed over to the "work guard," who, in order to frighten the newcomers, immediately shot several people. They formed us into rows, and took us to the factory, where they assigned us to various jobs.

The following Bilgoraj Jews were there: Geist, Israel; Zisman, Shmuel; Adler, Beinish; Zilberlicht, Shloime; Bendler, David; Shulman, Bonim, and others.

It was a weapons factory. We worked in shifts: two weeks day, and two weeks night. We worked there until May 1944. When the Russians arrived at the Vistula, at Warsaw, the Germans began to transfer the prisoners to Germany, and some to Czestochowa. Shmuel Zisman and I were sent to Czestochowa to a similar factory.

On January 15, 1945, I was working the dayshift, when I heard a commotion break out in the factory. We had already heard that the Russians were very near the city, yet our masters continued to abuse us as before. We heard that those due to work the night shift were going to be sent away. And Shmuel Zisman, who worked the nightshift, was sent away.

[Page 279]

Around three in the afternoon, it became clear that our German masters were slowly stealing away.

Knowing that the Russians were practically here, we looked for a way to hide ourselves to avoid being dragged along with the Germans.

Everybody managed to find a hiding place somewhere. There was not a German to be seen in the whole factory.

I hid with a large number of Jews in a cellar of the factory. We were there for a while. We heard the sound of windows breaking all over the factory, the detonations from the constant air bombardment, and shooting.

Lying there in great fear, we heard voices calling, "Out, out! The Russians are here!" People ran madly out of the cellar. We were greeted by Polish firefighters who said, "You are free! The Germans are gone." We all went out to the street and fell on each other's necks, embracing, kissing, weeping for joy. And then, we looked around, and realized that we were alone, cruelly separated from our loved ones.

I left the camp, and along with several friends from the camp, settled in Czestochowa. I remained there for 6 months, then went to Wroclaw, and from there to Israel where I was reunited with Shmuel Zisman.

————

Translator's footnote:

    1.   In Russia, village elder

[Page 281]

I Survived in Order to Take Revenge

by B. Wermuth (Australia)

Translated by Moses Milstein

I live now in Australia where I got the call from the surviving Jews of Bilgoraj who live in Israel, to help create a book about our home and the murders of our fathers, mothers, sisters and brothers. I have been waiting, with an aching heart, for ten years to put my sorrowful memories in writing. My two brothers–in–law, Benny Hochman and his son, and Hersh Silberfein and his daughter, survived with me at a certain Skoko of the Boyars, and I have undertaken the duty to relate a small part of the destruction of our city, Bilgoraj.

Before the Germans entered the city, they burned it down, and our Bilgorajers today are spread all over the world.

In 1940, the Germans sent 200 Jews, including my brother Eliezer and I, to the Turkowice labor camp. We suffered greatly there. The work was punishing, and there were beatings and murders. We were released after 6 months.

But that was not the end. The Germans needed fresh Jews in their camps, and they captured more people. This time I hid.

They finished with the small camps, and set to building larger ones. In 1942, the Germans captured Jews from all over Poland and sent them to Belzec and Dzikow to build fortifications for war with the Soviet Union.

They transported about 600 Jews from Bilgoraj. On the way, they shot Kalman Bendler and others. In these camps, the Germans began sentencing people to death, and many Bilgoraj Jews perished there.

[Page 282]

But we could not imagine that they were capable of much worse.

At the beginning of 1942, the Germans began to prepare death camps, but even though we were close to Belzec, we were ignorant of that knowledge.

One day, the Judenrat received an order to prepare a list of 1000 Jews who were to be deported for farm labor in the Ukraine. Each person was allowed to bring their belongings, and 1500 Zlotys. They selected all the older people, among them, my father, and mother, and my brother Eliezer, and my brother–in–law Hersh Silberfein. He, Hersh Silberfein asked my father whether he should show up, and my father told him to do what he thought best, so he went into hiding with his family. The Judenrat searched for him for a long time, but with time, things got quieter, and we went to work for the Germans in the forests.

In this way, the Germans annihilated 1000 people who were ostensibly traveling to the Ukraine to work. I had arranged with my parents that they should write as soon as they arrived as to whether the farm work was hard, whether one could survive there. If so, I would join them with our families at the next deportation. They released my brother, Eliezer. They needed young men for work.

From Tarnogrod and the surrounding cities, they brought about 1000 Jews to Bilgoraj, and transported all of them away. Right on the Zamosc road, they killed several hundred Jews claiming they were trying to escape. The remaining Jews in the city could not believe that they were being taken to be annihilated. Rumors went around town that letters had arrived from various of the deportees. When the supposed recipients were questioned, they said they had not received any such thing, but that they had heard that Yenkele Maimon's wife had received a letter.

[Page 283]

So they went to see her, but she said she had nothing. The whole thing came to nothing.

We heard there was a woman, Devorah, Hershke Hochman's daughter, who had been on the transport. She reported that, in Zwierzyniec, the German bandits ordered that everyone hand over their money and leave their belongings there, and whoever was found later with money would be shot.

From right to left: Moishe Silberman, Belke, Shloime Silbermintz, Hersh Yanower, Nuteh Kleinmintz, and Tauber's grandchild

They handed over everything, under blows from the German murderers. While the Germans were doing their murderous work, a terrible rain was falling, a veritable flood. All the Jews were driven into the wagons with blows from rifle butts, and the cars were sealed.

She described how she had to leave her young child and escape from there.

[Page 284]

But where our loved ones were taken, she did not know.

Later a train conductor, Sadowski's son–in–law, came and told me, "Baruch, you know that your people are being taken to Belzec. There is a crematorium there, and they are incinerated." I asked him how he knew about that, and he said that, as conductor, he had driven the train there twice already.

I reported this to Shmuel Arbesfeld, and Abraham Leichter. They warned me not to speak a word of this, that the conductor was an anti–Semite and that was why he was telling such tales.

A while later, Shebreshin[1] Jews were rounded up, loaded into freight cars, and taken away. A number of them jumped from the train, and from them we learned that the train was headed to Belzec. Two days later, a Jew returned form Belzec. He had hidden under the wagon they were brought in. He told us everything, and we finally began to believe.

In the meantime, the Gestapo continued to do its work. They grabbed innocent Jews, took them out to the Raper forest, and shot them. Among them: David Shlafrak, Leibish Grinboim, Motel Hodes' daughter, and others.

The heroism of the Bilgoraj youth was displayed by Mordechai Renner (Itzi Renner's son). When the Gestapo came for him he refused to go. He fought back, and beat them fiercely, until he was overwhelmed. They took him out to the same forest and shot him.

Things went on like this until the big aktion. I was evicted form my dwelling, and had to live in the ghetto on Third of May Street, or by the bridge.

[Page 285]

I did not want to live locked up, because the Germans could get me whenever they wanted. I went out to the Boyars, and hid in my own house with my wife and children, my sister, and my brother–in–law, Hershele.

One day, we heard loud shooting coming from the city. I, Hershele and Benieh with one son went to the mill. The women and children were supposed to have hidden themselves in the attic. But it was not to be. The Volksdeutsche who had taken my mill, chased them all away, and they fled to the forest.

Moishe Boim during the occupation

Moishe Boim and Fishel Kandel told me that that day was a horrible one in Bilgoraj. Blood ran like water in the streets. The dead were brought to Berach Hershman's place. A grave was dug there, and they were all buried. Among the first buried was Yekcle Leichter. He was still alive, begging them to shoot him.

[Page 286]

He was immediately approached by one of the murderers who said, "The dog is not dead yet? A pity to waste a bullet," but he shot him anyway.

The mayor came by, and asked that all the dead be buried in the Jewish cemetery. They brought Moishe Boim and Fishel Kandel from the ghetto to dig the graves.

Moishe Boim, and Fishel Kandel escaped from the Zamosc camp, and came to us to our bunker in the Boyars by a certain Skako. Moishe Boim died in the bunker from a hemorrhage. (from Consumption). Just when we were going to bury him, a raid took place, and his body stayed with us for several days. Later, we buried him.

Fishel Kandel, and his uncle, Yekl Perlmutter, left for Kapronie, near Frampol. Yekel Tauber and his family were there at a certain Jarmol. Towards the end, they all perished.

As I lay in the bunker, I often received news of who had been shot, and that the accomplices were the forester Blichasz, Tomaszewski, and the chief degenerate, Kolesza.

On July 22 1944, my brothers–in–law and I were freed from the bunker. When I returned to my old home on the Boyars, I found no trace of my loved ones. The Christian neighbors came to see us, and told me how my wife, and two children, sister and brother were killed.

Kolesza had found out where they were hiding. He informed the gendarmes, and at 5:00 am, he showed them the spot. He went straight up to the attic, dragged them out, and the Germans shot them, and left. He stayed behind to rob the bodies. He took everything and left them naked.

He took my brother, Laizer, to the river, and shot him.

[Page 287]

The first day after my liberation, I went up to the empty Bilgoraj marketplace. I didn't see any Jews or Christians. Everything was dead. I walked and asked myself, "To whom am I going, and who is mine?" Suddenly, I saw Kolesza coming towards me. I jumped as if I were standing on hot coals. I was overcome by one word, "Revenge!"

He came up to me and said, "Don't be mad at me. I'm not guilty. The Germans forced me to do it."

Translator's footnote:

1.   Szczebrzeszyn, about 30 km from Bilgoraj

[Page 289]

Shabbes in Bilgoraj

by Yoineh Chaim Kronenberg

Translated by Moses Milstein

> It was not only your beautiful
> scenery, Bilgoraj, that charmed
> me,
> Nor your level fields, mountains
> and valleys that affected me,
> And also not your shaded forests,
> meadows, waterfalls and rivers.

I loved you mostly for your
Jews:
Merchants, storekeepers, and
tradesmen.
Ach, how kind and sensitive they
were, your Jews!

Friday evening, absolute quiet
reigns in the city,
Shabbes candles shine from
every window.
And in the houses, a solemn
stillness.
The neighborhoods are quiet
everywhere.
Like a king in his kingdom, the
Jew hosts the Sabbath,
How heartily he sings the
"*Shalom Aleichem,*"
With which he greets the Shabbes
angels.
And how lovely is his singing of
the "*Eyshes Chayel.*"
Everyone's face is lit with holy
joy.

All the riches of the world cannot
satisfy the money hungry,
There is no limit to people's
striving and dreams,
And yet there are moments,
When a quiet corner, a plain
white tablecloth,
A dry piece of bread from one's
own efforts,
A warm glance from a loving
family
And that is enough.

Shabbes evening.
Women sit on benches in the side
streets and gossip.
The older ones—noses saddled
with glasses read the "*Tzeneh
Rehneh*[1]."

[Page 290]

The main street which cuts
through the city like a spine,
Is full of people strolling,

The whole city is walking.
Couples are strolling
Young men with their wives.
Young mothers with small
children.
A mother leads her daughter by
the hand, a father, his son.
Here a young woman in a wide
dress is walking.
A delicate fatigue in her face,
shame in her eyes.
Her heavy footsteps, how kind
and quavering are they?

The Shabbes angels disappear
with the last rays of the sun.
The red western horizon marks
the separation from the weekdays
that follow them.
A quiet, sentimental melody
comes from the Chasidim's
shtibl,
In the evening dark they celebrate
"*Shaleshudes*"
And they sing, among
other *zmires*, the *mizmor* "*Yedid
Nefesh Av Harachaman*,"
And the Chasidic melody spills
out mystically: "*Nafshi Cholet
Ahavtaich*."
Sometimes louder, sometimes
softer, as if it came out of a
distant stillness.

It is a heartfelt outpouring of
longing to something…
It is a mystery that cannot be
expressed and fills the heart…

And suddenly. A deeply sad
singing is heard from every house
--God of Abraham, Itzchak, and
Yakov,
Protect your beloved people
Israel and your exaltation…

Candles are shining in every
Jewish house.
By the red flames that light the
charming childish faces, the Jews
celebrate *Havdala*.

[Page 291]

With the singing of "*Hamavdil*"
the hard, week of toil begins
anew.
You were so dear to me,
Bilgoraj!
In the evening strolls in your
streets,
When the dew in the moonlight
covered the wet grass like a thin
blanket,
The emergence of the sun's
redness over your forests.
I loved you, Bilgoraj, for your
Jews
And hated your *kin's*
You were so close to me, and
also so far!

A wedding in Bilgoraj. Wolf Boim and his wife (live in Brazil), Israel Honigsfeld (lives in Israel). All the others perished.

Translator's footnote:

1.   Biblical writings in Yiddish

[Page 292]

Bilgoraj on the Eve of Destruction

by A. Yanower

Translated by Moses Milstein

By the first of November 1942, it was almost a certainty that in Bilgoraj too, a general liquidation would take place–in Shebreshin[1] it had already happened a month before–and Bilgoraj would become *judenrein*. We recognized it in the increasing efforts of the Judenrat. In reality, the Judenrat had ceased to exist by then. There was a certain H. Z. who represented himself as the Judenrat. He was always riding around in a *britchke*[2] with Nazi–bestowed importance. Anyone who could still scrape up a few zlotys for the Gestapo would greet him with a submissive, "Good morning." Whoever didn't have the means to give money, who had to subsist on potato peels, would hide from the eyes of H. Z., because he would readily pick him as a sacrifice for the filthiest, hardest work.

He would never tell us, as the previous Judenrat did, what to expect so we could hide. He did everything secretively, and precisely. That's why the *Kreizhauptman*[3] held him in such esteem.

One Saturday, an order came from the Gestapo, through the mediation of H. Z., to surround the three houses of Eliezer Kandel, Yantche Kantor, and Hersh Panzerman–all on Third of May Street–with barbed wire. Sunday night, the tradesmen, 70 of them, had to move to the ghetto.

It was clear to everyone that with this decree something terrible was going to happen, even though he assured us that nothing was going to happen, that everyone should stay in their houses, and spend the night there.

[Page 293]

At that time, there were about 3000 Jews in Bilgoraj. Many of them had been brought in from Josefow, Goraj, Frampol, and Tarnogrod, because those places were now *judenrein*. The majority of the Jews lived on Third of May Street, and some on the Lubliner road (the bridge).

That day, the Jews from the bridge street came to Third of May Street, to find out about the new decree. People stood around in circles and talked. When H.Z.'s *britchke* appeared, the groups quickly dispersed. He had forbidden any assemblies on the street, because, he said, the Gestapo could claim that we were preparing to revolt. As soon as he drove off, the circles reformed, and the talk was of what to do. No one believed anything he said.

Hours went by, evening fell, and the circles grew larger. People stood silently and watched as the tradesmen were moving their things into the bloc. They were to live there, and by day, work in Lipeh Wagshol's house.

**From right to left: Above, Golda Zoberman, Reizel Wermuth
Below, Rivkeh Susman, Sarah'tche Harman**

The bloc was allocated for the required workers, and everyone else lost the right to live.

The tradesmen entered the bloc, broken and miserable.

[Page 294]

They were not allowed to bring in their families. The few lucky ones were: Isaac Renner with his whole family; Todros Lang; and David Bendler. Hersh Zilberberg and his family remained living in Lipeh Wagshol's house.

That is how the day of the eve of destruction in Bilgoraj passed. When the sun went down behind the burned down skeleton of the shul, H. Z. hurriedly appeared, went into his house, stayed there a while, and quickly went out to the gate so that, God forbid, some "illegals" (non–tradesmen) wouldn't sneak in. He didn't trust the Jewish police, who were allowing a few "illegals" in.

He went in and searched the entire bloc, but the houses were built such that you could go in one side and out the other.

The ghetto was locked at the gate, but it was not guarded, so people in the ghetto could go about the city freely in the daytime. Only at night did they have to sleep in the ghetto. In that way, everyone had the opportunity to acquire food and various necessities. There were 70 tradesmen in the ghetto. But, in the attics, and cellars another 300 Jews were hiding. In Yantche Kantor's yard, there were Jews in hiding.

When the sun disappeared (many Bilgoraj Jews had not lived to see it rise), and darkness reigned on Third of May Street, a number of young people singly left the city, notwithstanding that it had been one year already since the decree was issued that any Jew found outside the city would be shot. Some went to the forest, some to Christians they knew on farms, anywhere, just not to be in the city. Older Jews said it was God's will, and there was no hiding from it. Many prayed for an end to their suffering. And so, the Bilgoraj Jews waited for the morrow.

[Page 295]

The sky was still dark when we heard shooting coming from all sides of the city. The bloc was sealed. Near the gate, lay old crates, rocks, and some boards which had, just yesterday, been used by the illegals to get into the bloc. I got up on one of the crates, and looked out, and saw Hershele Maler's son–in–law running over the ruins looking for someplace to hide. He didn't run far. He was hit by a bullet. Many more people were fleeing, but were felled almost immediately. There was no question that the liquidation of the Bilgoraj Jews was underway.

I heard loud banging at the gate. I looked for a hiding place because to go outside would be to go into a hail of bullets.

I ran up the stairs in Feivel Panzerman's house that led to a garret. In front of the door of the garret lay, shovels, sticks, and broken pieces of wood. It was impossible to get under the debris. In the meantime, the gendarmes and *schutzpolizei* had broken down the gate, and would have got here before I had had a chance to get under the wood. I was beginning to think it would be better to go with the others, when I heard my name being called. Avigdor Farshtendig , a furrier, who had been with the "legals" appeared and pointed to a hole in the ceiling of the garret which led to an attic space. It was really tight, he said, but what can you do? You have to save yourself. His father, he said, was downstairs and he would send him up. I was not to close up the hole until his father got there…

I had just managed to clamber up to the opening, when his father appeared ready to come up after me. His son boosted him up, and he climbed in. We covered the hole with a *lokshen* board, upside down so it would appear that it had been there for a while.

[Page 296]

There I found the owner of the house, and more people, men, women and little children, about 40 people.

The attic was so small and low ceilinged that we could only sit in the middle. On the sides, we had to lie down, and were pierced by the protruding nails of the shingles.

We, the two new ones, were given a place near the garret, because from there, you could see what was happening outside. Nobody wanted to see the horrors taking place outside. Secondly, it was so confined, that people lay on top of each other. Lying there, we could hear the heavy footsteps of the gendarmes on the stairs, their banging on the walls with their rifle butts. Everyone held their breath in deathly fear, waiting for what fate would bring.

**From right to left: (Seated) Chayah Panzerman, Ganik, Peseh Lichtenfeld
(Standing) Moishe Lichtenfeld, A. Danziger, and Yakov Tayer**

The assembly point (*umschlagplaz*) for the Jews caught outside the ghetto was at Berach Hirshman's place, opposite Lipeh Wagshol. Many people were shot in their houses, or while fleeing.

[Page 297]

All the captured Jews were brought to the assembly point under a hail of bullets. Many died right there. They were held there, in terror, until evening.

The gendarmes and the *schutzpolizei* guarded the Jews, and continuously taunted them. They would single out a Jew and force him to act clownish. They would order him to take off his shoes and prove that he had no gold hidden there, and when he bent down, they shot him in the back. They did this with women too.

The entire city resembled a slaughterhouse. Dead bodies everywhere. There was not one house on Third of May Street that didn't have dead victims. Jewish blood was spilled on the streets, the bridge, everywhere. And the murderers laughed when they shot a Jew.

When the *starosta* and the Gestapo chief arrived at the assembly point, the shooting stopped. We could hear the sound of shooting in the distance, in the Jewish houses. The *starosta* sent the "legals" back into the bloc.

In the evening, they were taken to horse stables that had been built on the old cemetery. There they were savagely treated, without food or water. Early Tuesday morning, the Bilgoraj Jews were driven on foot, under continuous firing, to Zwierzyniec for the train, and from there, to Belzec.

Several days later, through betrayal, about 80 Jews were caught who had been hiding in Yantche Kantor's yard. They were all shot there, and stacked in a pile in the middle of the yard. The ghetto continued for about 10 more weeks, and then they were sent to Zamosc, and from there, to Majdanek.

The Gestapo had withheld a few Jews to dig a mass grave at Baruch Hirshman's place, but Christian workers from city hall arrived who performed the work with joy.

[Page 298]

First, because they were burying Jews. Second, because they could plunder the bodies. They took money, watches, gold teeth, etc. There were soon plenty of Poles profiting off of the Jewish remains. They went from house to house, and took anything they could carry.

The attic, small though it was, was full of fear. It seemed that we were not in an attic but in a house of terror. Fear pressed in on us from all sides, from the shots and their echoes.

Aside from the constant fear, there were tense moments that threatened our hiding place. Soon after we got up to the attic, Pintche Farshtendig was looking through a crack in the attic. He saw a *schutz* policeman beating his daughter. (She had been hiding at Berich Hirshman's). He was hitting her on the head, and when she bent under the blows, a second man shot her in the neck. As she fell, Pintche Farshtendig forgot he was sitting in a house of fear, and shouted out at the shot. Feivel Panzerman quietly said to him, "Pintche, you are endangering so many little children!" And he covered his mouth with his sleeve.

Sometimes, at night, a patrol would go by and a child would begin to cry. It was a miracle that their heavy footsteps muffled the child's crying. Troubles were not lacking. Once, a Jew learned about the attic and wanted to be let up. But there was no place, and it resulted in acrimony.

Everyday, people came to the attic. Whoever heard about it came, until we ended up with 60 people.

One day a Jew came and asked to be let up. But since the attic was packed with people we could not accept him.

[Page 299]

As he left, he said, "You may live, but I can't?"

After this happened, I decided to leave the attic. I thought, no matter what happens, I can't take it here anymore.

Several hours after I left the attic, the Gestapo went straight to the spot, broke out the hole with the *lokshen* board, took everyone out, and shot them in the courtyard.

An aktion at the cemetery

There was a cellar in R' Eliezer Shneider's yard on Kosciusko Street, behind Yekele Maydener's apartment. There were never any stairs there. No one ever went in there except cats and rats making their wild cries.

[Page 300]

He was often asked, "R' Eliezer, why don't you fill in the cellar?" He would reply, "It doesn't matter. If it's there, let it be there," as if he knew that more than 50 Bilgoraj Jews would hide there for almost two months after the last aktion.

When R' Mendel Hurwitz was passing through the cellar, he paused for a minute in thought, and said, "Good, we will hide here."

He quickly hid the entrance with old planks, and rocks. He removed a board from the floor above, and made an entrance. He brought 50 people there, including women and children who ended up suffering for almost two months there.

R' Mendel Hurwitz's youngest son was then 12 years old. He was the runner and food getter. He was always out. Every night, he came with two sacks of bread. He carried out the buckets of waste that had accumulated throughout the day. He worked like this every night until late. Then he replaced the board in the floor, and covered it with straw left behind by the robbers of Jewish homes.

At the end of December, when the air was frosty already, the Jews in the cellar opened the floorboard a little to let in some fresh air. Two German gendarmes on patrol on Third of May Street came by. They became suspicious. They knew that Jews once lived there, but that there were no Jews anymore. Then where was this awful smell coming from? They approached closer and woke up the two Christians who were living in R' Eliezer Shneider's house. They went up to the hovel, and ordered them to remove the rocks and boards that R' Mendel Hurwitz had put there. And a dark grave was revealed to them from which they heard, "Shema Israel! Shema Israel!"

[Page 301]

The savage cries of "Heraus Juden!" mingled with the cries of, "Shema Israel." No one came out until a hand grenade put an end to the cries of "Shema Israel" issuing from the cellar. And even those who did come out did not run far before the bullets of the German murderers killed them.

And with this, Bilgoraj became *Judenrein*.

Berish Mintzer with his wife and family

From right to left: Standing: Sarah, Necheh, Frimet, Pesach Waxman and a child
Seated: Hersh Zotelman, his wife, Heneh and two children
Below: Chana and Shmuel–Leib

***Translator's footnotes*:**

1.   Szczebrzezsyn, 30 km NE of Bilgoraj
2.   Horse–drawn carriage
3.   German district head

[Page 302]

My Surviving the War

by Shmuel Sussman

Translated by Moses Milstein

With the coming of the Germans, the horrible chapter of pain and suffering began for the Bilgoraj Jews. They started seizing Jews for labor, beating them savagely throughout. They constantly demanded monetary contributions. They arrested well–to–do Jews, tortured them, and extorted ransoms.

The first deportation of Bilgoraj Jews occurred in April 1941. They exiled 800 Jews to Goraj. This particular forced deportation had no special goal. It was just a German strategy to terrorize the Jews. In a short time, all the Jews returned.

The Judenrat in Bilgoraj was a social institution as well. They established a low–cost kitchen in Eliezer Tayer's house, and the director was Nachum Wagner. They provided bread ration cards, and also monetary help.

Every Bilgoraj Jew could get a cheap lunch, which was an important thing in those days, and if they could not pay, they got it for free. Pesach, everybody was provided with matzes.

Nachum Wagner, on the way to Shebreshin[1] for food products, got trapped in an aktion there, and sent to Belzec. We learned this from a woman who had jumped from the same train he was on.

The Judenrat, putting their lives at risk, succeeded in getting many of the terrible decrees that poured down on the Jews repealed –for great sums of money, of course. This goal was further advanced by the protection of the former vice–*starosta*, Barszcz, who had a prominent place with the German authorities.

We hoped that we would be able to survive these horrible times. Then Hillel Yanower, the Judenrat head was shot. Hersh Zilberberg was nominated as his replacement.

The second deportation took place in summer, 1942. Belzec, the death camp, had already been built. They assured the Jews they were shipping them to work in the Ukraine. Everyone had to bring 400 Zl. They brought in carriages from the villages, seated the unfortunate Jews on them, and took them to Zwierzyniec. Freight cars were already waiting there for them. They were packed in, and sent to the death camp. Before the "loading in," they were subjected to various torments.

After this, there was a short breathing spell. No one died.

A Bilgoraj Jew in the time of the occupation.
(Perished)

In the last aktion, they assembled all the exhausted, tortured, half–dead Bilgoraj Jews, and marched them on foot to the Zwierzyniec station.

[Page 304]

Along the way, an SS man tore Shoshe Shechterman's child out of her arms, held it by its legs, and hit the half–dead walkers over the head with it, shouting, "Faster, Jews!"

One Sunday, an SS man seized 13 children, took them to Baruch Hershman's place, near Yeshiyahu Nuteh's pump, and started to shoot them there. In the middle of this ghastly work, he ran out of bullets. So he brought three little kids to the ghetto and ordered that they be well guarded. Then he ran and got more bullets, took the children, and shot them.

During this aktion in *Cheshvan* 1942, they held back the tradesmen, and their wives and children, and took them back to the ghetto. From there, they took all the men to jail, and left the women and children in the ghetto. Then an SS man appeared, and asked where all their belongings were. They answered that everything had been left behind in the ghetto. They quickly brought a truck, took several men along, and went to the ghetto to get the baggage. At the ghetto, they saw that all the women and children had been shot and were lying in a pile in the courtyard. Later, all the tradesmen were taken to Zamosc.

And in this way, the entire community, one that had endured for hundreds of years, was erased.

* * *

Hersh Tarm (Kras's son–in–law) was in the ghetto. His two children were hidden in Eliezer Kandel's house. While he was at work, his two children were caught. They asked them who they were and they told them. When Hersh Tarm returned from work, the Germans shot all three.

* * *

[Page 305]

After the last liquidation, the Volksdeutsche, Majewski, came to the ghetto, and proudly displayed the gold he had stolen from the murdered Jews.

* * *

Food provisions for a month in the ghetto were comprised of: 1 kg bread, 15 deca sugar, 10 deca honey, and a little marmalade.

* * *

There was a group of partisans in the forest: Itzik Porcelen, Sinai Shper, a son of Eliezer Shochet, Nuteh Kleinmintz, Shloime, Chaim Feiner's son, and Yosef Hirshenhorn. They frequently came to the ghetto, to try to persuade the youth to join them in the forest.

Once Itzik left the forest and encountered Germans. He began to shoot it out with them. He managed to get back to the forest, but was struck by a bullet there, and died.

Yosef Hirshenhorn

Yosef Hirshenhorn was caught by some peasants, who split his head open. With no medical help, maggots grew in the wound. He blundered around the forest for a while before he died.

[Page 306]

With great difficulty, we managed to get the Gestapo to accept Moishe Kornblit as a worker in the ghetto. He was overjoyed to get the news. Upon seeing how happy he was, the Germans shot him.

* * *

The Germans tied Hanieh Rosenboim to a horse and dragged her through the whole town. She died after much suffering.

* * *

Fishel Shulman was a painter. He always worked for the Germans, and became friendly with them. This gave him the opportunity to mitigate some of the worst torments inflicted on the Jews. There were cases that were life–threatening, but he ignored the danger, and put his own life at risk to save someone.

* * *

Abraham Rubinstein's family (Perished), daughter Chana Tarm and her son (lives in Israel)

[Page 307]

It was just before Chanukah. The Germans seized Jews, among them, Eliezer Shochet. They were harnessed to a wagon carrying a barrel to get water from the pump near Skarwiezak. They were savagely beaten and ordered to run faster, but not to allow one drop of water to spill from the barrel. After the work, they made them all stand with their faces to the wall. They were certain they were going to be shot. They let them stand there for a while, and then they let them go.

The Germans caught a group of Jews, and drove them, on the run, to work, all the time shooting at them. They hit Henoch Shier's son–in–law, Lumerman.

* * *

When a group of dragooned Jews were being driven to work, a German kicked Yosef Magram in the abdomen, rupturing his intestines. He died several days later.

Sarah Magram

* * *

After the last aktion, Yehuda Tauber was hiding in the "sands." The Germans captured him, but he escaped to the other side of the river. The Germans shot at him and killed him.

* * *

Zvieh Kolikstein ,David Manis's wife, and her child escaped during the last aktion. The Germans shot at her and hit her. She hid at the river below Maciocha, and lay there for several days in great suffering. Her groans could be heard from far. She and her child lay there in the snow until they both perished.

Leml Widerfelz

* * *

[Page 308]

When the Germans came for Zelig Weintraub during the last aktion, he grabbed an axe and killed a German on the spot. They shot him later.

Mordechai Mintz

* * *

Abraham Sharf had managed to hide under the gatar in his sawmill almost up to liberation. The Germans found him, led him to the plaza, and shot him.

* * *

Moishe Sharf had been in hiding in Radecznica The Germans caught him, took him out to the Shebreshiner road, and shot him.

* * *

Mordechai Zbinovitch, and his wife were shot in the middle of the street near Makarzec.

Yehuda Sharf

* * *

When Antshel Shur, and the Bilgoraj community were being led to their deaths, Antshel continuously spoke to them to encourage them. When the Germans asked what he was saying, he replied, "From the moment you undertook to exterminate the Jewish people, you had already lost the war." They shot him right there.

Translator's footnote:

1.   Szczebrzezsyn, about 30 km NE

———

[Page 309]

I Hid in a Bunker

by Ben–Zion Rosenboim

Translated by Moses Milstein

By 1940, Jews were forbidden from doing any sort of work. I succeeded in getting a position in Bilgoraj as a forestry worker for a German lumber company, Forfinkel and Richtenberg of Berlin.

Before that, I worked in Majdan Sieniawski, and at the end, at the "Rapa" station in Bilgoraj. Working with me were other Bilgoraj Jews including: Yakov Stern, Itzchak Meir Warshoviak, Chaim Feiner, and Hersh Tarm (Nuteh Kronenberg's son–in–law).

One day, Klinger, the supervisor came over, and began to yell at me that me my work was no good. He grabbed a wet stick, and gave me 10 lashes. I collapsed, and was laid up for weeks after.

Jews were not allowed to leave the city by then. Whoever was found outside without a work permit was shot on the spot.

Almost every day, the German murderers arrived with prisoners from the jail, in crates like dog kennels, and shot them at the Rapa station. Many had to dig their own graves, and were buried alive.

In March 1942, the Germans were transporting the Tarnogrod Jews through the "Raffes". Among the Jews, was R' Levi Stern. He was sitting on the truck in his *tallis*. "I know where they are taking me," he said, weeping.

Hershel Friend was also working for a German company when the first aktion took place in Bilgoraj.

[Page 310]

He was at work with Ben–Zion Rosenboim. Upon hearing that his family had been taken, he said he was going to go with his wife and children, and he perished with them.

On the way to Zwierzyniec during the deportation of November 1942, several people managed to escape, among others, Yosef Hirshenhorn, who I met later in the Bukownica Forest. I also met Nuteh Hirshenhorn there and his family.

Hiding in the bunker at Mikulski's: Perl Freiberg, Chaim Rosenboim, Weinberg, and Wakslicht

[Page 311]

Chaim Feiner, his son, and Perl Feinberg, and I, went to a Christian, Pieczkalan, in Bukownica, to spend the night. During the night, we heard him plotting to kill us. So we barred the door, and in the morning, we intended to go back to the Bukownica forest. As we were leaving, Pieczkalan asked us where we would be staying. Because we were afraid of him, we went to a different place.

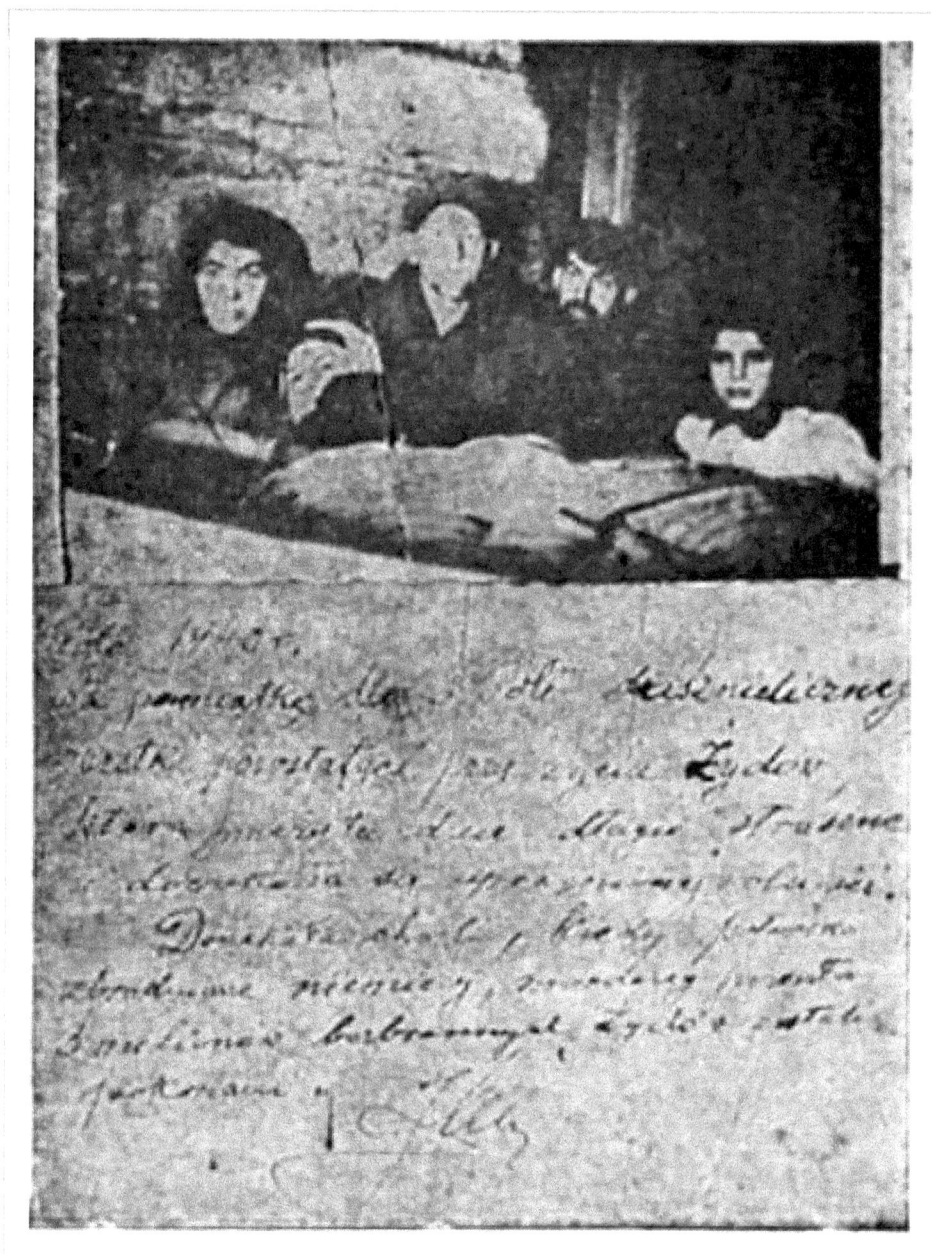

On our sleeping pallets in the bunker

[Page 312]

He looked for us in the Bukownica Forest, and stumbled upon Hersh Mercer, and Nathan Hirshenhorn with his wife and children, and others. He took all their money, and later, killed them all.

We soon had had enough of blundering around in the forest. Perl Freiberg wanted to go back to the city and turn herself in. I refused to let her. We kept walking until we came to Mikulski (the *Nadlieszna*). He took three people: Ben–Zion Rosenboim, Chaim Rosenboim, and Perl Freiberg. There we spent 9 months in the most tragic conditions.

He had no where to put us, so he built a hay stack, 12 meters high, and put us in there. We could not stay there. The heat from the hay was unbearable. So he put us in a small shed where he kept his rabbits. He pried opened the floorboards, and dug a hole for us. There were five of us; us three, and two new ones, Moishe Goldberg's grandchild, and a woman, Wakslicht, from Bagner Street.

We gave him everything we had. I also had *vloshanke* in the Rappes, which we brought him.

After being in the bunker for a while, Chaim Rosenboim, and I went to the forest in Ratwice. There we met Chaim Feiner and his son, and Laizer Fruchtlender. We had no bunker there. We sat in the forest summer and winter. With nothing else to eat, we stole potatoes from the farmers' cellars.

While we were in the forest, we heard from some Christians that Nechemiah and Berish Lang, were hiding at the Christian, Maciocha. They gave him a large sum of money, after which he poisoned them both. Before them, he also poisoned Machle Kolikstein, and Tzirl Kandel.

Once while we were lying in the bunker, gendarmes came and surrounded the house.

[Page 313]

Eating: Ben Zion Rosenboim, Perl Freiberg, and Chaim Rosenboim who fell in the Polish army near Berlin

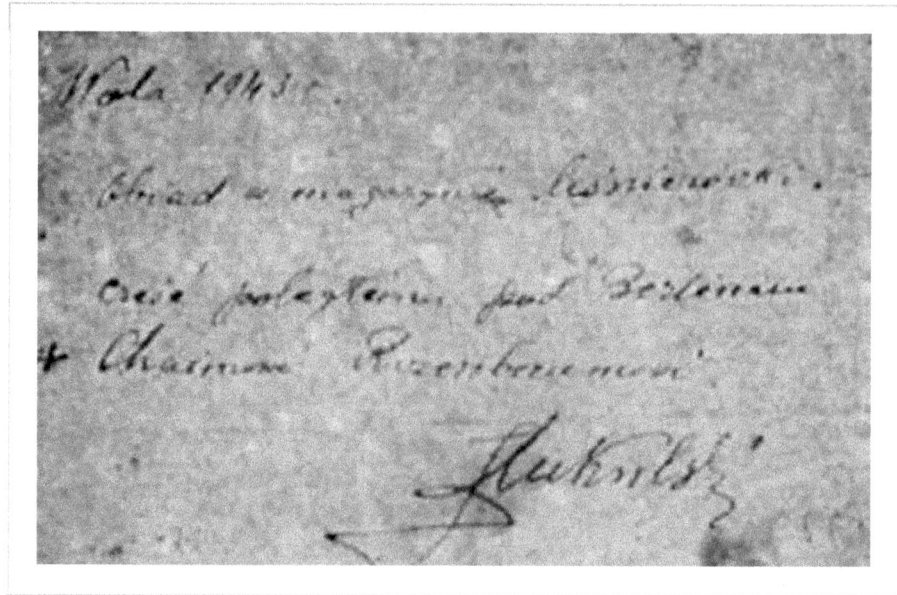

[Page 314]

We were sure we had been betrayed. Mikulski's daughter came and told us that they were all going to be sent away, and that we should poison ourselves with the strychnine that we had with us. A little later, after they had gone, she came and checked to see if we were still alive.

While in the forest, we heard that the Russian army was coming closer, and with its arrival we went to Bilgoraj. Upon seeing the destruction the Germans had created, we regretted having survived.

We walked around the ruins with downcast eyes. The Christians asked us where we had come from, but our pain was so great, we could not answer them.

Yakov Stern, and his wife were in Pulczanow at Cibulski's for one month. Then he tied them up and took them to the police.

It is interesting to note that, at the bottom of every picture, Mikulski has signed his own name.

[Page 315]

Exhumation

by Yehuda Sharf, Ben–Zion Rosenboim, Yoel Langburd, and Chaim Stern

Translated by Moses Milstein

The Bilgoraj Jews of the *She'erit Haplitah* added a worthy page to history, due to the initiative of the following people: Yehudah Sharf, Ben–Tzion Rosenboim from Wroclaw, Shloime Weinberg, Bran from the Diles of Lodz, Chaim Stern, Yoel Langburd, and Lemel Widerfeltz from Szczecin.

Notwithstanding the frequent attacks of the A.K . in the Bilgoraj area, they risked their lives to carry out the sacred work. *Koved* for the dead, and *Koved* for the survivors!

We arrived in Bilgoraj at the end of November 1948. The city was mostly burned down, the streets paved with Jewish tombstones, deserted. There was not a Jew to be seen, nor could one hear the ringing sounds of the laughter of Jewish children. The entire city was a wasteland. The cemetery was dug up, its walls were torn down, the synagogue and its *bes medreshes* lay in ruins. Everything had been erased, with no sign remaining of the hundreds–years old Jewish community.

We immediately set to work doing the holy work. We hired Christian workers to help us, and to show us where the bodies were buried. The first time, we retrieved about 90 bodies.

Gilewski, the carpenter, approached us, and said that he knew where Yekutiel Pest was buried. He had been buried right near the entrance to the Zamosc forest.

[Page 316]

In the Doler forest, which had been a work site for Majdanek, we exhumed about 27 people.

In the Boyar forest, we took out Mrs. Silberfein.

In the Koculkes, between the Smulskis, we found a grave covered by water, in which about 20 people were lying in rows, one upon the other. Because of the water, all the bodies had decayed and were mixed together, so we had to remove them with pitchforks. There lay Moishe Model with his wife and daughter, from the Taubers, Mrs. Dorenbust (the "fiefelech"), and others.

At the Bilgoraj cemetery

From right to left: Yehuda Sharf, Yoel Langburd, Ben–Zion Rosenboim, and Chaim Stern

Near the "Rapa" station, we took out about 40–50 dead.

[Page 317]

Near the "Rafer" station we exhumed Yakov Grinapfel's son (from the Oleyarnia).

The Second Time

Those taking part: Yehuda Sharf, Yoel Langburd, Abraham Glantz, Lemel Widerfeltz, Israel Silberzweig, and Hersheleh Silberfein.

Near Raznowiker yard, we exhumed Yehuda Tauber. Near Walliane's sawmill we took out one person. (It must have been Abraham Sharf).

At the Raznowkes, near the cement works, we found one body.

Past Maciocha at the river, with great difficulty, we took out Zviah Kolikstein, and a child. They had been shot there.

Burying the dead at the cemetery

[Page 318]

The Third Time

Taking part were: Yehuda Sharf, Yoel Broner.

Near the dogcatcher's we exhumed Hillel Yanower, and Shimon Bin.

Sholem Glicklech was exhumed near the *stok*.

In the "Rapess" at Zabatowski (Stemflupka), we disinterred Abraham Sharf's wife and daughter, Shmuel and Yantche, the Gerstenman's entire family. We found only bones there, the animals having eaten the bodies.

Past the Gramadas, we exhumed Moishe Boim.

In Fabricant's forest (the Sendlarkas), we exhumed Yekl Cohen Grinfal's son–in–law, and Leibtche Katzenberg.

All of these victims were collected together and buried in the Jewish cemetery.

[Page 319]

Necrology

Translated by Moses Milstein

The necrology is printed in the order in which the names arrived.

[Page 320]

The 13th memorial service for our martyrs, that took place in Tel Aviv with the participation of Isaac Bashevis[1]

Seated from R to L: Shloime Weinberg, Moishe Arbesfeld, Shimon Obligenhartz, Abraham Kronenberg, Moishe Tayer, Itzchak Bashevis (speaking), Shmai Fest

[Page 321]

Family of Nathan Nuteh Kroneberg, z"l.

My father, Nathan Nuteh Kronenberg, my mother, Ruchel'tshe. My sister, Miriam Torm, Baileh Hersh, and 3 children, my sister, Gitl Herman, and 1 child, sister Leah Frisherman, Baileh Shmuel, and 1 child, brother Avigdor Raphael.

Yoineh, Shmuel, and Abraham Kronenberg, Israel

[Page 322]

Family of Motl B"R Yehoshua Maimon, z"l

I memorialize with tears my family that was killed by the German murderers.

Nathan B"R Mordechai Maimon, his wife, Malkah, and 4 children.
Yehoshua B"R Motl Maimon, his wife, Yehudes, 3 children.
Hersh Sheinwald, his wife, Sarah and 1 child.
Yeshiyahu Shapiro, his wife, Hinde, and 2 children.
Eliezer Wermut, his wife, Finkl, and 2 children.
Golda Goldbrenner and 5 children.
Nathan B"R Yehoshua Maimon.
Gadliyahu Maimon, his wife, Freide, and 1 child.
Hersh Maimon, his wife Hindele, and 5 children.
Yaakov Maimon, his wife, Chinke, and 3 children.
Hersh Weissman, his wife, Feige, and 6 children.
Chaim Mordechai Hirshenhorn, his wife, Sarah, and 5 children.
Yehoshua Weissman, and his wife.
Shloime Shtarker, his wife, Hene, and 1 child

Yehoshua Reiz, Hadar-Yosef, Israel

[Page 323]

Memorial to the martyrs of the Geist family and relatives, z"l

Parents: Hershel Geist, and Roize Geist
Children: Shloime Geist, Gitl Geist, Chaye Geist, Rotze Geist
Abraham Moishe Geist
Grandfather, Shmuel Blander
Grandmother, Tobe Geist

Relatives:
Itchele Geist, wife, Shaindl, 5 children. Yoine Geist and his family.
Peretz Geist and family.
Mordechai Blander and family.
Yehoshua Blander and family.
Eliyahu Goldberg and wife, Ruchel, and 5 children.
Nachum Wagner, and wife Chana, and 4 children.
Nuteh Fink and wife, Hentshe, and 5 children.
Yosef Shmird, and wife, Chave, and children.
Yoineh Shmirer and wife and children.

[Page 324]

Family of Yosef Rapaport, z"l
My father, Yosef Rapaport.
My aunt, Perl, and 3 children.
My grandmother, Baile Rapaport.
My sister, Rivke Zetser, husband, Itzik, and 2 children.
My sister, Kressl Greenboim, husband, Alter, and 3 children.
My grandfather, Moishe Goldberg.
My grandmother, Chave
My uncle, Moishe Weinberg, his wife, Bashe, and 4 children.
My uncle, Abraham Harman, his wife, Dvoire'tshe.
My uncle, Abraham Brezl, wife, Ruchele, and 4 children.
My cousin, Zvi Herman, wife Rivke, and 2 children.
My cousin, Zvi Yechezkel Herman, wife and children

Mordechai Rapaport, Israel

[Page 325]

Family of Gitl Grossman, z"l

My grandmother, Gitl Groisman
My uncle, Yidl
My uncle, Shmuel Eliyahu Grosman, his wife, Sarah, their son, Moishe, their daughter, Chaye, their daughter, Dvoireh

Rivke Goldstein, Israel

[Page 326]

Family of Ephraim Bromberg, z"l

My father, Ephraim Bromberg, my mother, Feige, my sister, Beile, my brother, Leibl.
My brother, Shloime, his wife, Dina, and 3 children.
My sister, Esther Brik, husband, Shmuel, and 2 children.
My sister, Zvieh Weber, husband, Meier, and 2 children

Etl Bromberg, Israel

[Page 327]

Family of Israel Arbesfeld, z"l

My father Israel Arbesfeld.
My mother, Zvieh
My sister, Gitl Mermelstein, husband, Ben-Zion, 3 children.
My sister, Shaindl Shnitser, husband, Tzaddik, 5 children.
My sister, Kaileh, 1 child

Moishe Arbesfeld, Israel

[Page 328]

Family of Zvi Magram, z"l
My father, Zvi Magram.
My mother, Malkah (died)
My brother, Chaim, his wife, Chaveh, and 2 children.
My brother, Yosef, his wife, Dina, and 2 children.
My sister Leah Stockman, husband, Shmuel, and 4 children.
My sister, Fessl Zilberman, husband, Moishe and 1 child
My brother, Shloime.

Sarah Sharf, Israel

[Page 329]

Family of Moishe Yosef Gerstenblit, z"l

My father, Moishe Yosef Gerstenblit.
My mother, Rivkeh.
My brother, Leib, his wife, Perl, and a child.
My brother, Baruch.
My sister, Ruchel.
My brother, Zalman-Meier

Leml Gerstenblit, Israel

[Page 330]

Family of Mordechai Hodes, z"l

My father, Mordechai Hodes.
My mother, Lola.
My sister, Elke
My grandmother, Kineh

Yakov Hodes, Israel

[Page 331]

Family of Wolf Shatz z"l

My mother, Henne Shatz
My father, Wolf (died)
My brother, Moishe Chaim
My brother, Abraham Noach
My sister, Libe

Elimelech Shatz, America

[Page 332]

Family of Abraham Tauber, z"l

My father, Abraham Tauber, z"l
My mother, Frimet (died)
My sister, Sonja, husband and child
My brother, Yehuda
My sister, Tsirl
My sister, Yehudes

Yakov Tauber, Paraguay

[Page 333]

Family of Eliezer Buchbinder z"l

My father, Eliezer Buchbinder
My mother, Esther
My brother, Tzudik, his wife Feige, and 2 children
My sister, Mindl Frost, husband, Aharon Itzchak, 2 children
My brother, Shmuel, died in Russia

Shimon Buchbinder, Israel

[Page 334]

We place this memorial in the yizkor book of our Bilgoraj *kehile* for our beloved father, R' Israel Yakov Bron. Our beloved mother, Bashele, our beloved sisters, Ruchele, and Surele, and our beloved youngest brother, Chaimel, eleven years old at his death.

A monument on paper, with four pictures of faces, our only memento remaining of you. Only you, our beloved Chaimel, came like an unnoticed shadow into the world, and disappeared without a trace from this world.

No vestige, no memory, not even your tender likeness on a piece of paper, remained. Whenever we look at these four pictures of beloved parents and sisters we search for a fifth picture in our memory and imagination.

[Page 335]

We search for a photo of you, our once little Chaimel, little brother, the youngest, the liveliest, but we can't find it. We want to remember your little face, your slight body, certainly no taller than one stride. Your little head, the color of your hair, your hands and feet, your eyes were, it seems, light-blue, your voice soft like unplayed sounds, but everything dissolves, flees, hides, under the veil of the years, we lose your picture even in memory.

This was possibly the last picture of you taken when you went to your death.

And now, mother, father, sisters, and youngest brother lie in a mass grave in the far away Ukrainian earth, fathers and children together, a mass grave of the exterminated!...Perhaps grass has grown over it, and over the succulent grass sprouting, a curse, a last one! For the child-murderers who shed innocent blood.

May you rest in eternal peace!

Father, mother, beloved sisters and little brother.

Shalom and Shmuel Bron, Israel

[Page 336]

Family of Shloime Weinberg, z"l

My wife, Freide. My daughter, Golda Anger, her husband Yechiel, and 2 children. My son, Moishe, his wife Miriam. My son, Pinches, his wife, Yitke. My daughter, Gnendel and my granddaughter, Esther.

Shloime Weinberg, Israel

[Page 337]

Family of Israel Chaim Weinberg, z"l

My father Israel Chaim Weinberg. My mother Chantshe, my sister Miriam, my brother, Yechezkel Meier.

Basia Feder, Israel

[Page 338]

Family of Yosef Arye Putter, z"l

My grandmother Krasse Zoberman (died).
My father, Yosef Arye Putter. My mother, Esther Miriam and 3 children.
My aunt, Dintche Merzel, her husband, Feivel and 3 children. My aunt, Golde Tarm, her husband,
Hersh and 4 children. My uncle, Yakov Zoberman, his wife Gitl, 2 children.

Shmuel Putter, Israel

[Page 338]

Family of Chaim Zisman, z"l

Yocheved Dorfman;
husband, Eliyahu
Dorfman, and children

Chaim Zisman. Wife Esther
Malke, children, Gitl, Hersh-
Leib, Sarah, Matisyahu, Chana,
Alte, Raizel

Hinde
Kuperman

Shmuel Ziman, Israel

[Page 340]

Family of Eliyahu Zilberlicht, z"l

My father Eliyahu Zilberlicht, my mother, Nechameh, my brother, Hersh-Leib, his wife, Clara, and 2 children, my sister, Chaye Leah, my brother, Shmuel Zainvel.

Lippe Zilberlicht, Israel

[Page 341]

Dovid B"R Yehoshua Stern, z"l

After the war, he came to Lublin as a soldier with the Polish army. Sukkot, 1945, there was an attack by the A.K[2] groups. He was sent as a soldier to destroy the aggressors, and he fell there.

Chaim Stern, Israel

[Page 342]

Family of Yekutiel Kornblit, z"l

My mother, Malke Kornblit, my brother, Dovid, and his wife, Feige and 3 children. My brother, Leibl, his wife, Bashe and 1 child, my sister, Breindl Hochrad, her husband, Moishe, and 3 children; my sister, Hodes Zlotnick, and her husband Yosef and one child. My brother, Moishe.

Genedel Liebhober, America
Rechl Kronenberg, Israel
Chaim Stern, Israel

[Page 343]

Family of Abraham Yakov Bromberg, z"l[3]

My daughter Hodes Bendler, her husband, Yakov, 2 children. My son, Itzchak, his wife, Chaveh and 3 children. My daughter Necheh Donderstein, her husband, Eliyahu Yakov, and 1 child

Tzirl Bromberg, America

[Page 344]

Family of Shloime Rubinstein, z"l[4]

My father Shloime Rubinstein; my mother Batsheva; my sister Miriam Libe Warshaviak, her husband, Itzchak Meier, and 3 children; my sister Feige Hoffman, her husband, Levi, and 3 children; my sister, Malkeh

Tova Rubinstein, Israel

[Page 345]

Lichtenfeld Family, z"l

My mother, Chaye Sarah Lichtenfeld; my sister, Malye Feiner, her husband, Chaim, and children; my sister, Esther Yanower, and one child; my brother, Moishe.

Mordechai Lichtenfeld, Canada,
Lippe Lichtenfeld, Bolivia

[Page 346]

Family of Shaindl Boim, z"l

My mother, Shaindl Boim; my brother, Moishe, his wife Chinke, and one child; my sister Taube, my youngest sister

Wolf Boim, Brazil

[Page 347]

Rosenboim Family, z"l

My wife, Libe and 3 chidren; my sisiter Golde Twerski, her husband, Yehoshua, and 3 children; my sister-in-law Hanieh Rosenboim, and 2 sons; Shifra Glazberg and 1 child; Yitke Rubinstein with 1 son; their daughter Rivkeh and her husband Rali Singer, and 4 children. All perished in Bilgoraj on 10/2.1942

Ben-Zion Rosenboim, Israel

[Page 348]

Family of Matisyahu Feigenboim, z"l

My father, Matisyahu Feigenboim; my aunt, Breindl; my sister, Sarah Leah; my brother, Mendl.

Hershke Feigenboim, Israel

Translator's footnotes:

1. Isaac Bashevis Singer. Nobel prize winner for literature.
2. Armia Krajowa. Polish Home Army, putative anti-German Polish resistance group, notable for its anti-Semitism, and murder of Jews.
3. The photos on p. 343 and p. 344 are the same. This may be an error.
4. The photos on p. 343 and p. 344 are the same. This may be an error.

[Page 349]

List of the Dead

Translated by Moses Milstein

[Page 351]

Name	Wife/Husband	Children
Adler, Yakov Ber	Chayeh	5
Adler, Heneh		1
Adler, Shmai	Dvoireh	
Adler, Sarah		1
Obligenhartz, Libe Itte		
Obligenhartz, Chaim	Wife	5
Obligenhartz, Abraham	Wife	2
Obligenhartz, Malia		5
Obligenhartz, Shimon		
Oberhand, Dvoyre		2
Oberhand, Chaim	Chaveh	6
Oberhand, Naphtali		
Olander, Shmuel Lib	Raizel	4

Olive, Itzchak Lib	Basia	5
Olive, Ber	Ruchel	6
Olmer, Elyahu	Chaneh	2
Olmer, Yitzchak Yehoshua	Wife	1
Olmer, Avigdor		
Olmer, Chanina	Wife	1
Olmer, Yehoshua	Itta	2
Olmer, Pesach	Esther	2
Unker, Shloime	Chaneh	6
Unger, Neche		
Unker, Yakov	Wife	
Orbach, Leibish		
Attenberg, Andze		2
Eilboim, Abraham, Itzchak	Temeh	4
Eilboim, Chaim Gedalia	Goldeh	5
Eilboim, Mendl	Shaindl	3
Eilboim, Shloime	Wife	X
Eilboim, Moishe	Wife	
Eilboim, Zindl	Wife	2
Eilboim, Shloime	Mali	2
Eilboim, Yakov	Wife	X
Eilish, Chaim	Maltzie	
Eilish, Itzchak Meier		
Eilish, Leibel	Sheva	2
Eilish, Miriam Mechle		1
Eilboim, Ben Zion	Dvoireh	5
Ingber, Chaim	Goldeh	3
Ingber, Feivel		
Isser, Itzchak	Raizel	2
Isser, Abraham Yakov	Ytteh	6
Unger, Michal	Yocheved	3

Unger, Elke		2

[Page 352]

Ant, Abraham	Sarah	3
Ant, Chaim	Pesl	4
Ant, Nachum	Keileh	3
Ant, Shmuel	Chaveh	2
Ackerman, Arish	Chayeh	4
Ackerman, Ruchel		
Arbisfeld, Israel	Zviah	
Arbisfeld, Keile		
Arbisfeld, Yehoshua	Wife	2
Arbisfeld, David	Gitl	3
Arbisfeld, Chaim	Chaneh	2
Arbisfeld, Moishe	Chayeh	3
Arbisfeld, Menachem	Raizel	2
Arbisfeld, Yakov	Wife	2
Arbisfeld, Yakov daughter		1
Arbisfeld, Esther		
Bad, Moishe Ber	Wife	2
Bach, Israael Itzchak	Sarke	4
Boigen, Mordechai	Sarah	3
Boim, Moishe	Chinkeh	1
Boim, Moishe Lieb	Blimeh	3
Boim, Mendl	Nintzah	
Boim, Frida		2
Boim, Shaindl		2
Buchbinder, Eliezer	Esther	3
Buchbinder, Tzadok	Wife	2
Boxer, Gitl		4
Boxer, Shalom	Wife	

Boxer, Moishe Abraham		
Bin, Chayeh Alteh		
Bin, Wife of Yakov Lieb		
Bin, Shimon	Blimeh	3
Bin, Eliezer	Esther	10
Bin, Yehoshua	Wife	1
Birman, Benny	Blimeh	5
Bachar, Betsalel	Frida	2
Bachar, Moishe	Rivkeh	2
Blutman, Yosef	Chaveh	2
Bleiberg, Hersh	Sarah Nemi	2
Bleichman, Abraham Ozer	Yitkeh	6
Blinder, Shmuel		
Bendler, Wolf	Leahtche	3
Bendler, Leibish	Beileh	3
Belz, Shmuel	Sarah	2

[Page 353]

Baklman, Yokl	Chaneh	3
Berger, Abraham	Wife	3
Berger, Moishe	Nechameh	
Berger, Shmuel	Itteh	1
Berger, Dvoireh, Genedel, Sarah		
Berger, Ephraim	Wife	3
Berger, Isaak	Chaneh	2
Bergerfreind, Abraham		
Bergerfreind, Shmuel	Itteh	3
Bergerfreind, Wolf		3
Bergerfreind, Yenteh		
Bergerfreind, Moishe	Leah Gitl	5
Bergerfreind, Binem	Zisl	5

Bergerfreind, Benyomin	Wife	3
Bergerfreind, Yakov	Temmie	1
Bergerfreind, Eliyahu	Libeh	3
Bergerfreind, Isser	Wife	3
Bergerfreind, Rashi		
Bergerfreind, Zisl		2
Bergerfreind, Moishe	Wife	2
Bergman, Shimon	Liebeh	3
Bergstein, Abraham Yakov	Raitse	1
Bergstein, Binem	Chaneh	4
Bromberg, Zisl		1
Bromberg, Baruch	Zlateh	2
Bromberg, Chaim	Wife	3
Bromberg, Lieb	Nechameh	3
Bromberg, Abraham	Chaneh	4
Bromberg, Ephraim		1
Bromberg, Itzchak	Chaveh	3
Bromberg, Feileh daughter of Yehudit		
Bromberg, Shloime	Dineh	2
Broner, Abraham Hersh	Esther	
Bron, Israel Yakov	Basia	2
Braverman, Avigdor	Ruchel	2
Barzel, Reuben	Peshe	1
Barzel, Binyomin	Mechleh	2
Barzel, Abraham	Ruchel	3
Barzel, Mordechai	Fradel	
Barzel, Leibish	Wife	3
Barzel, Wife of Moti and daughter Blimeh		
Barzel, Pesach	Wife	2
Brick, Yosef	Chayeh	

Brick, Shmuel	Esther	2
Brick, Miriam Mindl		1
Brilintstein, Chaim	Wife	
Brilintstein, Michal	Ruchel	1
Brilintstein, Gedalia	2 sisters	

[Page 354]

Breyer, Abraham	Leah	2
Berlinerman, Kapl	Beileh Gitl	4
Brenner, Lippe	Wife	1
Brenner, lawyer		
Brenner, Itzchak	Rivkeh	4
Brenner, Shimon Mordechai	Zlateh	
Brenner, Yosef	Nechie	2
Bren, Chaim	Keileh	6
Brondwein, Hirsh	Beigeh	
Brondwein, Yeshiyahu	Wife	2
Brenner, Tsalvah		2
Brenner, David	Wife	3
Brofman, Brocheh		4
Gutman, Yehoshua	Wife	1
Guthart, Elke (Hodes)		1
Goldberg Wife of Eliezer		2
Goldberg, Itzchak Meier	Faige	1
Goldberg, Eliyahu	Ruchel	5
Goldberg, Moishe	Chaveh	
Goldberg, Yakov	Chantche	2
Goldberg, Itche	Mineh	1
Goldbrenner, Moishe	Chaveh	
Goldberg, Chaneh		
Goldberg, Moishe	Makeh	5

Geist, Hersh	Roize	4
Geist, Itzi	Shaindl	5
Gedacht, Liebe		
Golber, Abraham Itche	Chantche	1
Golber, Leibish	Esther Gitl	4
Golber, Nechamia	Chaneh	2
Glicklech, Sender	Golde	2
Glicklech, Rone		
Glicklech, Gershon	Etl	6
Glicklech, Shalom	Ruchel	6
Glicklech, Feige		3
Glicklech, Leibl	Wife	X
Glicklech, Moishe	Chaneh Ruchel	3
Glicklech, Abraham	Toibe	3
Glickman, Itzchak	Esther	
Glickman, Chaveh		
Glickman, Yosef	Dvoireh	2
Glanz, Itzchak Mendl	Wife	2
Glanz, Zainvel	Wife	2
Glanz, Simcheh	Wife	
Glanz, Yakov	Wife	2
Ganzenhot, Sarah		2
Ganzenhot, Nachum	Wife	2
Gerber, Chaim	Ruchel	
Gerber, Liebeh		2

[Page 355]

Groisman, Itzchak	Broche	3
Groisman, Gitl		
Groisman, Shmuel Eliyahu	Sarah	3
Groisman, Sarah		4

Grofman, Aharon	Dvoireh	2
Griner, Sheva		
Greenboim, Alter	Karsel	3
Greenboim, Leibish	Esther	2
Greenberg, Yosef	Ruche	
Greenfall, Yakov	Broche	2
Gerstenblit, Zvi and Perl		
Gerstenman, Shmue		
Gerstenman, Moishe	Rivkeh	X
Gerstenman, Itzchak	Wife	X
Dorenbust, Elimelech	Dvoireh	Blimeh
Dorenbust, Yehoshua		
Dorenbust, Zvi		1
Dorenbust, Itzchak	Sarah	2
Dorenbust, Sheharyahu	Chayeh	3
Dorenbust, Eliyahu Yakov	Necheh	1
Dorfman, Eliyahu	Yocheved	3
Dickler, Moishe	Blimeh	2
Damasti, Wolf	Hodes	3
Damfrucht, Mordechai	Wife	2
Hoberman, Zlati Esther		
Hoberman, Ruchek Leah		1
Hoberman, Yakov	Yehudes	1
Hoberman, Moishe Eliyahu	Brocheh	8
Hodes, Moishe	Mirl	
Hodes, Meier	Wife	
Hodes, Chaneh		1
Hodes, Motl	Lali	1
Hochman, Leibke	Feige	3
Hochman, Yechezkel	Wife	2
Hochman, Chanoch	Wife	5

Hochman, Alter	Wife	2
Hochman, Shaul	Wife	
Hochman, Broche		2
Hochman, Abraham	Dvoireh	2
Hochman, Ruchel		2
Hochman, Chaneh		2
Hochman, Alexander		2
Hochman, Chaim	Rikl	2
Hochman, Eliyahu	Rivkeh	3
Hochman, Yosef	Sarah	3
Hochman, Blimeh, Wife of Benny		2
Hochner, Yakov	Malke	2
Hochner, Chaim	Wife	X
Hon, Moishe	Itta	5
Honig, Berish	Wife	2
Honigboim, Nuteh	Tzippeh	
Honigboim, Feleh		1
Honigboim, Shepsl	Ruchel	2

[Page 356]

Hochner, Wife of Chaim		2
Hoff, Yehoshua	Goldeh	
Hoff, Moishe	Tova	1
Hoff, Sarah		
Hoff, Hersh	Hindeh	2
Horowitz, Mendl	Esther	4
Horowitz, Baruch	Nisl	
Hornfeld, Balche		2
Hornfeld, Chayeh		
Horndrexler, Wife of David		
Hirschenhorn, Chaim Mordechai	Sarah	3

Hirschenhorn, Israel	Wife	2
Hirschenhorn, Nathan	Mindl	3
Hirschenhorn, Yosef Hersh	Wife	2
Hirschenhorn, Itche	Bineh	
Hirz, Itzchak	Hadassah	4
Hirz, Eiyaahu	Miriam	
Hirschman, Beirech	Freidl	
Halpren, Mendl		
Halpren, Beileh		2
Hammer, Yakov	Mirl	2
Harman, Abraham	Dvoireh	
Harman, Hersh Yechezkel	Gitl	2
Harman, Chaim	Chaneh	
Harman, Zvi	Rivkeh	2
Harman, Motl	Wife	5
Harman, Motl B"R Itzik Hersh		
Weber, Meier	Zviyah	2
Wagner, Nachum	Temeh	3
Wagshul, Chayeh Leah		
Wagshul, Shimon	Rivkeh	1
Wagshul, Ephraim	Sarah	2
Widerplat, Gedalia	Malkeh	4
Weisenblut, Sarah		6
Weinberg, Zev	Liebeh	3
Weinberg, Freida	.	1
Weinberg, Moishe	Miriam	
Weinberg, Pinchas	Wife	
Weinberg, Moishe	Basia	3
Weinberg, Israel	Chantcheh	2
Weinberg, Aharon	Leah	
Weintroib, Yatzi		7

Weintroib, Zelig	Zelda	2
Weintroib, Wolf	Blimeh	1
Weintroib, Yosef	Wife	1
Walfish, Leibl	Wife	4
Waltz, Itzchak	Basia	5
Waltz, Moishe Aharon	Dineh	3
Weinman, Itzchak	Feige	3
Weinman, Itzchak	Wife	3
Weinman, Akiva	Temeh	
Weiss, Yoel	Rivkeh	5
Weissman, Zvi	Feige	3
Weissman, Yehoshua	Wife	
Weissman, Roizl		
Weissman, Yosef	Heneh	2
Weissman, Wolf	Wife	
Weissman, Yehuda	Chayeh	1
Weissman, Mendl	Wife	3
Weiser, Sarah		2
Weiser, Hershkeh	Wife	1
Wax, Yosef Hersh	Malkeh Perl	2

[Page 357]

Wachslicht, Yosef	Wife	2
Wachslicht, Shalom-Ber	Ruchel	3
Wachslicht, Yehuda	Wife .	
Wachslicht, Chaneh		2
Waxman, Hersh	Wife	3
Waxenfeld, Sender	Mali	2
Wermut, Shebach	Chaneh	1
Wermut, Eliezer	Goldeh	2
Wermut, Chaveh		2

Wurman, Gitl		
Wurman, Yosef		
Wurman, Tuvieh		1
Warshaviak, Itzchak Meier	Miriam Liebeh	3
Warshaviak, Leibl	Etke	2
Zokman, David	Chayeh	2
Zokman, Shloime	Roizeh	2
Zokman, Mordechai	Chayerh	1
Zokman, Necheh		1
Zotlman, Beileh		
Silverberg, Hersh	Faige	2
Zileh, Gitl	Yosef	
Zilberlicht, Yeshiyahu	Gitl	3
Zilberlicht, Dvoireh		
Zilberlicht, Hersh Lieb	Clara	2
Zilberlicht, Eliyahu	Nechama	2
Zilberlicht, Itzchak	Ruchel	
Zilberlicht, Yakov	Wife	1
Zilberlicht, Moishe wolf	Esther	2
Zilberlicht, Chaim	Hadassah	
Zilberlicht, Nathan	Gitl	6
Zilberlicht, Yehoshua	Wife	2
Zilberman, Itzchak	Tobeh	4
Zilberman, Chaneh		
Zilberman, Eliyahu	Pesheh	2
Zilberman, Moishe	Fesl	1
Zilbermintz, Etish		
Zilbermintz, Shloime	Tilleh	
Zilbermintz, Yakov		
Zilbermintz, Pinchas	Wife	2
Zilberzoig, Chaneh	Mother	

Zilberzoig, Shmuel	Wife	2
Zilberfein		1
Zilberfein, Goldeh		2
Zilber, Dvoireh and Beileh		
Zisman, Chaim	Esther	3
Zisman, Elchanan	Chaneh	3
Zipper, Yokl		4
Zaifer, Chaim Baruch	Wife	X
Ziperborsht, Moishe	Wife	2
Zaltzman, Eliezer	Sarah Ruchel	1
Zaltzman, Chaim	Leah	3
Zaltzman, Chaim	Ettl	6
Zamler, Hersh Leib		
Zamler, Eliezer	Perl	6
Zetzer, Itzchak	Rivkeh	2
Tauber, Ruchel		
Tauber, Abraham		4
Tauber, Yakov	Yocheved	3
Tauber, Abraham	Malkeh	2
Tauber, Shloime	Wife	4
Turbiner, Moishe	Henneh	

[Page 358]

Tabarski, Yehoshua	Goldeh	2
Turm, Hersh	Goldeh	2
Turm, Hersh	Miraim	3
Turm, Motl	Freide	
Toitman, Moishe	Wife	2
Tuch, Mendl	Feige	4
Tuch, Eliezer		1
Tuch, Itche	Esther Malkeh	3

Teicher, Yechezkel	Sarah	3
Teitlboim, Yakov	Mother	
Tintenfish, Yeshiyahu	Simeh	4
Tintenfish, Feivel	Esther	X
Tintenfish, Shmuel	Wife	2
Tintenfish, Azriel	Wife	1
Tintenfish, Mendl	Freide	2
Tintenfish, Moishe	Gitl	4
Teier, Yosef	Wife	3
Teier, Zev		
Teier, David	Rozeh	
Teier, Chiseh		
Teier, wife of Moishe		1
Teier, Nathan	Wife	2
Teier, Eliezer		1
Teier, David	Itta	2
Teier, Yakov	Chaneh	3
Teier, Shmai	Wife	1
Teier, Shloime	Leah	3
Teierstein, Abraham	Tsipoireh	2
Teierstein, David	Leah	2
Teller, Etl		
Tenenholtz, David	Leah	2
Tenenholtz, Nathan	Nechama	6
Treiber, Zelig	Chaneh	1
Yagergaren	Berish	1
Janower, Hillel	Roizeh	3
Janower, Esther		1
Judeski		
Katz, Abraham	Wife	6
Cohen, Pinchas	Wife	

Cohen, Aharon Ber	Wife	2
Cohen, Abraham, Itzchak	Chaveh	5
Cohen, Nachum	Wife	2
Cohen, Shloime	Beileh	3
Levi, Shifre		1
Lomerman, Zeli	Wife	1
Lustrin, Yukib	Wife	
Lurer, Moishe	Wife	
Lieber, Mordechai	Taube	3
Lieber, Israel	Rushe	1
Lieber, Ruchel		1
Lieberman, Leibish	Rivkeh	3
Leiter, Daniel	Wife	1
Lichtenfeld, Moishe	Mother	
Lichtenshein, Shloime	Wife	
Lichfeld, Moishe	Wife	3
Lichter, Tzirl		
Lichter, Chanoch	Ruchel	5
Lichter, Abraham		
Lichter, Yakov	Wife	2
Lichter, Yechiel		
Lipman, Zvi	Hentzi	3
Lipper, Yosef	Wife	1

[Page 359]

Lipper, Shloime	Wife	3
Lipper, Itzchak Mendl	Zeidl	1
Lang, Todros	Chaveh	3
Langfeld, Shloime Rafael	Tzarneh	2
Lemer, Itzchak	Roizeh	
Lemer, Asher	Henneh	3

Laks, Itzchak	Chayeh	2
Laks, Shalom	Rasheh	2
Laks, Moishe	Wife	1
Laks, Sarah Blimeh		2
Laks, Frieda		1
Lerman, Matl		
Magrom, Hersh		1
Magrom, Yosef	Dineh	2
Magrom, Chaim	Chaveh	2
Model, Shmuel	Wife	2
Model, Moishe	Wife	2
Model, Blimeh		
Model, Chaim		
Model, Hodes		
Mutterperl, Yakov	Fessl	
Milstein, Moishe	Wife	2
Milstein, Yechiel	Shprintze	2
Mintz, Leibish	Wife	X
Maimon, Motl		
Maimon, Nathan	Malke	2
Maimon, Yehoshua	Yehudis	2
Maimon, Zvi	Hindeh	5
Maimon, Gedalieh	Frieda	1
Maimon, Yakov	Minke	3
Mitzner, Moishe wolf	Sarah Ruchel	2
Mitzner, Abraham	Liebe	2
Mitzner, Itzchak	Wife	X
Mitzner, Chaim	Wife	X
Mitzner, Moishe ben Berl	Daughter, Matl	X
Mitzner, Leizer	Wife	3
Mitzner, Berish	Mashi	3

Mitzner, Itche	Wife	1
Mitzner, Hersh		1
Mitzner, Yakov	Wife	2
Mitzner, Moishe	Beileh	6
Mitzner, Israel	Chayeh	
Man, Esther		1
Mannis, Chaim	Adile	2
Mannis, Pinchas	Chaveh	Her brother
Mannis, Leib	Chaneh	1
Mannis, Shmuel Yakov	Leitchi	3
Mannis, David	Zviyah	2
Mannis, Baruch	Shoshe	3
Mannis, Rafael	Sarah	
Marinstein, Eliezer (shochet)	Chaneh	1
Marinstein, Motl	Tilleh	
Marinstein, Leib		
Marinstein, Leibish	Wife	2
Marinstein, Nachum	Wife	2
Marzel, rivkeh		2
Marmlstein, Yakov	Mirl	4
Mercer, Simche	Taube	2
Mercer, Nachum	Esther Mirl	1
Mercer, Chaim	Leah	2
Mercer	Chaveh	2
Mercer, Hersh	Gitl	2
Nirenberg, Nachum	Wife	X
Stempel, Tevl	Ruchel	3

[Page 360]

Dr. Potoker	Wife	1
Foigel, Yehoshua	Goldeh	1

Fuchs, Tevl	Reitzeh	1
Fuchs, Mordechai	Sarah	2
Fuchs, Leibish	Chaneh	1
Foxman, Shmuel	Goldeh	4
Foxman, Wolf	Wife	3
Foxman, Pinchas	Tzirl	
Pomeranc, Ephraim	Hodes	1
Porter, Israel	Leah	4
Porter, Moishe	Wife	1
Porter, Israel		
Porter, Nachman		
Porter, Yosef	Wife	3
Porter, Ruchel	Shalom Mordechai	
Porcelen, Shalom	Gitl	4
Furer, David	Wife	2
Feil, David	Wife	2
Feil, Asher	Wife	
Feil, Itzchak	Chaneh	2
Feil, Shmuel	Chayeh	2
Feil, Moishe	Goldeh	1
Feil, Baruch	Wife	2
Finger, Mendl		
Finger, Hersh	Wife	
Finger, Leizer	Maltzi	2
Fink, Nuteh	Hentzi	3
Feiner, Moishe	Esther	3
Feiner, Shimon	Leah	X
Feiner, Peretz	Wife	X
Feiner, Eliezer	Chaveh	
Feiner, Zlati Goldeh		
Feiner, Shalom	Bracha	2

Feiner, Chaim	Mali	3
Fireman, Feige		
Fireman, Leibl	Wife	
Fishbergen, Kalman	Goldeh	4
Fisher, Nachman	Fessl	
Fach, Sarah		2
Fach, Yeshiyahu		1
Fach, Charne		X
Fach, Abraham	Mindl	3
Fach, Yosef	Beileh	3
Fach, Eliezer	Leah	1
Fach, Henneh wife of Gedalia		1
Fach, Israel	Wife	2
Fach, Abraham'tche	Wife	
Fach, Shmuel	Wife	2
Ploc, Itteh		3
Ploc, Israel	Leah	2
Ploc, Itzchak	Dineh	
Ploc, Yechiel		
Ploc, Malke, and Beileh		1
Ploc, Pinchas	Wife	5
Ploc, Falik	Ruchel	
Ploc, Raizl		1
Ploc, Hersh	Sarah Dineh	6
Flug, Itzchak Meier	Rivkeh	1
Floimenboim	Abraham	
Floimenboim, Berish		
Flick, Mordechai	Rechel	2
Pelz, Chayeh Rivkeh		
Pantzer, Yehoshua	Wife	X
Pelz, Abish		

Felkser, Leibl	Feige	3
Panzerman, Leibish Pinchas	Wife	2
Panzerman, Hersh	Ruchel	2
Panzerman, Chaim Feivel	Raizel	6
Panzerman, Mendl	Chayeh	1
Panzerman, Moishe Mordechai		

[Page 361]

Feder, Zisl		
Furer, Mordechai	Wife	X
Panzerman, Chaye		1
Panzerman, Michal	Reitze	
Panzerman, Leibish Pinchas	Wife	5
Fast, Yekutiel	Batyeh	4
Feffer, Berish	Beileh	2
Freund, Zvi	Mindl	
Freund, Benyomin	Reitzeh	1
Fruchtlender, Todros	Fradl	3
Frost, Meier	Rechl	1
Frost, Aharon Itzchak	Mindl	2
Friling, Moishe	Shprintze	2
Friling, Freida Simeh		4
Frisherman, Shmuel	Leah	1
Pressburger, Chaneh		3
Pressburger, Feige		
Farshtendig, Pinchas	Chayeh Beileh	2
Farshtendig, Leibish	Wife	3
Ceber, Yehuda	Wife	1
Zilerman, Mordechai	Wife	3
Zilerman, Elimelech	Wife	2
Zilerman, Chaim Yosef	Wife	2

Zwicke, Yakov	Beileh	2
Zucker, Simche Meier	Chaneh	4
Zucker, Elchanan	Simeh	5
Zucker, Chaneh Raizl		4
Zucker, Rafael	Rivkeh	2
Zimring wife of Hersh Yosef		2
Zimring, Ephraim	Wife	2
Zimring, Yechezkel	Sarah	2
Zimring, Ber	Wife	
Zimring, Dvoireh		
Zimring, Beileh		
Kopf, Moishe	Wife	1
Kopf, Yidl	Henneh	
Cooperman, Goldeh		2
Korn, Taube		
Korn, Michal	Esther	2
Korn, Shmuel	Nechameh	4
Korn, Leah		
Korn, Moishe	Wife	
Korn, Leibish	Adile	2
Kornblit, Malkeh		
Kornblit, Moishe	Elke	
Kornstein, Yosef	Rivkeh	
Kornstein, Yehoshua	Chaneh	1
Kornstein, Leibl	Rivkeh	5
Kislovitz, Moishe	Rivkeh	2
Kislovitz, Hillel	Feige	3
Kitlnisser, Dvoireh		3
Kirshenfeld, Israael	Wife	2
Kirshenfeld, Baruch	Wife	1
Klotz, Eliezer	Ribah	

Klotz, Baruch		4
Klotz, Matut	Tisheh	2
Klotz, Leibish	Rivkeh	
Klotz, Yosef	Feige	2
Kleiner, Yentshi	Wife	2
Kleiner, Yekutiel	Wife	2
Kleiner, Serl		4
Kleinman, Shimshon	Chayeh	2
Kleinmintz, Sarah		Henneh
Kleinmintz, Mordechai	Malkeh	1
Kleinmintz, Moishe	Itte	2
Kleinmintz, Leibl	Wife	2
Kleinmintz, Yakov	Chaveh	1

[Page 362]

Kleinmintz, Leibl	Wife	1
Kleinmintz, Sarah		1
Kleinmintz, Yechekel	Sarah	2
Kleinmintz, Mechleh		
Kalminovitz, Fishl	Freida	3
Kaminer, Motl	Genieh	2
Kaminer, Berish	Sarah	1
Kaminer, Yakov	Wife	
Kaminer, Aharon	Wife	
Kaminer, Laizer		
Kandel, Shaul	Hesseh	4
Kandel, Yakov	Esther	3
Kandel, Reuben		
Kandel, Yechezkel	Hindeh	
Kandel, Avrumche	Wife	2
Kandel, Shepsl		

Kandel, Nathan	Itte	2
Kandel, Feige		
Kandel, Eliezer	Leah	2
Kandel, Benny Itche		
Kandel, Shloime	Gitl	4
Kandel, Fishl	Ruchel	2
Kantor, David	Raizl	2
Kantor, Leibl	Tzirl	8
Kantor, Yentchi	Bineh	5
Kantor, Arye	Wife	X
Knochen, Wolf	Hadassah	4
Konigsberg, Yosef	Wife	X
Konigsberg, Sender	Wife	1
Kassner, Moishe Wolf	Feige	3
Kassner, David		1 son
Kapenstock, Pinchas	Wife	2
Kapenstock, Yehoshua	Wife	1
Kapenstock, Hersh	Wife	
Katzenberg, Leibtchi	Charne	2
Kronenberg, Nathan Nuteh	Rechtche	
Kronenberg, Avigdor		
Krantz, Yoel	Esther	1
Kirschenfeld, Yosef	Wife	1
Rubinstein, Shloime	Sheba	1
Rubinstein, Leah		3
Rubinstein, Yakov	Wife	2
Dr. Rodarfer	Wife	1
Roizenblit, Gershen	Chaneh Esther	
Roizenblit, Yakov	Mindl	
Roizenberg, Nuteh	Gitl	2
Roizenboim, Chaneh		2

Roizenbach, Hersh Leib	Wife	
Roizenberg, Kaile		
Roit, Israel	Beileh	3
Rotenberg, Chanoch	Leah	3
Rotenberg, Leibl	Dvoireh	1
Rofer, Shalom	Ruchel	
Rofer, Yoineh	Hindeh	2
Rokeach, Bat-Sheva (rabbi's wife)		1
Ridler, Mordechai	Zlatie	2
Ridler, Shmuel	Perl	2
Ridler, Hersh	Wife	
Reich, Yechekel	Wife	2
Rindl, Yechiel	Wife	2
Ringler, Mendl		
Ringer, Wolf	Wife	1
Ritzer, David		2
Ritzer, Moishe	Wife	3
Renner, Israel-Itche	Ettl	1
Renner, Mordechai	Shoshe	1
Renner, David	Zlateh	4

[Page 363]

Renner, Isaak	Rivkeh	4
Renner, Zisl		1
Rapaport, Beileh		
Rapaport, Yosef	Perl	3
Rapaport, Breindl		
Shulman, Elke		1
Shulman, Lippe	Wife	2
Shulman, Fishl		
Shuldiner, Nechemieh	Zisl	2

Shuldiner, Zvi	Leah	2
Shuldiner, Moishe Elchanan	Esther Dvoireh	2
Shuldiner, Meier	Esther	2
Shulman (Olsh)	Wife	4
Shur, Antshl	Sarah	2
Shur, Mordechai	Wife	X
Shur, Moishe	Rasheh	1
Shtol, Shloime Israel	Hodes	2
Shtolman, Mordechai	Chaneh	3
Stockman, Shmuel	Leah	4
Shtender, Shloime	Gitl	3
Shtender, Leml	Feige	2
Stern, Levi	Sarah	
Stern, Leib	Fessl	2
Stern, Leahtche		1
Stern, Israel	Wife	
Stern, Baruch	Sheineh	2
Stern, Abraham	Wife	2
Stern, Shmuel Yakov	Wife	
Steinkohler, Michal	Wife	1
Steinkohler, Yonathan	Dineh	3
Steinkohler, Leah		
Shtruzar, Abraham, Itzchak	Itte	3
Shtruzar, Mordechai	Shaindl	4
Shtruzar, Zainvel	Wife	X
Starker, Pinchas	Wife	
Starker, Meier	Wife	2
Starker, Wolf		
Starker, Moishe	Esther	2
Starker, Shloime	Henneh	1
Strom, Itzchak		2

Scheinwald, Hersh	Sarah	1
Shibitz, Moishe	Wife	3
Shibitz, Matis	Wife	2
Shinsinger, Pesach	Wife	2
Shinsinger, Meier		Sarah
Shinsinger, Abraham	Wife	1
Schitz, Isser	Feige	2
Schitz, Hersh	Mechleh	5
Schitz, Yakov	Beileh	2
Shir, Avigdor	Feige	3
Shir, Hanoch	Ruchel	
Shir, Shmuel Eliyahu	Taube	3
Shir, Itzchak Meier	Itte	
Shleicher, Shloime	Ruchel	1
Shleicher, Nachum		
Shleicher, Odl		
Shleicher, Shloime	Malke	4
Shleicher, Itte		4
Schlachterman, Ephraim	Beileh Ruchel	3
Schlafrok, David	Tchippeh	2
Shnur, Hersh	Altie	1
Shnur, Moishe	Tzirl	2
Shnitscr, Yechiel	Sheva	2
Shnitser, Shloime	Zelda	3
Shnitser, Simcheh	Mindl	2
Shnitser, Basia		
Shnitser, Zev	Gitl 4	

[Page 364]

Shwerdsharf, Blimeh

Shwerdsharf, Nuteh

Shnitser, Yakov	Dvoireh	3
Shnitser, Nathan	Gitl	4
Shnitser, Tzaddok	Freidl	4
Shnitser, Shmuel	Reitzeh	6
Shnitser, Shloime	Wife	X
Shnitser, Shimon	Wife	X
Shpitzeisen, Rivkeh	Monish	
Shapiro, Alter	Chaneh Taube	2
Shapiro, Yeshiyahu	Hindeh	3
Sheffer, Isaak	Liebeh	3
Sheffer, Ephraim	Chaneh	6
Sheffer, Nuteh	Wife	
Schatz, Mendl	Miriam	2
Schatz, Yeshiyahu	Ruchel	4
Schatz, Sarah		
Schatz, Sender	Wife	1
Schatz, Henneh	Hindeh	4
Schatz, Yeshiyahu	Tsarneh Ruchel	4
Sharf, Yocheved		3
Sharf, Israel	Wife	
Sharf, Moishe	Wife	3
Sharf, Abraham	Wife	2
Sharf, Yosef	Wife	2
Sharfman, Blimeh		1
Sharfman, Motie		
Sharfman, Esther		2
Sharfman, Chayeh		
Anger, Yechiel	Goldeh	2
Brenner, Tsipeh		3
Bergerfreind, Kaileh		1
Barziel, Leibish	Wife	X

Grauer, Israel	Wife	X
Gliklich, Yakov	Wife	X
Gropman, Miriam		
Gropman, Chayeh		
Gropman, Leah		
Gropman, Chaim		
Gerstenbust, Leah		
Harman, Gitl	Yechezkel	
Lichter, Rivkeh		
Mitzner, Kalman	Chaneh	3
Sofer, Nuteh	Wife	X
Farshtendig, Mendl	Wife	X
Farshtendig, Bruch	Wife	X
Panzerman, Shloime	Leah	3
Feigenboim, Matisyahu	Breindl	2
Biberman, Hersh	Roizeh	2

[Page 365][1]

Bilgoraj Jews who Perished in Other cities

Translated by Moses Milstein

Mizocz

Abraham Brezel and his family–David Teier and his family, Hershke Goldbrenner and his family, Honigsfeld Shepsl and his family, Pinchas Weinberg and his wife, Eilboim Moishe, and his family, Eilboim Shloime, Reuben Brezel and his family, Tenenholz David, and his family, Hersh Zutelman and 2 children.

Berdychew

Moishe Mintz, Henech Leichter and his family, Dorfman Eliyahu, and his family, Tintenfish Leah.

Ludmir

Shloime Zilbermintz, and his wife, Binem Bergstein, and his family, Dvoireh Zimring and her husband, Ber Zimring and his wife, Hersh Yosef Zimring's wife.

Romanow

Israel Yakov Bron, and his wife, and 3 children.

Zdolbuniv

Mendl Weissman, and his family

Oluka (in the Radziwill court)

Hersh Sheinwald, and his family, Alter Shapiro and his family, Yeshiyahu Shapiro and his family.

Hurchow

Hersh Weissman, and his family, Shloime Starker, and his family, Kuperschmid Leibel, and his family.

Kirowgrad

Nuteh Honigboim, and his family, Abraham Yakov Bergstein, and his family. Leibel Warshaviak and his family, Henech Rotenberg and his family, Leibel Rotenberg and his family.

Translator's footnote:

1.   Incorrectly printed as 265

[Pages 321-348]

List of Martyrs extracted from the Necrology

Transliterated by Moshe Steinberg

Edited by Yocheved Klausner

Family names(s)	First name(s)	Maiden	Sex	Marital Status	Father's name	Mother's name	Name of spouse	Additional family	Family name(s) of eulogizer 1
KRONENBERG	Natan Nuta		M	Married			Rukhltshe		KRONENBERG
KRONENBERG	Rukhltshe		F	Married			Natan Neta		KRONENBERG
TORM	Miriam	KRONENBERG	F	Married	Natan Neta	Rukhltshe	Hersh	3 children	KRONENBERG
TORM	Hersh		M	Married			Mirjam	3 children	KRONENBERG
HARMAN	Gitl	KRONENBERG	F		Natan Neta	Rukhltshe		child	KRONENBERG
FRISHERMAN	Lea	KRONENBERG	F	Married	Natan Neta	Rukhltshe	Shmuel	child	KRONENBERG
FRISHERMAN	Shmuel		M	Married			Lea	child	KRONENBERG
KRONENBERG	Refael Avigdor		M		Natan Neta	Rukhltshe			KRONENBERG
RAPAPORT	Yosef		M			Beila			RAPAPORT
RAPAPORT	Perl		F			Beila		3 children	RAPAPORT
RAPAPORT	Beila		F						RAPAPORT
ZETSER	Rivka	RAPAPORT	F	Married	Yosef		Itzik	2 children	RAPAPORT
ZETSER	Itzik		M	Married			Rivka	2 children	RAPAPORT
GRINBAUM	Kresl	RAPAPORT	F	Married	Yosef		Alter	3 children	RAPAPORT
GRINBAUM	Alter		M	Married			Kresl	3 children	RAPAPORT
GOLDBERG	Moshe		M	Married			Chava		RAPAPORT
GOLDBERG	Chava		F	Married			Moshe		RAPAPORT
WEINBERG	Moshe		M	Married			Bashe	4 children	RAPAPORT
WEINBERG	Basha		F	Married			Moshe	4 children	RAPAPORT
HERMAN	Avraham		M	Married			Dvorhtshe		RAPAPORT
HERMAN	Dvorhtshe		F	Married			Avraham		RAPAPORT
BREIZIL	Avraham		M	Married			Rachela	4 children	RAPAPORT
BREIZIL	Rachela		F	Married			Avraham	4 children	RAPAPORT
HARMAN	Tzvi		M	Married	Avraham	Dvorhtshe	Rivka	2 children	RAPAPORT
HARMAN	Rivka		F	Married			Tzvi	2 children	RAPAPORT
HARMAN	Yechezkel Tzvi		M	Married				children	RAPAPORT
HARMAN			F	Married			Yechezkel Tzvi	children	RAPAPORT
GROISMAN GROSMAN	Gitl		F						GOLDSTEIN
GROISMAN GROSMAN	Yidl		M			Gitl			GOLDSTEIN
GROISMAN GROSMAN	Eliahu Shmuel		M	Married		Gitl	Sara		GOLDSTEIN
GROISMAN GROSMAN	Sara		F	Married			Shmuel Eliahu		GOLDSTEIN
GROISMAN GROSMAN	Moshe		M		Eliyahu Shmuel	Sara			GOLDSTEIN
GROISMAN GROSMAN	Chaia		F		Eliyahu Shmuel	Sara			GOLDSTEIN
GROISMAN GROSMAN	Devorah		F		Eliyahu Shmuel	Sara			GOLDSTEIN
BROMBERG	Efraim		M	Married			Feiga		BLUMENFELD
BROMBERG	Feiga		F	Married			Efraim		BLUMENFELD

First name(s) of eulogizer 1	Relationship of eulogizer to victim	Residence of eulogizer 1	Family name of eulogizer 2	First name of eulogizer 2	Residence of eulogizer 2	Remarks	Page
Yona	son	Israel	KRONENBERG	Shmuel	Israel	Photograph	321
Yona	son	Israel	KRONENBERG	Shmuel	Israel	Photograph	321
Yona	brother	Israel	KRONENBERG	Shmuel	Israel	Photograph	321
Yona	brother-in-law	Israel	KRONENBERG	Shmuel	Israel	Photograph	321
Yona	brother	Israel	KRONENBERG	Shmuel	Israel	Photograph	321
Yona	brother	Israel	KRONENBERG	Shmuel	Israel	Photograph	321
Yona	brother-in-law	Israel	KRONENBERG	Shmuel	Israel	Photograph	321
Yona	brother	Israel	KRONENBERG	Shmuel	Israel	Photograph	321
Mordechai	son	Israel					324
Mordechai	nephew	Israel					324
Mordechai	grandson	Israel					324
Mordechai	brother	Israel					324
Mordechai	brother-in-law	Israel					324
Mordechai	brother	Israel					324
Mordechai	brother-in-law	Israel					324
Mordechai	grandson	Israel					324
Mordechai	grandson	Israel					324
Mordechai	nephew	Israel					324
Mordechai	nephew	Israel					324
Mordechai	nephew	Israel					324
Mordechai	nephew	Israel					324
Mordechai	nephew	Israel					324
Mordechai	nephew	Israel					324
Mordechai	nephew	Israel					324
Mordechai	nephew	Israel					324
Mordechai	nephew	Israel					324
Rivka	granddaughter	Israel				Photograph	325
Rivka	niece	Israel				Photograph	325
Rivka	niece	Israel				Photograph	325
Rivka	niece	Israel				Photograph	325
Rivka	niece	Israel				Photograph	325
Rivka	niece	Israel				Photograph	325
Rivka	niece	Israel				Photograph	325
Etel	daughter	Israel					326
Etel	daughter	Israel					326

Family names(s)	First name(s)	Maiden	Sex	Marital Status	Father's name	Mother's name	Name of spouse	Additional family	Family name(s) of eulogizer 1
BROMBERG	Beila		F		Efraim	Feiga			BLUMENFELD
BROMBERG	Leibl		F		Efraim	Feiga			BLUMENFELD
BROMBERG	Shlomo		M	Married	Efraim	Feiga	Dina	3 children	BLUMENFELD
BROMBERG	Dina		F	Married			Shlomo	3 children	BLUMENFELD
BRICK	Ester	BROMBERG	F	Married	Efraim	Feiga	Shmuel	2 children	BLUMENFELD
BRICK	Shmuel		M	Married			Ester	2 children	BLUMENFELD
WEBER	Tzvia	BROMBERG	F	Married	Efraim	Feiga	Meir	2 children	BLUMENFELD
WEBER	Meir		M	Married			Tzvia	2 children	BLUMENFELD
ARBESFELD	Israel		M	Married			Tzvia		ARBESFELD
ARBESFELD	Tzvia		F	Married			Israel		ARBESFELD
MERMELSTEIN	Gitl	ARBESFELD	F	Married	Yisrael	Tzvia	Ben Tzion	3 children	ARBESFELD
MERMELSTEIN	Ben Tzion		M	Married			Gitl	3 children	ARBESFELD
SNITZER	Freidl	ARBESFELD	F	Married	Yisrael	Tzvia	Tzadok	5 children	ARBESFELD
SNITZER	Tzadok		M	Married			Freidl	5 children	ARBESFELD
	Keilah	ARBESFELD	F		Yisrael	Tzvia		child	ARBESFELD
MAGROM	Tzvi		M	Widower			Malka		SHARF
MAGROM	Chaim		M	Married	Tzvi	Malka	Chava	2 children	SHARF
MAGROM	Chava		F	Married			Chaim	2 children	SHARF
MAGROM	Yosef		M	Married	Tzvi	Malka	Dina	2 children	SHARF
MAGROM	Dina		F	Married			Yosef	2 children	SHARF
MAGROM	Lea	MAGROM	F	Married	Tzvi	Malka	Shmuel	4 children	SHARF
MAGROM	Shmuel		M	Married			Lea	4 children	SHARF
SILBERMAN	Pesl	MAGROM	F	Married	Tzvi	Malka	Moshe	child	SHARF
SILBERMAN	Moshe		M	Married			Pesl	child	SHARF
MAGROM	Shlomo		M		Tzvi	Malka			SHARF
GERSCHTENBLIT	Yosef Moshe		M	Married			Rivka		GERSCHTENBLIT
GERSCHTENBLIT	Rivka		F	Married			Moshe Yosef		GERSCHTENBLIT
GERSCHTENBLIT	Leib		M	Married	Yosef Moshe	Rivka	Perel	child	GERSCHTENBLIT
GERSCHTENBLIT	Perel		F	Married			Leib	child	GERSCHTENBLIT
GERSCHTENBLIT	Barukh		M		Yosef Moshe	Rivka			GERSCHTENBLIT
GERSCHTENBLIT	Rakhel		F		Yosef Moshe	Rivka			GERSCHTENBLIT
GERSCHTENBLIT	Meir Zalman		M		Yosef Moshe	Rivka			GERSCHTENBLIT
HODES	Mordechai		M	Married			Lala		HODES
HODES	Lala		F	Married			Mordechai		HODES
HODES	Elka		F		Mordechai	Lala			HODES
HODES	Kine		F						HODES
SCHATZ	Hene		F	Widow			Wolf		SHATZ
SCHATZ	Chaim Moshe		M		Wolf	Hana			SHATZ

First name(s) of eulogizer 1	Relationship of eulogizer to victim	Residence of eulogizer 1	Family name of eulogizer 2	First name of eulogizer 2	Residence of eulogizer 2	Remarks	Page
Etel	sister	Israel				Photograph	326
Etel	sister	Israel				Photograph	326
Etel	sister	Israel				Photograph	326
Etel	sister-in-law	Israel					326
Etel	sister	Israel					326
Etel	sister-in-law	Israel					326
Etel	sister	Israel					326
Etel	sister-in-law	Israel					326
Moshe	son	Israel				Photograph	326
Moshe	son	Israel					327
Moshe	brother	Israel					327
Moshe	brother-in-law	Israel					327
Moshe	brother	Israel					327
Moshe	brother-in-law	Israel					327
Moshe	brother	Israel					327
Sara	daughter	Israel					328
Sara	sister	Israel					328
Sara	sister-in-law	Israel					328
Sara	sister	Israel					328
Sara	sister-in-law	Israel					328
Sara	sister	Israel					328
Sara	sister-in-law	Israel					328
Sara	sister	Israel					328
Sara	sister-in-law	Israel					328
Sara	sister	Israel					328
Lemel	son	Israel				Photograph	329
Lemel	son	Israel				Photograph	329
Lemel	brother	Israel				Photograph	329
Lemel	brother-in-law	Israel				Photograph	329
Lemel	brother	Israel				Photograph	329
Lemel	brother	Israel				Photograph	329
Lemel	brother	Israel				Photograph	329
Yakov	son	Israel				Photograph	330
Yakov	son	Israel				Photograph	330
Yakov	brother	Israel				Photograph	330
Yakov	grandson	Israel					330
Elimelech	son	America					331
Elimelech	brother	America					331

Family names(s)	First name(s)	Maiden	Sex	Marital Status	Father's name	Mother's name	Name of spouse	Additional family	Family name(s) of eulogizer 1
SCHATZ	Noach Avraham		M		Wolf	Hana			SHATZ
SCHATZ	Libe		F		Wolf	Hana			SHATZ
TAUBER	Avraham		M	Widower			Frimet		TAUBER
	Sonia	TAUBER	F	Married	Avraham	Frimet		husband and child	TAUBER
TAUBER	Yehuda		M		Avraham	Frimet			TAUBER
TAUBER	Tzirl		F		Avraham	Frimet			TAUBER
TAUBER	Yehudit		F		Avraham	Frimet			TAUBER
BUCHBINDER	Eliezer		M	Married			Ester		BUCHBINDER
BUCHBINDER	Ester		F	Married			Eliezer		BUCHBINDER
BUCHBINDER	Tzadok		M	Married	Eliezer	Ester	Feiga	2 children	BUCHBINDER
BUCHBINDER	Feiga		F	Married			Tzadok	2 children	BUCHBINDER
FROST	Mindl	BUCHBINDER	F	Married	Eliezer	Ester	Ahron Itzchak	2 children	BUCHBINDER
FROST	Yitzhak Aharon		M	Married			Mindl	2 children	BUCHBINDER
BUCHBINDER	Shmuel		M		Eliezer	Ester			BUCHBINDER
BRAN	Yakov Yisrael		M	Married			Bashele		BRAN
BRAN	Bashele		F	Married			Yakov Israel		BRAN
BRAN	Ruchele		F		Yakov Israel	Bashele			BRAN
BRAN	Surale		F		Yakov Israel	Bashele			BRAN
BRAN	Chaiml		M		Yakov Israel	Bashele			BRAN
VEINBERG	Freida		F	Married			Shlomo		WEINBERG
ANGER	Golda	WEINBERG	F	Married	Shlomo	Freida	Yechiel	2 children	WEINBERG
ANGER	Yechiel		M	Married			Golda	2 children	WEINBERG
WEINBERG	Moshe		M	Married	Shlomo	Freida	Miriam		WEINBERG
WEINBERG	Miriam		F	Married			Moshe		WEINBERG
WEINBERG	Pinchas		M	Married	Shlomo	Freida	Yetka		WEINBERG
WEINBERG	Yetka		F	Married			Pinchas		WEINBERG
WEINBERG	Genendel		F						WEINBERG
WEINBERG	Ester		F			Gnendel			WEINBERG
WEINBERG	Chaim Yisrael		M	Married			Chanatshe		FEDER
WEINBERG	Chantshe		F	Married			Chaim Israel		FEDER
WEINBERG	Miriam		F		Chaim Israel	Chanatshe			FEDER
WEINBERG	Meir Yechezkel		M		Chaim Israel	Chanatshe			FEDER
PUTER	Arye Yosef		M	Married			Miriam Ester	3 children	PUTER
PUTER	Miriam Ester		F	Married			Arye Yosef	3 children	PUTER
MERZEL	Dinatshe		F	Married			Feivel	3 children	PUTER
MERZEL	Arye Yosef		M	Married			Dinatshe	3 children	PUTER

First name(s) of eulogizer 1	Relationship of eulogizer to victim	Residence of eulogizer 1	Family name of eulogizer 2	First name of eulogizer 2	Residence of eulogizer 2	Remarks	Page
Elimelech	brother	America				Photograph	331
Elimelech	brother	America				Photograph	331
Yakov	son	Paraguay				Photograph	332
Yakov	brother	Paraguay				Photograph	332
Yakov	brother	Paraguay				Photograph	332
Yakov	brother	Paraguay				Photograph	332
Yakov	brother	Paraguay				Photograph	332
Shmuel	son	Israel				Photograph	333
Shmuel	son	Israel					333
Shmuel	brother	Israel					333
Shmuel	brother-in-law	Israel					333
Shmuel	brother	Israel					333
Shmuel	brother-in-law	Israel					333
Shmuel	brother	Israel				Died in Russia. Photograph	333
Shalom	son	Israel				Photograph	334
Shalom	son	Israel				Photograph	334
Shalom	brother	Israel				Photograph	334
Shalom	brother	Israel				Photograph	334
Shalom	brother	Israel				Aged 11	334
Shlomo	husband	Israel				Photograph	336
Shlomo	daughter	Israel				Photograph	336
Shlomo	father-in-law	Israel				Photograph	336
Shlomo	son	Israel				Photograph	336
Shlomo	daughter-in-law	Israel				Photograph	336
Shlomo	son	Israel				Photograph	336
Shlomo	daughter-in-law	Israel				Photograph	336
Shlomo	daughter	Israel				Photograph	336
Shlomo	grandfather	Israel				Photograph	336
Basia	daughter	Israel				Photograph	337
Basia	daughter	Israel				Photograph	337
Basia	sister	Israel				Photograph	337
Basia	sister	Israel				Photograph	337
Shmuel	son	Israel				Photograph	338
Shmuel	son	Israel				Photograph	338
Shmuel	nephew	Israel				Photograph	338
Shmuel	nephew	Israel				Photograph	338

Family names(s)	First name(s)	Maiden	Sex	Marital Status	Father's name	Mother's name	Name of spouse	Additional family	Family name(s) of eulogizer 1
TROM	Golda		F	Married			Hersh	4 children	PUTER
TROM	Hersh		M	Married			Golda	4 children	PUTER
ZUBERMAN	Yakov		M	Married		Krase	Gitl	2 children	PUTER
ZUBERMAN	Gitl		F	Married			Yakov	2 children	PUTER
KUPERMAN	Hinda		F						SUSMAN
SUSMAN	Chaim		M	Married			Malka Ester		SUSMAN
SUSMAN	Malka Ester		F	Married			Chaim		SUSMAN
SUSMAN	Gitl		F		Chaim	Ester Malka			SUSMAN
SUSMAN	Leib Hersh		M		Chaim	Ester Malka			SUSMAN
SUSMAN	Sara		F		Chaim	Ester Malka			SUSMAN
SUSMAN	Matitiahu		M		Chaim	Ester Malka			SUSMAN
SUSMAN	Chana		F		Chaim	Ester Malka			SUSMAN
SUSMAN	Alte		F		Chaim	Ester Malka			SUSMAN
SUSMAN	Reisel		F		Chaim	Ester Malka			SUSMAN
DORFMAN	Yocheved		F	Married			Eliyahu	children	SUSMAN
DORFMAN	Eliyahu		M	Married			Yocheved	children	SUSMAN
SILBERLICHT	Eliyahu		M	Married			Nachman		SILBERLICHT
SILBERLICHT	Nachman		F	Married			Eliyahu		SILBERLICHT
SILBERLICHT	Leib Hersh		M	Married	Eliyahu	Nechama	Klara	2 children	SILBERLICHT
SILBERLICHT	Klara		F	Married			Leib Hersh	2 children	SILBERLICHT
SILBERLICHT	Lea Chaya		F		Eliyahu	Nechama			SILBERLICHT
SILBERLICHT	Zeinvil Shmuel		M		Eliyahu	Nechama			SILBERLICHT
STERN	David		M		Yehoshua				STERN
KORNBLIT	Malka		F						LIEBHABER
KORNBLIT	David		M	Married		Malka	Feiga	3 children	LIEBHABER
KORNBLIT	Feiga		F	Married			David	3 children	LIEBHABER
KORNBLIT	Leibl		M	Married		Malka	Basha	child	LIEBHABER
KORNBLIT	Basha		F	Married			Leibl	child	LIEBHABER
KORNBLIT	Breindl	KORENBLIT	F	Married		Malka	Moshe	3 children	LIEBHABER
KORNBLIT	Moshe		M	Married			Breindl	3 children	LIEBHABER
ZLOTNIK	Hudes	KORENBLIT	F	Married		Malka	Yosef	child	LIEBHABER
ZLOTNIK	Yosef		M	Married			Hudes	child	LIEBHABER
KORNBLIT	Moshe		M			Malka			LIEBHABER

First name(s) of eulogizer 1	Relationship of eulogizer to victim	Residence of eulogizer 1	Family name of eulogizer 2	First name of eulogizer 2	Residence of eulogizer 2	Remarks	Page
Shmuel	nephew	Israel				Photograph	338
Shmuel	nephew	Israel					338
Shmuel	nephew	Israel					338
Shmuel	nephew	Israel					338
Shmuel		Israel				Photograph	339
Shmuel		Israel				Photograph	339
Shmuel		Israel					339
Shmuel		Israel					339
Shmuel		Israel					339
Shmuel		Israel					339
Shmuel		Israel					339
Shmuel		Israel					339
Shmuel		Israel					339
Shmuel		Israel					339
Shmuel		Israel				Photograph	339
Shmuel		Israel					339
Lipa	son	Israel					340
Lipa	son	Israel				Photograph	340
Lipa	brother	Israel					340
Lipa	brother-in-law	Israel					340
Lipa	brother	Israel					340
Lipa	brother	Israel					340
Chaim		Israel				Fell in battle as a Polish soldier in Prague, October 1945. Photograph	341
Genendl	daughter	America	KRONENBERG	Rechl	Israel	Photograph	342
Genendl	sister	America	KRONENBERG	Rechl	Israel	Photograph	342
Genendl	sister-in-law	America	KRONENBERG	Rechl	Israel	Photograph	342
Genendl	sister	America	KRONENBERG	Rechl	Israel	Photograph	342
Genendl	sister-in-law	America	KRONENBERG	Rechl	Israel	Photograph	342
Genendl	sister	America	KRONENBERG	Rechl	Israel		342
Genendl	sister-in-law	America	KRONENBERG	Rechl	Israel		342
Genendl	sister	America	KRONENBERG	Rechl	Israel		342
Genendl	sister-in-law	America	KRONENBERG	Rechl	Israel		342
Genendl	sister	America	KRONENBERG	Rechl	Israel		342

Family names(s)	First name(s)	Maiden	Sex	Marital Status	Father's name	Mother's name	Name of spouse	Additional family	Family name(s) of eulogizer 1
BENDLER	Hudes	BROMBERG	F	Married	Yakov Avraham	Tsirl		2 children	BROMBERG
BENDLER	Yakov		M	Married			Hudes	2 children	BROMBERG
BROMBERG	Itzchak		M	Married	Yakov Avraham	Tsirl	Chava	3 children	BROMBERG
BROMBERG	Chava		F	Married			Itzchak	3 children	BROMBERG
DONNERSTEIN	Necha	BROMBERG	F	Married	Yakov Avraham	Tsirl	Yakov Eliyahu	child	BROMBERG
DONNERSTEIN	Yakov Eliyahu		M	Married			Necha	child	BROMBERG
RUBINSTEIN	Shlomo		M	Married			Bat Sheva		RUBINSTEIN
RUBINSTEIN	Bat Sheva		F	Married			Shlomo		RUBINSTEIN
WARSHOVIAK	Myriam Liba	RUBINSTEiN	F	Married	Shlomo	Bat Sheva	Meir Itzchak	3 children	RUBINSTEIN
WARSHOVIAK	Meir Itzchak		M	Married			Myriam Liba	3 children	RUBINSTEIN
HOFMAN	Feiga	RUBINSTEiN	F	Married	Shlomo	Bat Sheva	Levy	3 children	RUBINSTEIN
HOFMAN	Levy		M	Married			Feiga	3 children	RUBINSTEIN
RUBINSTEIN	Malka		F		Shlomo	Bat Sheva			RUBINSTEIN
LICHTENFELD	Sara Chaia		F						LICHTENFELD
FEINER	Malea	LICHTENFELD	F	Married		Chaia Sura	Chaim	children	LICHTENFELD
FEINER	Chaim		M	Married			Malea	children	LICHTENFELD
	Pesia	LICHTENFELD	F	Married		Chaia Sura		husband	LICHTENFELD
JANOVER	Ester	LICHTENFELD	F			Chaia Sura		child	LICHTENFELD
LICHTENFELD	Moshe		M			Chaia Sura			LICHTENFELD
BAUM	Sheindl		F						BAUM
BAUM	Moshe		M	Married		Sheindl	Chinka	child	BAUM
BAUM	Chinka		F	Married			Moshe	child	BAUM
BAUM	Taube		F			Sheindl			BAUM
BAUM			F			Sheindl			BAUM
ROSENBAUM	Liba		F	Married			Ben Tzion		ROSENBAUM
TVERSKY	Golda	ROSENBOIM	F	Married			Yehoshua	3 children	ROSENBAUM
TVERSKY	Yehoshua		M	Married			Golda	3 children	ROSENBAUM
ROSENBAUM	Henia		F						ROSENBAUM
ROSENBAUM			M			Henia			ROSENBAUM
ROSENBAUM			M			Henia			ROSENBAUM
GLASBERG	Shifra		F					child	ROSENBAUM
RUBINSTEIN	Yetka		F						ROSENBAUM
RUBINSTEIN			M			Itka			ROSENBAUM
ROKEACH			F	Married				husband	ROSENBAUM
SINGER	Rale		F	Married				4 children	ROSENBAUM

First name(s) of eulogizer 1	Relationship of eulogizer to victim	Residence of eulogizer 1	Family name of eulogizer 2	First name of eulogizer 2	Residence of eulogizer 2	Remarks	Page
Tsirl	mother	America				Photograph	343
Tsirl	father-in-law	America				Photograph	343
Tsirl	mother	America				Photograph	343
Tsirl	daughter-in-law	America				Photograph	343
Tsirl	mother	America					343
Tsirl	father-in-law	America					343
Tova	daughter	Israel				Photograph	344
Tova	daughter	Israel				Photograph	344
Tova	sister	Israel				Photograph	344
Tova	sister-in-law	Israel				Photograph	344
Tova	sister	Israel					344
Tova	sister-in-law	Israel					344
Tova	sister	Israel					344
Mordechai	son	Canada	LICHTENFELD	Lipa	Bellevue	Photograph	345
Mordechai	brother	Canada	LICHTENFELD	Lipa	Bellevue	Photograph	345
Mordechai	brother-in-law	Canada	LICHTENFELD	Lipa	Bellevue	Photograph	345
Mordechai	brother	Canada	LICHTENFELD	Lipa	Bellevue		345
Mordechai	brother	Canada	LICHTENFELD	Lipa	Bellevue		345
Mordechai	brother	Canada	LICHTENFELD	Lipa	Bellevue		345
Wolf	son	Brazil				Photograph	346
Wolf	brother	Brazil				Photograph	346
Wolf	brother-in-law	Brazil					346
Wolf	brother	Brazil					346
Wolf	brother	Brazil					346
Ben Tzion	husband					Died in Biłgoraj	347
Ben Tzion	brother					Died in Biłgoraj	347
Ben Tzion	brother-in-law					Died in Biłgoraj	347
Ben Tzion	brother-in-law					Died in Biłgoraj	347
Ben Tzion	uncle					Died in Biłgoraj	347
Ben Tzion	uncle					Died in Biłgoraj	347
Ben Tzion	brother-in-law					Died in Biłgoraj	347
Ben Tzion	brother-in-law					Died in Biłgoraj	347
Ben Tzion	brother-in-law					Died in Biłgoraj	347
Ben Tzion	brother-in-law					Died in Biłgoraj	347
Ben Tzion	brother-in-law					Died in Biłgoraj	347

Family names(s)	First name(s)	Maiden	Sex	Marital Status	Father's name	Mother's name	Name of spouse	Additional family	Family name(s) of eulogizer 1
SINGER			M	Married			Rale	4 children	ROSENBAUM
FEIGENBAUM	Matitiahu		M						FEIGENBAUM
FEIGENBAUM	Breindl		F						FEIGENBAUM
FEIGENBAUM	Lea Sara		F		Matitiahu				FEIGENBAUM
FEIGENBAUM	Mendel		M		Matitiahu				FEIGENBAUM

First name(s) of eulogizer 1	Relationship of eulogizer to victim	Residence of eulogizer 1	Family name of eulogizer 2	First name of eulogizer 2	Residence of eulogizer 2	Remarks	Page
Ben Tzion	brother-in-law					Died in Biłgoraj	347
Hershke	son						348
Hershke	nephew						348
Hershke	brother						348
Hershke	brother						348

NAME INDEX